CITIZENS DIVIDED

The Tanner Lectures on Human Values

CITIZENS DIVIDED

Campaign Finance Reform and the Constitution

ROBERT C. POST

With Commentary by

PAMELA S. KARLAN

LAWRENCE LESSIG

FRANK MICHELMAN

NADIA URBINATI

Harvard University Press

Cambridge, Massachusetts
London, England
2014

Library of Congress Cataloging-in-Publication Data

Post, Robert, 1947– author.
Citizens divided : campaign finance reform and the constitution / Robert C. Post ; with commentary by Pamela S. Karlan, Lawrence Lessig, Frank Michelman, Nadia Urbinati.
pages cm
Includes bibliographical references and index.
ISBN 978-0-674-72900-1 (alk. paper)
1. Campaign funds—Law and legislation—United States.   2. Law reform—United States.
3. Constitutional law—United States.   4. Election law—United States.   5. Elections—United
States.   I. Title.
KF4920.P67 2014
342.73'078—dc23   2013040590

To Reva

così de l'atto suo, per li occhi infuso
ne l'imagine mia, il mio si fece

CONTENTS

CITIZENS DIVIDED

I

THE LECTURES

1

FIRST LECTURE: A SHORT HISTORY
OF REPRESENTATION AND
DISCURSIVE DEMOCRACY

Campaign finance reform is among the most vexing constitutional issues of our time. All sides agree that the stakes are momentous. For reformers, regulation is necessary to preserve the integrity of the Republic; for opponents, regulation threatens the freedom of speech necessary for democratic self-governance. The constitutional arguments slide past one another with scarcely a moment of mutual engagement. If constitutional law is meant to affirm common principles of agreement, the debate over campaign finance reform could not be more disheartening.

The decisions of the Supreme Court exemplify the problem. From the beginning the Court has been nothing but confused on the issue. Its first major opinion on the topic, *Buckley v. Valeo*,[1] attempted a grand strategic compromise. Lacking a coherent intellectual foundation, the compromise quickly foundered,[2] leaving the Court bitterly divided, sometimes leaning in favor of reform, sometimes against.

In recent years, the Court has tilted decidedly against efforts to control campaign spending. Its recent opinion in *Citizens United v. Federal Election Commission*[3] can fairly be described as expressing profound suspicion of efforts to control campaign expenditures.[4] Although *Citizens United* was from the beginning a highly controversial and unpopular decision,[5] the Court plainly believed that it was merely reaffirming self-evident and fundamental principles of freedom of speech. "[U]nder our law and our tradition," Anthony Kennedy wrote for the Court, "it seems stranger than fiction for our Government to make . . . political speech a crime. Yet this is the statute's purpose and design."[6] Authoring a dissent

3

for four justices, John Paul Stevens affirmed with equal conviction: "The Court's ruling threatens to undermine the integrity of elected institutions across the Nation."[7]

Intensity and eloquence notwithstanding, there was precious little common ground between the majority and the dissent. The decision reflected a country divided, not united. The two sides seemed to inhabit entirely different constitutional universes.[8] There are many reasons for this horrifying disjunction, including the intense ideological and political divisions that have plainly shaped debate on the topic of campaign finance reform. From the narrow perspective of constitutional law, however, the sharp discord among the justices reflects disturbing imprecision in the formulation of constitutional issues inevitably raised by efforts to regulate campaign contributions and expenditures.

Two issues in particular have proved difficult for the Court. First, the Court lacks a disciplined and coherent explanation of its own First Amendment jurisprudence. Because its First Amendment opinions are marred by overreaching rhetoric and clumsy doctrinal tests, the Court is ill equipped to think carefully about how campaign finance reform might be reconciled with fundamental First Amendment principles. Second, proponents of campaign finance reform have failed to advance justifications for regulation that can be inosculated with basic First Amendment principles.[9] They have instead promoted justifications like "distortion"[10] or "equality,"[11] which are inconsistent with essential premises of First Amendment doctrine. It is surprisingly difficult to express the fundamental republican value of "the integrity of elected institutions" in a manner that can be reconciled with the structure of received First Amendment thought.

My hope, and it is a modest hope, is to use these Tanner Lectures to propose a solution to these two difficulties. By constructing a careful, disciplined account of our First Amendment jurisprudence, I shall try to illuminate how certain state interests in campaign finance reform may be reconciled with traditional constitutional commitments. I shall argue, in brief, that a primary purpose of First Amendment rights is to make possible the value of self-government, and that this purpose requires public trust that elections select officials who are responsive to public opinion. Government regulations that maintain this trust advance the constitutional purpose of the First Amendment.

I shall not in these lectures propose a particular agenda of practical reform. I shall leave that project to those better versed than I in the actual dynamics of American politics.[12] Nor shall I address how change can be mobilized and achieved. I shall leave that effort to those more capable than I in such matters.[13] Instead I shall seek to elaborate a constitutional framework of analysis in which First Amendment doctrine and campaign finance reform can be connected to each other in a coherent and theoretically satisfactory manner. My hope is that in the future this framework may serve as a basis for actual dialogue between the parties to this vital but acrimonious controversy.

I.

From its inception, the government of the United States has been built on the premise of self-government. We were founded upon a belief in the value of self-determination. In American history this value has taken two distinct forms: republican representation and democratic deliberation. In republican representation, the value of self-determination is realized when the people elect representatives who govern. In democratic deliberation, the value of self-determination is realized when the people actively participate in the formation of public opinion.

Although a republic and a democracy each seek to embody the value of self-government, they do so in different ways. Republican principles can sometimes reinforce democratic principles, and they can sometimes contradict democratic principles. The Court in *Citizens United* builds on democratic principles, which in contemporary constitutional law are embedded in First Amendment doctrine. The Court explains that "[s]peech is an essential mechanism of democracy, for it is the means to hold officials accountable to the people. The right of citizens to inquire, to hear, to speak, and to use information to reach consensus is a precondition to enlightened self-government and a necessary means to protect it."[14] The Court infers from these principles that "laws that burden political speech are 'subject to strict scrutiny,' which requires the Government to prove that the restriction 'furthers a compelling interest and is narrowly tailored to achieve that interest.' "[15]

The dissent in *Citizens United* also insists on the principle of self-government. But whereas the Court imagines self-government as a process of citizens communicating among themselves, the dissent instead envisions self-government as a structure of representation. It imagines that self-government happens when people select representatives who engage in the actual practice of lawmaking. It is of crucial importance for the dissent, therefore, "to assure that elections are indeed free and representative,"[16] "because in a functioning democracy the public must have faith that its representatives owe their positions to the people, not to the corporations with the deepest pockets."[17] The dissent associates this faith with "compelling governmental interests in 'preserving the integrity of the electoral process.' "[18]

The crux of the constitutional issue for the dissent is the relationship between the people and their representatives, a relationship that is mediated by the institution of elections. The crux of the constitutional issue for the Court is the capacity of the people freely to participate in public discussion, a capacity that is not mediated by elections. The Court and the dissent agree that constitutional analysis must turn on the value of self-government, but they differ in how they conceive this constitutional value.

I have been teaching First Amendment doctrine for almost thirty years. I have in the past done my best to avoid addressing the Court's campaign finance decisions, because I have never achieved clarity about how these decisions should be understood. The need for freedom of political speech appears self-evident, but so also does the need for electoral integrity. Each seems indispensable, and yet in cases like *Citizens United* they appear incompatible.

Buckley v. Valeo attempted to split the difference between these two ideals by proposing an arbitrary distinction between campaign *contributions* and independent campaign *expenditures*.[19] Regulations of the former were permitted to protect electoral integrity, but regulations of the latter were prohibited to safeguard freedom of speech. Although this compromise has endured for over a third of a century, it is now fast unraveling. Because the compromise lacks theoretical structure, there is little to stop the slide into chaos.

The fundamental question posed by the campaign finance decisions is how our republican tradition may be reconciled with our commitment to discursive democracy. My goal in these Tanner Lectures is to provide a constitutional account of how these two distinct paths to self-governance may be integrated, one with the other. We shall begin with a quick and stylized survey of the history of self-government in the United States. In this first lecture, I shall discuss how our nation's initial commitment to republican self-government evolved in the opening decades of the twentieth century into a foundational commitment to "political deliberation by ordinary citizens."[20] This history suggests why principles of campaign finance reform may be in tension with received First Amendment jurisprudence, and it also intimates how this tension may be doctrinally resolved. In my second lecture, I shall discuss the implications of this history for the constitutional reasoning adopted by the Court in *Citizens United*. I shall propose how *Citizens United* might have been decided in a manner that is truer to our fundamental constitutional commitment to self-governance.

II.

The American Revolution was fought to achieve "the blessings and security of self-government."[21] The Colonies boldly proclaimed that "Governments . . . instituted among Men" derive "their just powers from the consent of the governed,"[22] that "all lawful government is founded on the consent of those who are subject to it."[23] They sought to create a government in which "*all authority is derived from the* PEOPLE."[24] "The people were in fact, the fountain of all power."[25] "It is evident that no other form would be reconcilable with the genius of the people of America," wrote James Madison, "[than] to rest all our political experiments on the capacity of mankind for self-government."[26]

The Framers were aware of ancient democracies in which people physically met to deliberate and decide on governmental action. They regarded such democracies as societies "consisting of a small number of citizens, who assemble and administer the government in person."[27] But as societies "increased in population and the territory extended, the simple democratical form became unwieldy and impracticable."[28] In the vast stretches of the new continent, the people could never physically assemble to govern themselves. They could "never act, consult, or reason together, because they cannot march five hundred miles, nor spare the time, nor find a space to meet."[29]

How might the ideal of self-government be maintained under these new and modern conditions? The answer, "the pivot" on which Americans sought to build their new republic, was "the principle of representation."[30] "Representation was an expedient by which the meeting of the people themselves was rendered unnecessary."[31] It was "an expedient by which an assembly of certain individuals chosen by the people is substituted in place of the inconvenient meeting of the people themselves."[32] The Framers sought to create a new form of self-government in which "all authority of every kind *is derived by* REPRESENTATION *from the* PEOPLE, *and the* DEMOCRATIC *principle is carried into every part of the government.*"[33]

It is not obvious how the principle of representation can be reconciled with the ideal of self-government. Already by 1762 Rousseau had published his famous critique of representation. He had argued that "[t]he sovereign cannot be represented, for the same reason that it cannot be alienated: its essence is the general will; and that will must speak itself, or it does not exist. . . . The deputies of the people are of course not their representatives; they can only be their commissioners, and as such are not qualified to conclude upon any thing definitively."[34] Rousseau observed that "the people of England deceive themselves, when they fancy they are free: they are so, in fact, only during the interval between a dissolution of one parliament and the election of another; for, as soon as a new one is elected, they are again in chains, and lose all their virtue as a people."[35]

The answer to Rousseau's challenge was to forge a living connection between the people and their representatives. Americans believed that "representation" required a "chain of communication between the people, and those, to whom they have committed the exercise of the powers of government. This chain may consist of one or more links; but in all cases it should be sufficiently strong and discernible."[36] The chain of communication needed to be "sufficiently strong and discernible" to sustain the popular conviction that representatives spoke for the people whom they purported to represent. Only in this way could the value of self-government be maintained.

The Founders had personally experienced the failure of this chain of communication. In protesting British taxes, they had contended "that parliamentary authority is derived SOLELY from representation— . . . those who are bound by Acts of Parliament, are bound for this ONLY reason, because they are represented in it."[37] They contended that British taxes were unjustified because the colonists were not represented in the British parliament. "*Those* who are *taxed* without their own consent, expressed by themselves or their representatives, are *slaves. We are taxed* without our own consent, expressed by ourselves or our representatives. *We* are therefore—SLAVES."[38]

The British were puzzled by this argument. From their perspective the colonists were "subjects of Great Britain," and therefore "The King, Lords, and Commons are their representatives; for to them it is that they have delegated their individual rights over their lives, liberties, and property; and so long as they approve of that form of government, and continue under it, so long do they consent to whatever is done by those they have intrusted with their rights."[39]

Conceding that the colonists did not actually vote for members of the British parliament, British apologists dryly observed that neither did "Nine Tenths of the People of *Britain*," for "the Right of Election is annexed to certain Species of Property, to peculiar Franchises, and to Inhabitancy in some particular Places."[40] The colonists were "in exactly the same situation" as the vast majority of the British population: "None of them chuse their Representatives; and yet are they not represented in Parliament? Is their vast Property subject to Taxes without their Consent?"[41] The question answered itself: "All *British* Subjects are . . . virtually represented in Parliament; for every member of Parliament sits in the House, not as Representatives of his own Constituents, but as one of that august Assembly by which all the Commons of *Great Britain* are represented."[42]

The colonists rejected the British claim to virtual representation.[43] In their experience, "the People of these Colonies are not, and from their local Circumstances cannot be, Represented in the House of Commons in *Great-Britain*."[44] In attempting to explain why this was true, the colonists began to construct a theory of successful representation, representation that actually embodies the value of self-government. They articulated two prerequisites for successful representation. The first was consent.[45] The Stamp Act Congress affirmed "That the only Representatives of the People of these Colonies, are Persons chosen therein by themselves."[46] "Not one *American* ever gave, or can give, his suffrage for the choice of any of these pretended representatives [in Parliament]. . . . How can a colony, shire, city or borough be represented, when not one individual inhabitant ever did the least thing towards procuring such representation? . . . If we are not their constituents, they are not our representatives."[47]

The second was commonality of interests. The colonists claimed that they were "not represented, and from their local and other circumstances, cannot properly be represented in the British parliament."[48] "Why was America so justly apprehensive of Parliamentary injustice?" Madison asked the members of the constitutional convention. "Because G. Britain had a separate interest real or supposed, & if her authority had been admitted, could have pursued that interest at our expense."[49] "There is not that intimate and inseparable relation between the *Electors of Great-Britain* and the *Inhabitants of the Colonies*, which must inevitably involve both in the same Taxation; on the contrary, not a single *actual* Elector in *England,* might be immediately affected by a Taxation in *America,* imposed by a Statute which would have a general Operation and Effect, upon the Properties of the Inhabitants of the Colonies."[50]

Constructing a framework of representation that would meet these conditions was the great challenge of the Constitution. "The great difficulty lies in the affair of Representation," Madison told the delegates to the constitutional convention, "and if this could be adjusted, all others would be surmountable."[51] In thrashing out the structure of the Constitution, the Framers thought long and hard about how to construct a "chain of communication" between the people and their representatives that would preserve "the necessary sympathy between [the people] and their rulers and officers."[52] They fiercely debated whether persons, states, or property ought to be represented, the size of electoral districts, the periodicity of elections, the qualifications for suffrage, and so on.[53] In the controversy surrounding the Constitution's ratification, a major point of contention would be whether "our representation in the proposed government ... would be merely virtual, similar to what we were allowed in England, whilst under the British government."[54] In the end, the nation came to accept the Constitution's complicated and carefully balanced structures of representation as an authentic expression of self-government.

III.

The founding generation believed in "the democratic principle of the Govt."[55] It was, as James Madison observed, "essential to every plan of free Government," which "would be more stable and durable if it should rest on the solid foundation of the people themselves."[56] Yet the founding generation also feared "the fury of democracy."[57] They were apprehensive of "the amazing violence & turbulence of the democratic spirit," which can seize "the popular passions" and "spread like wild fire, and become irresistible."[58] They believed that "democratic communities may be unsteady, and be led to action by the impulse of the moment."[59]

They sought, therefore, to form "a republican government" that would avoid both "despotism" and "the extremes of democracy."[60] The Founders took the difference between a republic and a democracy quite seriously.

In his biography of George Washington, for example, John Marshall praised Washington for being "a real republican. . . . But, between a balanced republic and democracy, the difference is like that between order and chaos."[61] The Framers carefully designed a system that, in Madison's words, involved *the total exclusion of the people in their collective capacity from any share*" in the government.[62]

The Framers conceived a republic to be a form of government that checked and channeled the unstable force of popular sentiment. Republics used laws and constitutional structures to protect rights and to divide power into a multitude of competing centers. Republics deployed the principle of representation, which was itself an antidote to the possibility of democratic chaos.

In *Federalist 10,* Madison observed that "a pure democracy," by which he meant "a society consisting of a small number of citizens, who assemble and administer the government in person,"

> can admit of no cure for the mischiefs of faction. A common passion or interest will, in almost every case, be felt by a majority of the whole; a communication and concert result from the form of Government itself; and there is nothing to check the inducements to sacrifice the weaker party or an obnoxious individual. Hence it is that such Democracies have ever been spectacles of turbulence and contention; have ever been found incompatible with personal security or the rights of property; and have in general been as short in their lives as they have been violent in their deaths.[63]

The mischiefs of faction, Madison famously argued, are best addressed by "a republic, by which I mean a government in which the scheme of representation takes place."[64] Representation could tame the turbulence of democracy in two ways.

First, public officials in republics are elected, which means that republican government can "refine and enlarge the public views, by passing them through the medium of a chosen body of citizens, whose wisdom may best discern the true interest of their country, and whose patriotism and love of justice will be least likely to sacrifice it to temporary or partial considerations. Under such a regulation, it may well happen that the public voice, pronounced by the representatives of the people, will be more consonant to the public good than if pronounced by the people themselves, convened for the purpose."[65]

Second, republics allow for an extended sphere of governance. Republican officials could thus be elected by a large number of citizens, which would make it correspondingly "more difficult for unworthy candidates to practice with success the vicious arts by which elections are too often carried."[66] An extended sphere of governance would make it more likely that the "suffrages of the people" would "centre in men who possess the most attractive merit, and the most diffusive and established characters."[67]

Implicit in eighteenth-century American republicanism was the effort to reconcile the principle of self-government with a social system that reflected "hierarchies . . . as resilient as they were soft."[68] Eighteenth-century American republicans expected a system of representation to select for leaders of the better sort, elites with "the most attractive merit and the most diffusive and established characters." The larger the electoral districts established by the Constitution, the more such elites would stand out, identified and trusted by deeply ingrained habits of social deference. Elites would temper the vulgarity of democratic sentiment by refining and enlarging the views of a democratic public.

The Framers' commitment to elite representation was tested almost immediately after the founding of the nation. In 1789 Thomas Tudor Tucker of South Carolina moved in the first Congress to amend the proposed text of the First Amendment to provide that "the people should have a right to instruct their representatives."[69] Several states at the time provided for a right of instruction in their state constitutions.[70] The obvious argument in favor of a right of instruction was that it "was strictly compatible with the spirit and the nature of the Government; all power vests in the people of the United States."[71] "Instruction and representation in a republic" were for this reason "inseparably connected."[72]

Those who opposed the amendment, however, believed that "Representation is the principle of our Government; the people ought to have confidence in the honor and integrity of those they send forward to transact their business."[73] The instruction of representatives was said to be "a most dangerous principle, utterly destructive of all ideas of an independent and deliberative body, which are essential requisites in the Legislatures of free Government; they prevent men of abilities and experiences from rendering those services to the community that are in their power."[74] "[W]hen the people have chosen a representative," Representative Roger Sherman of Connecticut argued, "it is his duty to meet with others from the different parts of the Union and consult and agree with them to such acts as are for the general benefit of the community. If they were to be guided by instructions, they would be no use in deliberation; all that a man would have to do would be to produce his instructions."[75]

The first Congress rejected the motion to include a right to instruct in the First Amendment.[76] The right was deemed inconsistent with the independence required of true representatives. That very independence, however, was potentially in tension with the "chain of communication" necessary to connect representatives to their constituents. How could representatives speak for the people, if the people could not control their representatives?

In part the answer lay in the First Amendment itself. By protecting freedom of speech, the First Amendment established a chain of communication that would connect the people to their representatives.[77] As James Madison pointed out on the floor of the House, the amendment gave "the people . . . a right to express and communicate their sentiments and wishes. . . . The right of freedom of speech is secured; the liberty of the press is expressly declared to be beyond the reach of this Government; the people may therefore publicly address their representatives, may privately advise them, or declare their sentiments by petition to the whole body."[78] With such freedoms, Madison concluded, there was no need for a distinct right of instruction.

Yet for the Framers the communicative freedoms of the First Amendment were by themselves insufficient to sustain "the necessary sympathy between [the people] and their rulers and officers."[79] The maintenance of this sympathy depended upon "the right of electing the members of the government," which "constitutes more particularly the essence of a free and responsible government."[80] The founding generation regarded "frequency of elections" as "the great bulwark of our liberty";[81] elections were "necessary to preserve the good behavior of rulers."[82] Elections empowered the people to "choose" their representatives and thereby to affirm a commonality of interests with those whom they decided to select. The Framers believed that "the elective mode of obtaining rulers is the characteristic policy of republican government."[83]

The Constitution structured the House of Representatives as the branch of government most dependent upon, and most responsive to, public opinion. "It is essential to liberty that the government in general should have a common interest with the people, so it is particularly essential that the [House of Representatives] should have an immediate dependence on, and an intimate sympathy with, the people. Frequent elections are unquestionably the only policy by which this dependence and sympathy can be effectually secured."[84] Elections were necessary to establish "a due connection between [the people's] representatives and themselves."[85] Elections created "such a limitation of the term of appointments as will maintain a proper responsibility to the people."[86] To serve this function, elections had to occur with an appropriate frequency,[87] by the appropriate electors,[88] and within a framework that produced the correct number of representatives to maintain a suitable relationship between representatives and their constituents.[89]

The great debate over the ratification of the Constitution turned in part on whether the proposed federal government created a structure of elections adequate to sustain the viability of representative institutions. The prominent anti-federalist Brutus argued that "if the people are to give their assent to the laws, by persons chosen and appointed by them, the manner of the choice and the number chosen, must be such, as to possess, be disposed, and consequently qualified to declare the sentiments of the people; for if they do not know, or are not disposed to speak the sentiments of the people, the people do not govern, but the sovereignty is in a few."[90]

The Constitution explicitly provided that the first House of Representatives would contain sixty-five representatives (and that no future House could contain more representatives than one for every thirty thousand). Brutus argued that sixty-five was too small a number, because "One man, or a few men, cannot possibly represent the feelings, opinions, and characters of a great multitude. . . . Sixty-five men cannot be found in the United States, who hold the sentiments, possess the feelings, or are acquainted with the wants and interests of this vast country."[91] The House of Representatives therefore could "not possess the confidence of the people. . . . [R]epresentation in the legislature is not so formed as to give reasonable ground for public trust."[92]

In electoral districts so large, moreover, it would be "impossible the people of the United States should have sufficient knowledge of their representatives" to satisfy themselves that their representatives were persons who could "manage the public concerns with wisdom" and who would be "men of integrity, who will pursue the good of the community with fidelity; and will not be turned aside from their duty by private interest, or corrupted by undue influence."[93] In districts so large, only "the rich and *well-born*" could possibly gain election, and they would "not be viewed by the people as part of themselves, but as a body distinct from them, and having separate interests to pursue."[94]

In *Federalist 57*, Madison defended the Constitution's electoral structure. He argued that it would create "such a limitation of the term of appointments, as will maintain a proper responsibility to the people."[95] He stressed that the biennial election cycle of the House would impose a "restraint of frequent elections" that would create in representatives "an habitual recollection of their dependence on the people."[96] Members of the House of Representatives could "make no law which will not have its full operation on themselves and their friends, as well as on the great mass of the society," and this mutuality of position should be "deemed one of the strongest bonds by which human policy can connect the rulers and the people together. It creates between them that communion of interests and sympathy of sentiments . . . without which every government degenerates into tyranny."[97]

The contretemps between Madison and Brutus is worth careful attention, for it reveals aspects of representation that continue to be relevant to our own debates, more than two centuries later. Madison and Brutus agree that a representative government can fulfill the promise of self-government only if there is a close connection between representatives and their constituents. Madison and Brutus were each aware of the failed claims of the British Parliament to represent the people of America. They each knew that representative institutions can fulfill the ideal of self-government only if there is "reasonable ground for public trust" that representatives speak for the people who elect them.

In theorizing how representative institutions could be organized to create such trust, Madison stressed structural features like biennial elections and general legislation. He believed that such features would create incentives for representatives to connect with their constituents.[98] By contrast, Brutus argued that something more was needed, some personal connection between constituents and their representatives, or, failing that, some guarantee that the legislative body "should resemble those who appoint them—a representation of the people of America" that constitutes "a true likeness of the people."[99] Brutus feared that in the absence of a true likeness, the claim to representation "will not possess the confidence of the people."[100]

If Madison conceptualized representation from the perspective of the representative, Brutus did so from the perspective of the constituent. Brutus asked what would lead constituents to trust and identify with their representatives. Madison by contrast asked what would lead representatives to establish "that communion of interests and sympathy of sentiments . . . without which every government degenerates into tyranny." What is important for our purposes is that Madison and Brutus each agree that a successful system of representation depends upon a particular kind of *relationship* between representatives and constituents. They each agree that representative government cannot embody the value of self-government without trust and confidence between representatives and constituents,[101] such that the latter believe that they are indeed "represented" by the former.

I shall call this relationship *representative integrity*. Madison and Brutus each agree that representative integrity is necessary for a republic to fulfill the value of self-government. They each agree that representative integrity is a contingent empirical question, dependent in part upon the institutional design of elections.

IV.

In the first third of the nineteenth century, the framework of representative government in the United States was forced to adjust to the remarkable and unexpected collapse of the system of deference and hierarchy that had characterized the founding generation.[102] It is hard to overstate "the miraculous transformation" and the sheer "discontinuity" implied by this shift.[103] The rambunctious, egalitarian, and uncontrollable world so pungently described by Alexis de Tocqueville in *Democracy in America* could not remotely have been anticipated in 1789.

Having committed themselves to the principle of self-government, the Framers were prepared to accept the importance of public opinion. In his famous essay on the subject, James Madison candidly affirmed: "Public opinion sets bounds to every government, and is the real sovereign in every free one."[104] But Madison imagined public opinion as a two-way street. "As there are cases where the public opinion must be obeyed by the government, so there are cases where, not being fixed, it may be influenced by the government."[105] Madison believed that influencing public opinion was the task of "the class of literati," who "are the cultivators of the human mind—the manufacturers of useful knowledge—the agents of the commerce of ideas—the censors of public manners—the teachers of the arts of life and the means of happiness."[106]

An elite among elites, Madison "looked to the most thoughtful and virtuous citizens to keep the people informed about political activity at the seat of government."[107] This aspiration was inseparable from the republican stress on divided power, which gave time and opportunity for elites to inform and shape public opinion. As Hamilton put it candidly in *Federalist 72:*

> The republican principle demands that the deliberate sense of the community should govern the conduct of those to whom they intrust the management of their affairs; but it does not require an unqualified complaisance to every sudden breeze of passion, or to every transient impulse which the people may receive from the arts of men, who flatter their prejudices to betray their interests. It is a just observation, that the people commonly INTEND the PUBLIC GOOD. This often applies to their very errors. But their good sense would despise the adulator who should pretend that they always REASON RIGHT about the MEANS of promoting it. They know from experience that they sometimes err; and the wonder is that they so seldom err as they do, beset, as they continually are, by the wiles of parasites and sycophants, by the snares of the ambitious, the avaricious, the desperate, by the artifices of men who possess their confidence more than they deserve it, and of those who seek to possess rather than to deserve it. When occasions present themselves, in which the interests of the people are at variance with their inclinations, it is the duty of the persons whom they have appointed to be the guardians of those interests, to withstand the temporary delusion, in order to give them time and opportunity for more cool and sedate reflection.

By the time Tocqueville visited America in 1831, this relationship between representatives and constituents had been fundamentally undermined. As the democratic publicist William Leggett put it, "For our own part, we profess ourselves to be democrats in the fullest and largest sense of the word. . . . We are for a strictly popular Government. We have none of those fears, which some of our writers, copying the slang of the English aristocrats, profess to entertain of an 'unbalanced democracy.' We believe [in] when government in this country shall be a true reflection of public sentiment."[108] "It is really true," Leggett wrote, "that popular intelligence and virtue are the true source of all political power and the true basis of Government."[109]

The new faith in public sentiment reflected changes in "the social condition of the Americans," which had become "eminently democratic" and egalitarian.[110] During the Jacksonian era, the movement for universal white male suffrage triumphed.[111] Because the "superior classes of society" were "carefully exclude[d]" by the people "from the exercise of authority,"[112] Tocqueville theorized that "the power of the majority in America" became "not only preponderant, but irresistible."[113]

The overpowering tide of equality meant that in Jacksonian America "the people is . . . the real directing power; and although the form of government is representative, it is evident that the opinions, the prejudices, the interest, and even the passions of the community are hindered by no durable obstacles from exercising a perpetual influence on society."[114] As George Bancroft put it in his famous oration of July 4, 1826: "The popular voice is all powerful with us; this is our oracle; this, we acknowledge, is the voice of God."[115]

In the Framers' conception of representation, the people were most definitely not "the voice of God." The Framers assumed that representatives could earn the trust of their constituents because they were persons of independent means, public merit, and established character, whose calm reason would tame the impulsive passions of the people by filtering unsteady popular sentiments. But this framework of representation could not survive the new egalitarianism of the Jacksonian period, which exhibited a "faith in public opinion" that was downright hostile to the independent "intellectual authority" of right reason.[116] As the *United States Magazine and Democratic Review* proclaimed in its opening manifesto, "The general diffusion of education; the facility of access to every species of knowledge important to the great interests of the community; the freedom of the press, . . . make the pretensions of those self-styled 'better classes' to the sole possession of the requisite intelligence for the management of public affairs, too absurd to be entitled to any other treatment than an honest, manly contempt."[117]

If representatives could no longer depend upon the respect and deference of social inferiors, how might they maintain the trust and confidence of their constituents? They could become transparent instruments of the public will. In the words of Jacksonian congressman Thomas R. Mitchell, representatives should act "in accordance with the will of the People, in their representative capacity, and with representative responsibility."

What is the meaning of the word Representative? Does it not, *ex vi termini*, imply a power to create that Representative, and to govern and direct his action—he having no will but a political will, and that derived alone from those who invested him with the power of action? And, in view of our Government, the Representative is presumed, yea, intended, to do for the People that thing that the People would do were they personally present. But, if a Representative is to act according to his own will, in opposition to that of his constituents, whom does he represent, sir? He can only be the representative of himself. If the latter is the true meaning of the word Representative, I call upon the fathers and professors of literature to expunge the term from our vocabulary.[118]

Jacksonians fundamentally altered the Framers' concept of representative government. "Representative government necessarily implies the supremacy of the constituents over the agents to whom they have delegated their authority, and entrusted the management of their concerns. When it emanates, freely and in just proportions, from the whole people, it is as much a government of the people, as the more simple form of an immediate democracy. The only difference is, that in the one case the people act personally; in the other, by their substitutes."[119]

If individual representatives should become more like delegates, instructed by their constituents, then government as a whole ought also to become more responsive to the will of the majority. Yet this imperative ran headlong into the Founders' careful partition of power into "separate departments" to prevent the "abuse [of] what is granted."[120] The Founders had sought to reduce the vulnerability of government to the instability of popular opinion and to give time for elite representatives to assess and improve public sentiment. By the 1830s this calculated scheme of separation of powers had come to seem more like an unjustified impediment to the popular will. President Jackson himself proclaimed that "experience proves that in proportion as agents to execute the will of the people are multiplied there is danger of their wishes being frustrated. . . . [P]olicy requires that as few impediments as possible should exist to the free operation of the public will."[121]

The Framers' design for the federal government "was not by intention a democratic government. In plan and structure it had been meant to check the sweep and power of popular majorities."[122] By the 1830s the pressing question was no longer how to check popular majorities, but instead how to unleash the "popular power,"[123] how to make "all . . . dependent with equal directness and promptness on the influence of public opinion; the popular will should be equally the animating and moving spirit of them all, and ought never to find in any of its own creatures a self-imposed power, capable . . . of resisting itself, and defeating its own determined object."[124]

Jacksonian egalitarianism thus posed two deep challenges to the existing structure of representation. First, how could the people identify representatives who deserved their trust and confidence? The social distinctions assumed by the Framers to mark those most worthy of election had been swept away in the democratic tide of the 1830s.[125] All candidates for public office were now of potentially equal worth. Every candidate could claim to be a man of the people, with a background that mimicked the great democratic masses. It was during this time that the log cabin emerged as the symbol of popular authenticity for political candidates.[126] With the growth in national population, moreover, the electorate could not possibly possess firsthand experience of the individual quality of particular candidates. On what basis, then, could the electorate select representatives with whom they could sustain a "due connection"? How could representative integrity be maintained?

Second, how could even the most trustworthy representatives retain the confidence of the people, if their ability to affect government action was constrained by the separation of powers? If representatives needed to make government responsive to popular opinion in order to maintain a suitable "communion of interests and sympathy of sentiments" with their constituents, and if government responsiveness was paralyzed by the mechanical checks and balances so lovingly fashioned by the Framers, how could the connection between representation and self-government be sustained?

The invention of the second American party system proved a solution to both these challenges.[127] The Jacksonian era witnessed an upwelling of organized and disciplined political parties, replete with partisan rivalry and "party warfare."[128] "The Jacksonians . . . created the first mass democratic national political party in modern history."[129]

Elections were the crucial events for this new democracy, toward which all organizing efforts led. But elections were only the culmination of a continual effort to draw together the faithful. In place of the discarded nominating caucuses, the Jacksonians substituted a national network of committees, reaching up from the ward and township level to the quadrennial national convention, each a place where, at least in principle, the popular will would be determined and ratified. The political ferment continued almost year-round, with local committees calling regular meetings to approve local nominations, pass public resolutions, and mount elaborate processions.[130]

By the end of Jackson's second term, "Whigs and Democrats everywhere were nominated, campaigned, and were elected to Congress with their position on the [banking] issue known by everyone and with the expectation that they would later act accordingly."[131]

The new political parties functioned to connect voters directly with their representatives. Voters could choose among representatives based upon the platform and principles to which candidates were committed. Elections would thus turn less on the merit of individual candidates than on the political principles that candidates were pledged to support. These principles increasingly connected voters to representatives.[132]

"We call upon every man who professes to be animated with the principles of the democracy, to assist in accomplishing the great work of redeeming this country from the curse of our bad bank system," cried Democratic party publicist William Leggett.[133] Indignant that a party formed to protect "the labouring classes in vindication of their political principles" had been attacked as a "danger to the rights of person and property," Leggett asked:

> Is not this a government of the people, founded on the rights of the people, and instituted for the express object of guarding them against the encroachments and usurpations of power? And if they are not permitted the possession of common interest; the exercise of a common feeling; if they cannot combine to resist by constitutional means, these encroachments; to what purpose were they declared free to exercise the right of suffrage in the choice of rulers, and the making of laws?[134]

Building on theoretical work by Edmund Burke more than half a century earlier, Leggett defended "the importance and even dignity of party combination" because it furnished "the only certain means of carrying political principles into effect. When men agree in their theory of Government, they must also agree to act in concert, or no practical advantage can result from their accordance."[135]

Parties could also solve the problem of government responsiveness. Writing at the dawn of the twentieth century, Woodrow Wilson observed that the Framers' constitutional commitment to separation of powers had so successfully prevented "the will of the people as a whole from having at any moment an unobstructed sweep and ascendency,"[136] that democratic aspirations for responsiveness could succeed only through "the closely knit imperative discipline of party, a body that has no constitutional cleavages and is free to tie itself into legislative and executive functions alike by its systematic control of the *personnel* of all branches of the government."[137] Parties were "absolutely necessary to . . . give some coherence to the action of political forces,"[138] for without parties "it would hardly have been possible for the voters of the country to be united in truly national judgments upon national questions."[139] "It is only by elections, by the filling of offices, that parties test and maintain their hold upon public opinion."[140]

During the Jacksonian era, political parties became the medium through which "the absolute sovereignty of the majority" could exercise its dominion.[141] The implications for institutions of representation were profound. The invention of party nominating conventions, together with presidential electors selected by political parties pledged in advance to vote for party candidates, "wrested control of the presidency away from Congress by forging an independent, popular electoral base for the President."[142] Party affiliation became inseparable from the "chain of communication" connecting constituents to representatives. Voters no longer needed to possess personal knowledge of the character and beliefs of individual candidates, as Brutus had imagined. Voters could instead select representatives based upon their party principles. The party vouched for the integrity of its candidates. By voting for a party, the electorate could seek to make government responsive to the principles espoused by the party.

The voter, Robert La Follette would later say, "gives support to that party which promises to do the specific things that he regards of the highest importance to the state and to the welfare of every citizen. . . . Upon its promise and his support the party has become the custodian of his political rights. . . . [T]he party is bound to keep its pledged word. . . . This measures its value as a power for good in representative government."[143] Upon this mutual understanding, political parties became a solution for the problem of representative integrity.[144] They enabled representatives and constituents to maintain the "communion of interests and sympathy of sentiments" necessary for representative government to fulfill the ideal of self-government.*

V.

No doubt there are multiple ways in which parties can enable constituents to identify with their representatives. A movement party, capable of mobilizing mass appeal through its distinctive platform and principles, might be one such structure. Examples would include the Democratic Party of Andrew Jackson and Franklin Roosevelt, or the Republican Party of Abraham Lincoln or Ronald Reagan.

---

* From the perspective of representatives, the Jacksonian era marked the moment when party discipline became an indispensable proxy for popular sentiment. In practice this meant that representatives became beholden not only to their constituents but also to their party. The dual loyalty could become especially confusing in moments when public opinion and party loyalty diverged. And of course the responsibility of representatives to exercise their own independent judgment had never (and could never) entirely disappear. Consider in this regard the dilemma of poor Congressman Gayton Osgood, a Democrat from Massachusetts:

> Mr. Osgood said it was always an unpleasant task for a Representative to oppose the wishes of any portion of his constituents. Considering himself as the organ of their will, he cannot, without many painful sensations of regret, find his own sentiments in opposition to theirs. But the diversity of human opinion . . . must often render it necessary for him to gratify the wishes of one part of his constituents at the risk of displeasing the rest. Nor will he always be able to find out what the wishes of a majority of his constituents really are. As to the general course of his official duties, if he has openly avowed his adherence to a political party, if he has been chosen with a knowledge on the part of his constituents of his political predilections, he may safely conclude that a concurrence with the measures of his party will not be obnoxious to those who elected him. But a new state of things may arise, unexpected events may happen, unforeseen measures may be proposed, a different course of policy may be instituted, and the vote that sanctioned his adherence to his party at the time of his election may fail to sustain him in this new junction of events, and he will be compelled to resort to some other criterion to determine the wishes of his constituents. If . . . the measure proposed . . . rouse into opposition the adherents of a political party, he will be liable to be led astray by the overheated exertions of its opponents, and to mistake the noisy clamor of a few zealous partisans for the real, sober, and permanent sense of the community. And when the excitement has passed away, and the momentary passions which created it have subsided, he will find, to his mortification and regret, that in obeying the instructions of self-constituted conventions, and in listening to the dictations of interested memorialists, he has overlooked the opinions of the less obtrusive, but not the less enlightened portion of his constituents—that he has gone contrary to the wishes, and, what is more, to the welfare of his district.

Cong. Globe, 23d Cong., 1st Sess. 363–364 (1834).

In the decades after the Civil War, however, American political parties began to lose their character as ideological movements. Although political parties remained necessary to connect elected officials to their constituents,[145] they came increasingly to seem organizations devoted chiefly to maintaining their own hold on power. National parties deployed ever more effective networks of local political operatives to oversee polling places, compose and print party tickets, turn out voters, and ensure that voters elected the right candidates.[146] These party functionaries required support, which in turn required the distribution of patronage jobs.[147] Reconstruction-era reformers bemoaned the grip of patronage-driven party organizations.[148] Stripped of the raiment of ideological mobilization, parties came ever closer to appearing as organizations devoted merely to "the interests of getting or keeping the patronage of the government."

> The great parties are the Republicans and the Democrats. What are their principles, their distinctive tenets, their tendencies? Which of them is for tariff reform, for the further extension of civil service reform, for a spirited foreign policy, for the regulation of railroads and telegraphs by legislation, for changes in the currency, for any other of the twenty issues which one hears discussed in the country as seriously involving its welfare?
>
> This is what a European is always asking of intelligent Republicans and intelligent Democrats. He is always asking because he never gets an answer. The replies leave him in deeper perplexity. After some months the truth begins to dawn upon him. Neither party has, as a party, anything definite to say on these issues; neither party has any clean-cut principles, any distinctive tenets. Both have traditions. Both claim to have tendencies. Both have certainly war cries, organizations, interests, enlisted in their support. But those interests are in the main the interests of getting or keeping the patronage of the government. Distinctive tenets and policies, points of political doctrine and points of political practice, have all but vanished. They have not been thrown away, but have been stripped away by Time and the progress of events, fulfilling some policies, blotting out others. All has been lost, except office or the hope of it.[149]

The Gilded Age was nevertheless a period of "strong partisan loyalties and massive voter turnout."[150] It "was distinguished by the dominance of political parties."[151] "[P]arties shaped campaigns and elections into popular spectacles featuring widespread participation and celebration.

Three-quarters of the nation's adult male citizens voted in presidential elections and nearly two-thirds also participated in off-year contests. Most of them cast straight tickets conveniently supplied by the party organizations. . . . [I]t is probable that the great majority of adult males voted honestly, enthusiastically, and partisanly."[152]

Party loyalty was composed of many factors, including "ethnoreligious" identification and the distribution of "resources and privileges to individuals and groups."[153] Journalist William L. Riordon records of Tammany district leader George Plunkitt that it was "his belief that argument and campaign literature have never gained votes."[154] Tammany instead maintained partisan fidelity by offering a steady stream of constituent services.[155]

We shall probably never settle on an explanation of how party identification was sustained during the Gilded Age. The point I wish to stress, however, is that parties of the time could not have solved the problem of representative integrity unless they *in fact* maintained this identification. Without party identification, political parties cannot ensure the "necessary sympathy between [the people] and their rulers and officers" which alone transforms representation into an effective instrument of self-governance.

The point is illustrated by the periodic eruptions of third-party mobilization that broke out during the Gilded Age. A "common element" of such movements was the "preponderance of *anti*-party thought and culture."[156] Third parties characteristically denounced "the political machinery of the dominant party used to defeat the will of the people."[157] In 1886 Henry George's insurgent platform announced that "Independent political action affords the only hope of exposing and breaking the extortion and speculation by which a standing army of professional politicians corrupt the public whom they plunder."[158]

Even when third parties managed to elect members of Congress, they discovered that institutional rules, created by the two dominant parties, effectively rendered them "unable to speak on the floor, to gain assignments to important or relevant committees, to introduce measures, have them reported, or bring them to a vote."[159] One Iowa Populist newspaper wondered "whether it will ever again be possible for the people to govern themselves through representatives,"[160] concluding bitterly in another article that "representative government is a failure."[161] The very "intense partisanship, party patronage, and distributive policy making" that made possible "the regime of party government"[162] during the Gilded Age functioned to deny self-government to those who felt excluded from that regime.

It is commonly accepted that the framework of party government that characterized the Gilded Age collapsed sometime around the closing years of the nineteenth century. "[B]etween the 1890s and the 1920s, the lights dimmed in the great showcase of nineteenth century democracy: the extraordinary public outpourings to electioneer and to elect. In national contests, turnouts declined from around 80 percent of the eligible voters in 1896 to under 50 percent in 1924."[163] "As turnout declined, a larger and larger component of the still-active electorate moved from a core to a peripheral position, and the hold of the parties over their mass base appreciably deteriorated," causing a "revolutionary contraction in the size and diffusion in the shape of the voting universe," affecting "both the national and state levels."[164]

In part, the loss of voters was the result of deliberate "efforts to disfranchise alleged discordant social elements" by enacting "measures to restrict suffrage."[165] Southern exclusion of black voters is exemplary, but states everywhere sought to curtail voting through strict registration requirements, poll taxes, and the like.[166] For our purposes, however, the most important dimension of the altered political universe of the twentieth century was its deep disillusion with political parties as a medium of self-governance. Like the many third parties of the Gilded Age, like the Mugwumps who were their direct intellectual and social predecessors,[167] Progressives came to see parties as an obstruction to self-government.

Political parties had saved representative institutions in the United States in the 1830s. When the electorate lost confidence in political parties at the turn of the century, representative institutions were profoundly threatened. The Progressive era was marked by a "growing popular distrust of the representative system whereon both federal and State governments are based."[168] "The American people are drifting towards a general loss of faith in representative government. . . . One of the most universal causes of complaint is the tendency [of legislative assemblies] to play party politics instead of regarding purely the welfare of the whole community."[169]

Whereas in an earlier political universe the political party had connected voters to government, in the Progressive era the party came to be viewed as a mere "political machine": "It rules caucuses, names delegates, appoints committees, . . . dictates nominations, makes platforms, dispenses patronage, directs state administrations, controls legislatures, stifles opposition, punishes independence and elects United States Senators. . . . Having no constituency to serve, it serves itself."[170] And, most troubling to Progressives, "the corporation now makes terms direct with the machine."[171]

The analysis of the influential political scientist J. Allen Smith is illustrative. He wrote that the political party "professes of course, to stand for the principle of majority rule, but in practice it has become . . . one of the most potent checks on the majority."[172] Smith observed that the American system of separation of powers, in contrast to European parliamentary systems, meant that a political party could only rarely achieve "control of the government"[173] and hence could "not be held accountable for failure to carry out its ante-election pledges."[174] As a consequence the party platform "ceases to be a serious declaration of political principles. It comes to be regarded as a means of winning elections rather than a statement of what the party is obligated to accomplish."[175] Parties are thus essentially "misrepresentative."[176] Lacking popular discipline, they fall under the sway "of the professional politician who, claiming to represent the masses, really owes his preferment to those who subsidize the party machine."[177]

Smith spoke for his age when he characterized the political party as a machine for cynically attracting the votes necessary to justify its own continued subsidy and support.[178] By controlling nominations to public office, by controlling the actions of public officials, the party came to be regarded as a vehicle for "unscrupulous politicians" to sell protection to "corporate wealth."[179] "The party, though claiming to represent the people, is not in reality a popular organ. Its chief object has come to be the perpetuation of minority control, which makes possible protection and advancement of those powerful private interests to whose co-operation and support the party boss is indebted for his continuance in power."[180] Hence "the growth of that distinctively American product, the party machine, with its political bosses, its army of paid workers and its funds for promoting or opposing legislation, supplied by various special interests which expect to profit thereby. . . . We encounter its malign influence every time an effort is made to secure any adequate regulation of railways, to protect the people against the extortion of the trusts, or to make the great privileged industries of the country bear their just share of taxation."[181]

Progressivism was an effort to master the consequences of the immense economic growth that had engulfed the nation. Smith's analysis exemplified an essential progressive insight, which was that "businessmen systematically corrupted politics."[182] The problem was not merely "the product of misbehavior by 'bad' men," but the predictable "outcome of identifiable economic and political forces."[183] "There is not one of our states which has not, to a very considerable extent, come under the baneful influence of this system, by means of which the political life of the people is dominated and exploited for private ends by rich working corporations in alliance with professional party politicians."[184]

The eminent Wisconsin sociologist Edward A. Ross laid down the basic principle: *"The force devoted to wresting government from the people will correspond to the magnitude of the pecuniary interest at stake."*[185] The incentives to undermine popular sovereignty grew precisely as did the "magnitude of the interest affected by the action of government."[186] "The railroads want to avert rate regulation and to own the State board of equalization. The gas and street railway companies want . . . the authorization of fifty-year franchises and immunity from taxation of franchises. . . . Manufacturers want the unrestricted use of child labor. Mining companies dread short-hour legislation. . . . The baking-powder trust wants rival powders outlawed. . . . The shipping interests are after subsidies."[187] The list was endless. Corporations sought to prosper in brutally competitive markets by using political parties to produce laws that would give them an economic edge.[188]

Progressives offered a two-pronged approach to counter the economic capture of representative government. They sought to regulate business and they sought to restructure politics.[189] Jacksonians concerned about the possible corruption of politics by corporations had insisted that government withdraw completely from entanglements with business. Progressives did not have this option, because they could not ignore the massive and pervasive consequences of economic development.

With regard to business, therefore, Progressives pushed for a "regulatory revolution" in order to establish "effective regulatory boards—progressivism's most distinctive governmental achievement."[190] As a means of insulating regulation from the control of the party machine, they sought to distinguish administration from politics, a strategy that Woodrow Wilson had advocated as early as 1887.[191] Progressives conceived regulation as a form of administration answerable to expertise rather than to public opinion. "Administration lies outside the proper sphere of *politics*. Administrative questions are not political questions. Although politics sets the tasks for administration, it should not be suffered to manipulate its offices."[192] In contrast to the Jacksonians, and analogously to the founding generation, Progressives placed their faith in the intelligence and competence of an educated minority.

With regard to politics, Progressives pursued multiple strategies for preserving representative integrity. On the most basic level, they sought to sever ties between corporations and politics, enacting statutes that were the direct ancestors of the legislation found unconstitutional a century later in *Citizens United*.[193] As early as 1894, the irreproachable Elihu Root, a "conservative of conservatives,"[194] had proposed amending the New York State Constitution to prohibit corporate campaign contributions and expenditures. "The idea," Root said,

> is to prevent the great moneyed corporations from furnishing the money with which to elect members of the legislature of this state, in order that those members of the legislature may vote to protect the corporations. It is to prevent the great railroad companies, the great insurance companies, the great telephone companies, the great aggregations of wealth, from using their corporate funds, directly or indirectly to send members of the legislature to these halls, in order to vote for their protection and the advancement of their interests as against those of the public.
>
> It strikes . . . at the constantly growing evil in our political affairs, which has, in my judgment, done more to shake the confidence of the plain people of small means in our political institutions, than any other practice which has ever obtained since the foundation of our government. . . .
>
> It is precisely because laws aimed directly at the crime of bribery so far have been ineffective, that we deem it advisable to provide limitations short of the actual commission of the crime. . . . I think it will be a protection to corporations and to candidates against demands made upon them.[195]

Root's motion failed, but in 1909 New York enacted a statute "substantially in the words" of Root's original proposed amendment.[196] In 1910 in his famous address on the New Nationalism in Osawatomie, Kansas, Theodore Roosevelt was equally explicit:

> The Constitution guarantees protection to property, and we must make that promise good. But it does not give the right of suffrage to any corporation. . . .

The citizens of the United States must effectively control the mighty commercial forces which they have themselves called into being.

There can be no effective control of corporations while their political activity remains. . . . It is necessary that laws should be passed to prohibit the use of corporate funds directly or indirectly for political purposes; it is still more necessary that such laws should be thoroughly enforced. Corporate expenditures for political purposes, and especially such expenditures by public service corporations, have supplied one of the principal sources of corruption in our political affairs. . . .

If our political institutions were perfect, they would absolutely prevent the political domination of money in any part of our affairs. We need to make our political representatives more quickly and sensitively responsive to the people whose servants they are. . . .

One of the fundamental necessities in a representative government such as ours is to make certain that the men to whom the people delegate their power shall serve the people by whom they are elected, and not the special interests. I believe that every national officer, elected or appointed, should be forbidden to perform any service or receive any compensation, directly or indirectly, from interstate corporations; and a similar provision could not fail to be useful within the states.[197]

Progressives sought not merely to staunch the flow of money from business into politics; they sought also to diminish the role of political parties in political governance.[198] The movement for the direct election of senators should be regarded in this light.[199] So should the movement for direct primaries,[200] which empowered voters "to select directly candidates without intervention of caucus or convention or domination of machines."[201] The effort was to bring candidates "face to face" with the voter, so that politicians would be "directly accountable to the citizen" and not to "the political machine of his party."[202] "The chief object of direct primaries and of other proposals for the democratization of the party is to break up the alliance between corrupt business and corrupt politics."[203] Signature innovations of the Progressive era like the referendum, the initiative, and the recall also sought to liberate politics from the control of political parties.[204]

In all these reforms, Progressives expressed their "distrust in representative government."[205] They were "part of the great movement which has been going on now in these recent years throughout the country, and in which our people have been drifting away from their trust in representative government."[206] Underlying this distrust was the loss of faith in parties as faithful vehicles of popular will.[207] The hope was to "abate the rigor of our party system, break the crushing and stifling power of our great party machines, and give freer play to the political ideas, aspirations, opinions and feelings of the people."[208] Progressives sought to create institutional forms in which public opinion could directly express itself, without the need of intermediation.[209] They hoped to fashion a government efficiently and transparently responsive to majority will.[210] In Richard Hofstadter's famous formulation, Progressives "wanted to bring about direct popular rule, break up the political machines, and circumvent representative government."[211]

The pathos of Progressive reforms, however, is that they were advanced within a structure of government that would inevitably remain representative. Every official nominated directly by the people in a primary would remain, after election, a representative. Every senator directly elected by the people would remain, after election, a representative. And all recognized that initiatives and referenda could never substitute for the routine and ordinary legislation that would remain securely in the hands of elected representatives.[212]

Although they sought to connect government more directly with the people, Progressives could not escape the challenge of representation. They could not avoid the problem of how representatives might preserve the trust and confidence of their constituents. The question that loomed large at the outset of the twentieth century was how the necessary "chain of communication" between representatives and the people could be sustained in the absence of political parties. How could self-government survive?

VI.

The answer to this question emerged from the Progressive era in a manner that was neither anticipated nor designed. It took the form of a fundamental constitutional transformation that has proved so pervasive, so quiet, so unassuming, that it has scarcely been noticed. The transformation underlies a contemporary decision like *Citizens United*, although in that decision, as in most modern constitutional law, the transformation is inhabited as if it were without history or context.

Tocqueville knew that in a democratic society, public opinion must rule. He conceived public opinion as pressing "with enormous weight upon the mind of each individual; it surrounds, directs, and oppresses him; and this arises from the very constitution of society, much more than from its political laws."[213] A half century later James Bryce also realized that "in no country is public opinion so powerful as in the United States,"[214] so much so that America could aptly be termed a "government by public opinion," in which "the will of the people acts directly and constantly upon its executive and legislative agents."[215]

Bryce observed that "Government by popular opinion exists where the wishes and views of the people prevail, even before they have been conveyed through the regular law-appointed organs, and without the need of their being so conveyed."[216] He conceded that public opinion might be difficult to ascertain,[217] but he nevertheless insisted that "public opinion can with truth be said not only to reign but to govern. . . . The . . . sovereign is not the less a sovereign because his commands are sometimes misheard or misreported. In America every one listens for them. Those who manage the affairs of the country obey to the best of their hearing."[218] He noticed that although "opinion declares itself legally through elections," it "is at work at other times also, and has other methods of declaring itself."[219] Elections are only an "intermittent mechanism," whereas public opinion is "constantly active" and "in the long run" can exercise "a great and growing influence."[220]

Most importantly, government by public opinion altered the attitude of the American public. Their "habit of breathing as well as helping to form public opinion . . . cultivates, develops, trains the average American. It gives him a sense of personal responsibility stronger, because more constant, than exists in those free countries of Europe where he commits his power to a legislature."[221] In contrast to Tocqueville, Bryce conceived public opinion as liberating rather than as oppressive. The average American "has a sense of ownership in the government, and therewith a kind of independence of manner as well as of mind very different from the demissness of the humbler classes of the Old World."[222]

The "sense of ownership" observed by Bryce can be said to underwrite "that communion of interests and sympathy of sentiments . . . without which every government degenerates into tyranny," which Madison long ago knew to be essential for self-government. The "sense of ownership" connected Americans to their government, in much the same way that political parties aimed to do. And it did so through a medium that was independent of the institutional organization of elections.

So long as public officials were continuously attuned to the content of public opinion, and so long as Americans actively participated in the formation of public opinion, Americans could imagine their government, and its elected officials, as responsive to them.[223] Bryce did not suggest that public opinion formation could displace the accountability created by a regular election process, but he did emphasize that it was an independent avenue for forging a direct relationship of ownership with the state.

Progressives like John Dewey[224] and M. P. Follett[225] would eventually develop and theorize this insight. But it was the cofounder of the *New Republic,* Herbert Croly, who most explicitly pondered its implications for self-government.[226] Croly stressed the distinction "between the 'electorate' and the 'people.' "[227] The electorate is necessary because "in a democracy organized for action some agency must be provided to decide what immediate action is to be taken."[228] But elections are neither the beginning nor the end of self-government. "The finality of any particular decision must not be taken too seriously. The decisions of an electorate are frankly tentative and revocable. . . . The really effective sovereign power is to be found in public opinion, and public opinion is always in the making. It is always, that is, essentially active. Its sovereignty is wholesome in so far as its activity is determined by a sufficiency of information, the ability to understand and face the really pertinent facts, and real integrity of purpose."[229]

In the eighteenth century, when people had to physically assemble in order to create an informed public opinion, democratic self-government may not have been possible. But now advances in communication have enabled people to keep

in constant touch with one another by means of the complicated agencies of publicity and intercourse which are afforded by the magazines, the press and the like. The active citizenship of the country meets every morning and evening and discusses the affairs of the nation with the newspaper as an impersonal interlocutor. Public opinion has a thousand methods of seeking information and obtaining definite and effective expression which it did not have four generations ago. . . . Under such conditions the discussions which take place in a Congress or a Parliament no longer possess their former function. They no longer create and guide what public opinion there is. Their purpose rather is to provide a mirror for public opinion, to advertise and illuminate its constituent ideas and purposes, and to confront the advocates of those ideas with the discipline of effective resistance and, perhaps, with the responsibilities of power. Phases of public opinion form, develop, gather to a head, assert their power and find their place chiefly by the activity of other more popular unofficial agencies.[230]

Elihu Root, who believed profoundly in the virtues of representative government, had advised citizens that their "first and chief duty" is "to serve in the ranks" of political parties, so that they can make "the difference between popular self-government and popular submission to an absolute monarch."[231] For Croly, by contrast, active citizenship involved effective participation in the formation of public opinion,[232] which can create an immediate form of self-governance "which is, or may become, superior to that which . . . formerly obtained by virtue of occasional popular assemblages."[233] Government by public opinion does not require parties, because it creates an independent mechanism by which the public can instruct their government and hold it accountable.

Croly perceived that participating in the formation of public opinion could create a kind of self-government that was different from a representative republic. He used the term "direct democracy" to characterize this form of self-government,[234] because it involved a direct relationship between each citizen and the state, a relationship unmediated by elected officials. But because he also sensed that public opinion was itself incapable of any sustained action other than "being educational,"[235] of maintaining its own "ultimate social cohesion" through "popular intelligence, sympathy and faith,"[236] he concluded that direct democracy could not entirely displace representative institutions. There would always be a need for "some method of representation which will be efficient and responsible enough to carry out a social policy."[237]

Croly ultimately determined that America needed "both an efficient system of representation and an efficient method of direct popular supervision."[238] "The two different methods of government [are] supplementary and mutually interdependent. . . . Direct government has come to stay and is entitled to stay, but it cannot dispense with the use of representative agencies."[239] The challenge facing the nation was to structure the "phases of the relationship which ought to obtain between direct and representative government."[240]

Lodging self-governance in public opinion solved two great theoretical difficulties of representative government. First, it explained how the people could come to identify with specific candidates for office. Public opinion established a "chain of communication" through which the public could hold candidates accountable. Elected officials could be expected, in Bryce's words, to obey public opinion "to the best of their hearing." The task was to fashion institutions that would encourage such attentiveness. Among these institutions were elections, which would reward representatives who were responsive to public opinion and punish those who were not.

Second, identifying self-government with public opinion could solve the problem of separation of powers. Like political parties, public opinion addressed the entire government. By simultaneously affecting all public officials, it could create its own form of immanent coordination across the divided branches of government. Croly himself believed that a strong executive was institutionally best suited to serve the "proper and natural function of giving effective expression to the will of the temporarily preponderant weight of public opinion,"[241] and that it was therefore necessary to "increase . . . executive authority and responsibility."[242] His thinking in this regard, as in many others, was deeply prescient of political developments in the last century.

Croly's discussion of the relationship between self-government and public opinion consists of distinct logical strands that should be carefully separated. On one level, Croly believed that public opinion offered a solution to the specific problem of representative integrity. Public opinion could connect representatives to their constituencies, even in the absence of party identification.[243] Defining representative integrity in terms of responsiveness to public opinion is particularly attractive when partisan identities promoted by political parties are weak and insubstantial.[244] At another level, however, Croly understood that attributing the "really effective sovereign power" to public opinion made possible forms of self-governance that bypassed representative institutions and so transcended the very idea of representative integrity. Croly envisioned the possibility of specifically *democratic* versions of self-government. Croly and his generation of American Progressives were drawn to the possibility that the people could speak directly in their own voice.

Croly was attracted to two distinct and incompatible versions of democratic self-government. Sometimes Croly meant by direct democracy the capacity of the people to act in an unmediated fashion, as when public opinion is translated directly into law through the institution of the initiative. At other times Croly meant by direct democracy the capacity of the people to participate in an "essentially active" public opinion that is "always in the making." Used in this latter sense, direct democracy does not refer to government action but to communicative processes in which an ever-changing population continuously articulates its ever-evolving experience. I shall henceforth reserve the term *direct democracy* for the first meaning, which denotes government institutions capable of directly enacting public will. I shall use the term *discursive democracy* to refer to the second meaning, which conceives public opinion as "always in the making" rather than as decisive.

Direct democracy is familiar to students of progressivism. It is exemplified by institutions like initiatives, referenda, and recalls. The ambition of direct democracy is to unleash the unmediated authority of popular judgment.[245] But because direct democracy cannot displace ordinary mechanisms of electoral representation, because "great communities cannot be governed by permanent town meetings,"[246] the scope of direct democracy is intrinsically limited and quite circumscribed. It can exercise the authority of self-government only episodically and intermittently. Although laws may occasionally be enacted by popular initiatives, the vast bulk of quotidian government business must remain in the hands of ordinary representative institutions.

By contrast *discursive democracy* imagines that, as Bryce put it, public opinion "rules as a pervading and impalpable power, like the ether which . . . passes through all things. It binds all the parts of the complicated system together and gives them whatever unity of aim and action they possess."[247] Within discursive democracy, public opinion is conceived as a process that is constantly in flux. Like Heraclitus's river, it is a stream that is always moving and never twice repeated. Understood in this way, public opinion is unremitting and ubiquitous. It surrounds and envelops government, holding it continuously but indirectly accountable. Public opinion is the incessant muffled voice that elected officials always strain to hear and interpret.[248]

Discursive democracy postulates that by participating in the ongoing and never-ending formation of public opinion, and by establishing institutions designed to make government continuously responsive to public opinion, the people might come to develop a "sense of ownership" of "their" government and so enjoy the benefit of self-government. This ownership is not confined to the episodic ritual of elections but is, in Bryce's words, "constantly active" and always influencing "executive and legislative agents." I shall henceforth call this ongoing process of ownership *democratic legitimation*.[249]

Herbert Croly, like most Progressives, was quite comfortable with the idea of direct democracy.[250] He could easily imagine institutions capable of yielding pure and unmediated representations of popular will. Progressives supported "direct nominations, the recall, the initiative, the referendum," because of "the directness of their appeal to the rule of the majority."[251] But Progressives of Croly's generation could never quite grasp the basic implications of discursive democracy.[252] At root this is because prewar Progressives were interested primarily in "a democracy organized for action."[253]

Public opinion can direct state action only if it is represented in an explicit and definitive way. Within direct democracy, we construct the identity of public opinion with this goal in mind. We conduct elections or polls, and we let the results of these interventions stand metonymically for the decisive substance of public opinion. But if public opinion is instead imagined as "always in the making," it must necessarily elude any such clear and static representation. A poll or an election can at most offer a glimpse of what public opinion may once have been at some moment in the past. If public opinion is constantly changing, the representations of a poll or of an election are outdated from the instant of their release. Such representations, moreover, can never capture the full complexity of public opinion. Polls and elections are merely schematic and partial instruments, profoundly influenced by the questions they pose, by the choice of candidates they offer, by the timing of their intervention, and so on. That is why the significance of elections or polls is always subject to further debate and controversy.

Within discursive democracy, therefore, public opinion can be known only indirectly. Although within discursive democracy public opinion is omnipresent and pervasive, its influence on governance is inherently mediated. There are always contested interpretations about what the true substance of public opinion actually is. Because a continuously evolving public opinion is for this reason not a fit instrument for concrete decision making, discursive democracy remained of secondary interest for Croly and other prewar Progressives. They could glimpse the theoretical possibility of conceiving public opinion as a continuous process, but they could never concentrate on it long enough to appreciate its institutional entailments.

At least some of these entailments have now become apparent to us. If participation in the ongoing formation of public opinion is to serve as a foundation for democratic self-government, all must have an equal right to participate in the communicative processes by which public opinion is formed.[254] All must be entitled to participate "in deliberation" because "political decisions are characteristically imposed on all."[255] We enshrine these entitlements in constitutional communicative rights, which we regard as distinct from, and as more essential than, any particular or momentary representation of public opinion. We use communicative rights to define the processes that produce public opinion *as such*.

Like most of his Progressive peers, Croly in the years before World War I was quite hostile to the notion of entrenched constitutional rights.[256] He remained instead entranced by the ideal of direct democracy, enamored of the possibility of an unobstructed and undistorted representation of majority will. This ideal became increasingly less attractive as the twentieth century matured, and as fascist and totalitarian regimes, claiming the authority of popular acclamation, began to corrupt the very communicative processes necessary to create public opinion. Those who looked to public opinion as a foundation for self-government responded by advocating for communicative rights as a check against these aggrandizing tendencies of direct democracy. They began to conclude that the authority of public opinion lies less in its immediate expression than in the integrity of the processes by which it is formed. The consequent focus on rights to define this integrity signified a turn to the paradigm of discursive democracy.

In the United States this process of disenchantment began suddenly in the years after World War I, when massive government censorship[257] and propaganda[258] starkly revealed the vulnerability of public opinion to official manipulation. The startling vulnerability made salient and convincing the need to reestablish "freedom of discussion, for without freedom of discussion there is no public opinion that deserves the name."[259] In the decades after World War I, a consensus began to form around the proposition that freedom of discussion, which is the essence of self-government, could be guaranteed only through constitutional rights.[260] Progressives began to recognize, as John Dewey and James Tufts wrote in the second (but not the first 1908) edition of their volume *Ethics,* "Liberty to think, inquire, discuss, is central in the whole group of rights which are secured in theory to individuals in a democratic organization."[261]

It is at this time that justices of the Supreme Court first recognized judicially enforceable First Amendment rights.[262] Although the United States had always enjoyed a robust civic culture celebrating freedom of speech,[263] judicial protection for First Amendment rights did not begin to emerge until the decades after World War I. Before that time "the overwhelming majority of . . . decisions in all jurisdictions rejected free speech claims, often by ignoring their existence. No court was more unsympathetic to freedom of expression than the Supreme Court, which rarely produced even a dissenting opinion in a First Amendment case."[264]

The dominant nineteenth-century interpretation of the First Amendment, summarized in 1907 by Justice Oliver Wendell Holmes, was that its "main purpose . . . is 'to prevent all such previous restraints upon publications as had been practised by other governments,'" and that it did "not prevent the subsequent punishment of such as may be deemed contrary to the public welfare."[265] In his 1893 book *Lectures on the Constitution of the United States,* Justice Samuel Miller did not even bother to comment on the freedom of speech provisions of the First Amendment, preferring instead to offer a few sentences on freedom of religion.[266] It was not until the pathbreaking dissent of Justice Holmes in November 1919 in *Abrams v. United States* that a coherent and sustained judicial theory of the First Amendment began to develop.[267]

In explaining the basis for First Amendment rights, Holmes used rhetoric that emphasized the necessity of a "free trade in ideas," because "the best test of truth is the power of the thought to get itself accepted in the competition of the market."[268] Holmes always wrote in the context of the suppression of political opinion, so his theorization of First Amendment rights should be understood as bounded by the circumstances of political deliberation. The point is not so much that First Amendment rights are necessary for the cognitive attainment of truth as that a free trade in ideas is necessary for determining what a democracy ought to do.[269]

The connection between First Amendment rights and the principle of self-governance was first explicitly discussed in 1920 in a Supreme Court opinion by Justice Louis Brandeis, who in dissent wrote:

> The right of a citizen of the United States to take part, for his own or the country's benefit, in the making of federal laws and in the conduct of the government, necessarily includes the right to speak or write about them; to endeavor to make his own opinion concerning laws existing or contemplated prevail; and, to this end, to teach the truth as he sees it. Were this not so, "the right of the people to assemble for the purpose of petitioning Congress for a redress of grievance or for anything else connected with the powers or duties of the national government" would be a right totally without substance. . . . Full and free exercise of this right by the citizen is ordinarily also his duty; for its exercise is more important to the nation

than it is to himself. Like the course of the heavenly bodies, harmony in national life is a resultant of the struggle between contending forces. In frank expression of conflicting opinion lies the greatest promise of wisdom in governmental action; and in suppression lies ordinarily the greatest peril.[270]

Brandeis is clear that freedom of speech is a pathway to self-government. Freedom of speech allows each citizen personally "to endeavor to make his own opinion concerning laws existing or contemplated prevail." So long as "governmental action" is responsive to "the resultant of the struggle between contending forces," each citizen can directly take part "in the conduct of the government." In effect, Brandeis imagines communicative rights as establishing the form of self-governance associated with discursive democracy. Seven years later Brandeis would defend First Amendment rights as "essential to effective democracy."[271] "Those who won our independence believed . . . that public discussion is a political duty; and that this should be a fundamental principle of the American government."[272]

It was on the foundation of Brandeis's conception of the First Amendment that the Court in the 1930s began to erect the structure of First Amendment doctrine. In the spare and muscular prose of Chief Justice Hughes's pioneering 1931 opinion in *Stromberg v. California*: "The maintenance of the opportunity for free political discussion to the end that government may be responsive to the will of the people and that changes may be obtained by lawful means, an opportunity essential to the security of the Republic, is a fundamental principle of our constitutional system."[273]

For the last eighty years, First Amendment jurisprudence has been founded on the premise that "speech concerning public affairs is . . . the essence of self-government."[274] The Court has repeatedly emphasized that the First Amendment exemplifies a "profound national commitment" to the principle that "debate on public issues should be uninhibited, robust, and wide-open."[275] "Speech on public issues occupies the 'highest rung of the hierarchy of First Amendment values' and is entitled to special protection,"[276] because "discussion of public issues and debate on the qualifications of candidates are integral to the operation of the system of government established by our Constitution."[277] "[T]he First Amendment serves to ensure that the individual citizen can effectively participate in and contribute to our republican system of self-government."[278]

The First Amendment protects speech not primarily to sustain representative integrity but instead, as Brandeis contemplated, to enable persons to become directly involved "in the conduct of the government." To understand First Amendment doctrine, therefore, and especially the kind of doctrine that is relevant to a decision like *Citizens United,* we must conceive First Amendment rights as designed to protect the processes of democratic legitimation required for discursive democracy.[279] As the Court just recently affirmed, "rights protected by the First Amendment" safeguard "our Nation's commitment to self-government" by defining "'an open marketplace' in which differing ideas about political, economic, and social issues can compete freely for public acceptance without improper government interference."[280]

The precise nature and scope of First Amendment rights are of course controversial. We debate endlessly about how the First Amendment ought to apply to particular circumstances. If the historical account I have just offered is accurate, however, these controversies should be adjudicated according to the needs of democratic legitimation. When we argue about the content of First Amendment rights, we debate how best to advance the value of self-government in the context of ongoing public discussion.

It is for this reason that we celebrate the First Amendment "as the guardian of our democracy"[281] even though we use the First Amendment chiefly to strike down legislation that has been enacted according to representative procedures that are otherwise majoritarian and "democratic." The First Amendment can remain the guardian of our democracy only so long as we interpret its requirements to promote the value of self-determination. Discursive democracy requires that the "demanding communicative presuppositions . . . that regulate the flow of discursive opinion- and will-formation"[282] be defined so as to facilitate democratic legitimation. At a minimum, First Amendment rights must guarantee that "[e]very citizen is a potential participant, a potential politician. The potentiality is the necessary condition of the citizen's self-respect."[283]

This is now all so obvious that we never pause to ask why First Amendment doctrine did not emerge until the aftermath of World War I. By the time the Court came to decide *Citizens United* in 2010, the foundational status of First Amendment rights was simply assumed. The Court did not ask why First Amendment rights should trump the interests of representative integrity that were advanced to justify the campaign finance reform measures at issue in *Citizens United*. If the Court were pressed, however, it would have had to explain that the discursive democracy established by First Amendment rights takes precedence over representation as a pathway for American self-government.

Why might this be so? We might regard the question as obtuse, for in our government constitutional rights take precedence over mere legislation. But for more than a century the nation did not understand the First Amendment to entail judicially enforceable rights. In a decision like *Citizens United,* the Court was forced to choose whether the nation's commitment to self-governance would be better realized through institutions of representation or through the discursive democracy established by First Amendment rights. The Court selected the latter path, even though we have been committed to structures of representation for far longer than we have aspired to democratic self-government. Why did the nation in the decades after World War I turn to discursive democracy as the constitutionally preferred avenue to self-government?

From a historical perspective, it seems significant that First Amendment rights arose concomitantly with the growth of American pluralism.[284] Americans have believed since the Progressive era that government should be directly responsive to the advocacy of citizens and their expressive associations.[285] As Arthur Bentley famously observed in 1908, politics in the United States can be understood only if we "strike much deeper" than the "level" of political parties to identify private groups and their interests.[286] American politicians are continuously tempted to abandon "party loyalty in order to tend to the demands of organized constituencies."[287]

Within the sphere of public opinion formation, individuals join groups and constituencies, which range from unions to the NRA, just as they might join a political party within the sphere of representative government. The primacy of discursive democracy in the United States corresponds to the primacy of political debate occurring outside the strict domain of representation. Americans now expect their government to be responsive to that debate. The unique power of American First Amendment rights may in this way be connected to the unique weakness of American political parties,[288] which characteristically forces Americans to engage in open battles for public opinion outside representational structures of governance.

Tomorrow I shall discuss the nature of the communicative rights guaranteed by the First Amendment. These rights are connected to self-government only if the actions of the state are understood to be responsive to public opinion. In my second lecture, I shall inquire why we might believe that the state is responsive to public opinion. This is not an inquiry pursued by the Court in *Citizens United*. Instead the Court applied First Amendment doctrine as though it were a repository of abstract and categorical rules. Because the Court never asked what these rules are designed to accomplish, it could not begin to explain how discursive democracy might be connected to the representative integrity that campaign finance reform seeks to sustain.

It is to that question that I shall turn in tomorrow's lecture.

2

SECOND LECTURE: CAMPAIGN FINANCE REFORM AND THE FIRST AMENDMENT

In *Citizens United v. FEC,*[1] the Supreme Court, by a bitterly divided vote of five to four, struck down long-standing federal regulation of independent corporate campaign expenditures. Due to its extraordinarily broad rationale, the decision sent shock waves through the world of campaign finance regulation, as well as through First Amendment jurisprudence generally.

At stake in *Citizens United* is the nature of the state's authority to regulate campaign finances. The Court in *Citizens United* is explicit that the First Amendment is implicated in campaign finance reform because "Speech is an essential mechanism of democracy, for it is the means to hold officials accountable to the people. The right of citizens to inquire, to hear, to speak, and to use information to reach consensus is a precondition to enlightened self-government and a necessary means to protect it."[2] The First Amendment therefore "'has its fullest and most urgent application to speech uttered during a campaign for political office.'"[3]

Citizens United squarely imagines the First Amendment as protecting the value of what in yesterday's lecture I called *discursive democracy.* The constitutional challenge of the case is how this value may be reconciled with the requirements of representative government, which campaign finance regulations seek to serve.

Constitutional restraints enforced by nondemocratically accountable courts are always serious business in a free country. The application of constitutional rights must be carefully tailored to their underlying purposes. The need for such judicial discipline is especially acute in the context of the First Amendment.

By its terms, the First Amendment protects "the freedom of speech." Human interaction everywhere characteristically occurs through the medium of communication. "We are men," Montaigne writes, "and we have relations with one another only by speech."[4] On their face, therefore, First Amendment rights apply to almost all human transactions. This means that First Amendment rights can potentially constitutionalize vast stretches of social life. They can become an irrepressible engine of judicial control, wresting authority from democratic institutions in virtually any circumstance. It is thus particularly important that First Amendment rights be carefully construed lest "self-rule" succumb, in Justice Scalia's pungent formulation, to a "black-robed supremacy."[5]

I.

Before analyzing *Citizens United* in light of the history we discussed yesterday, it is necessary to clear away a preliminary claim that has received much attention. In its first major campaign finance decision of the modern era, the Court held in *Buckley v. Valeo* that legislative efforts to regulate campaign contributions and expenditures implicate core First Amendment values, because "discussion of public issues and debate on the qualifications of candidates are integral to the operation of the system of government established by our Constitution."[6] Some have contended that this conclusion is misguided because "money is property" rather than "speech."[7] Those who adopt this position argue that it is inappropriate to invoke "the First Amendment" when evaluating "campaign finance regulations."[8] The argument is that statutory bans on campaign expenditures should not trigger any First Amendment scrutiny at all.

I regard this argument as untenable. As a general matter, First Amendment review of legislation can be triggered *either* by the purpose of legislation *or* by the objects that legislation regulates.[9] The claim that money is not speech at most seeks to characterize the object of campaign finance legislation. It does not and cannot address the question of whether the purpose of campaign finance legislation is consistent with First Amendment principles.

If legislation were to prohibit campaign expenditures by Democrats but not Republicans, no one would deny that a serious First Amendment question would be raised. This is because the legislation would naturally arouse suspicion that it is motivated by the improper purpose of distorting the free formation of public opinion. Even if the legislation applies only to expenditures, no one would deny that its improper purpose would render the legislation rightfully subject to strict First Amendment review.

The example illustrates that the First Amendment restrains government action that is enacted for constitutionally improper purposes.[10] About such legislation one does not ask whether it applies to speech or to conduct. If a law prevents Democrats but not Republicans from buying ink or newsprint, it should fall under the First Amendment, whether or not we would describe the proscribed purchases as speech.[11] Even if it is assumed that money is "not speech," therefore, it does not follow that campaign finance regulation is immune from First Amendment scrutiny.

The underlying assumption that money is "not speech," moreover, is far from obvious. When speech is dependent upon the resources necessary to create and disseminate it, proscription of the latter should be regarded as suppression of the former. It should make little constitutional difference whether legislation bans films directly or instead proscribes the celluloid on which films are printed. In either case, judicial First Amendment scrutiny is warranted.

There are important precedents for the proposition that legislative suppression of the financial resources necessary to create or publish speech is constitutionally equivalent to suppression of the speech itself.[12] These precedents are entirely defensible. Legislation prohibiting the sale of books containing the biographies of current political figures should properly be regarded as effectively prohibiting the biographies themselves.

Even if a law is enacted for an unquestionably proper purpose, it may nevertheless trigger First Amendment scrutiny if its impact on public opinion formation is sufficiently consequential. Consider a law that bans newsprint in order to save trees. The purpose of the law may be entirely legitimate, but its effect would be to eliminate an important medium for the communication of ideas. First Amendment scrutiny would accordingly be triggered.[13] If the regulation of campaign finance expenditures sufficiently diminishes the exchange of ideas believed necessary for the formation of public opinion, the regulation should trigger First Amendment review.[14]

For these reasons, the question before us is not whether First Amendment scrutiny should apply to campaign finance regulations of the kind reviewed in *Citizens United*. The question is how this scrutiny should be conducted.

II.

At issue in *Citizens United* was the constitutionality of § 441b of the Bipartisan Campaign Reform Act of 2002 (BCRA), which prohibited independent expenditures by the treasury funds of corporations "for speech defined as an 'electioneering communication' or for speech expressly advocating the election or defeat of a candidate."[15] The opinion for the Court in *Citizens United* is not a model of clarity, and it is difficult to discern the decisive line of the Court's constitutional reasoning.

It is nevertheless clear that the Court was deeply concerned by the government's failure to articulate a compelling government interest to justify the prohibition contained in § 441b. The Court held that § 441b is "subject to strict scrutiny," which means that it is constitutional only if it "'furthers a compelling interest and is narrowly tailored to achieve that interest.'"[16] A major portion of the Court's opinion in *Citizens United* is devoted to demonstrating that § 441b does not further any compelling interest.

Three major state interests have traditionally been advanced to support restrictions on campaign expenditures. These are interests in promoting equality, in removing distortion, and in eliminating corruption. Each of these interests makes good constitutional sense within the logic of representation. Each offers a cogent justification of why an effective system of representation might wish to control independent campaign expenditures. But none of these justifications translates easily into the context of First Amendment rights and the discursive democracy that it seeks to preserve.

A.

We construct elections to equalize the potential influence of each citizen. That is why, with the notorious exception of the United States Senate, the Constitution is interpreted to require the franchise to be distributed according to the formula of one person, one vote. As the Court famously said in *Reynolds v. Sims*: "Full and effective participation by all citizens in state government requires . . . that each citizen have an equally effective voice in the election of members of his state legislature."[17] If the Constitution *demands* that citizens be given an equally effective voice in elections, why would it not also *permit* government to regulate campaign financing so as to promote the equal influence of all?[18]

The principle of equality is given full-throated expression in Canadian law. Canada imposes stringent restrictions on all campaign contributions and expenditures. Rejecting a challenge to these restrictions, the Canadian Supreme Court affirmed that "individuals should have an equal opportunity to participate in the electoral process" and that "wealth is the main obstacle to equal participation."[19] "[T]he egalitarian model of elections adopted by Parliament is an essential component of our democratic society," the Court explained; it "promotes an electoral process that requires the wealthy to be prevented from controlling the electoral process to the detriment of others with less economic power."[20]

In sharp contrast to the Canadian approach, the United States Supreme Court in *Buckley* firmly rejected the idea that a "governmental interest in equalizing the relative ability of individuals and groups to influence the outcome of elections" can "justify" restrictions on campaign expenditures.[21] In a famous passage, the Court asserted that "the concept that government may restrict the speech of some elements of our society in order to enhance the relative voice of others is wholly foreign to the First Amendment, which was designed 'to secure "the widest possible dissemination of information from diverse and antagonistic sources,"' and '"to assure unfettered interchange of ideas for the bringing about of political and social changes desired by the people."'"[22] The Court conceded that persons may have "an equal right to vote for their representatives regardless of factors of wealth or geography," but it insisted that "the principles that underlie invalidation of governmentally imposed restrictions on the franchise do not justify governmentally imposed restrictions on political expression."[23]

Regulations of the "franchise" must comply with the logic of representation, whereas regulations of "political expression" must comply with the logic of discursive democracy. The logic of representation ultimately turns on decision making; elections are institutions that decide the identity of representatives.[24] Insofar as elected officials represent persons, and insofar as persons are regarded as having an equal interest in the identity of their representatives, it makes perfect sense to allocate the vote equally to all persons.[25] The rule of equality expresses the moral judgment that in a democracy each person should have an equal right to influence the outcome of the decision.

By contrast, the logic of discursive democracy does not turn on decision making. Discursive democracy inheres in continuous communicative processes that are incompatible with decision making. Because discursive democracy regards public opinion as constantly evolving, there is never an "outcome" with respect to which each affected person can be entitled to equal influence. Instead each person is entitled to the equal right to participate in the ongoing dialogue that constitutes public opinion. The right to participate is equally distributed, but not the influence caused by that participation. This distinction reflects a fundamental difference between the logic of representation and the logic of discursive democracy.

Following the terminology of the Court, I shall use the term *public discourse* to describe the communicative processes by which persons participate in the formation of public opinion.[26] The First Amendment ensures that the opportunity to participate in public discourse is equally distributed to all because all are potentially affected by government actions taken in response to public opinion. In a democracy in which all citizens are equal before the law, each citizen is equally entitled to the *opportunity* to participate in public discourse.

But First Amendment rights do not ensure that each citizen can exercise equal *influence* on government action. The First Amendment does not protect direct democracy; within discursive democracy, public opinion should not be analogized to an initiative. The point of First Amendment rights is instead to guarantee that each person is equally entitled to the possibility of democratic legitimation.[27] First Amendment rights institutionalize the hope that affording each person the opportunity to participate in public discourse can create the "communion of interests and sympathy of sentiments" between persons and their government that is the foundation of self-government.[28]

Democratic legitimation occurs when persons believe that government is potentially responsive to their views. If they do not believe this, if they become alienated from their government and lose the experience of ownership, government ceases to be democratically legitimate with respect to them. Democratic legitimation therefore depends upon what people actually believe.

A government cannot enjoy democratic legitimacy unless it carries the trust and confidence of its people. If a government possesses the trust and confidence of its people, it will be democratically legitimate, even if the impartial verdict of reason declares that the people ought to withdraw allegiance from their government. Conversely, if persons are persuaded to forfeit confidence in their government, their government will *pro tanto* lose democratic legitimacy, even if impartial reason might suggest a different conclusion.

The subjective nature of democratic legitimacy underwrites the nature of First Amendment rights. We live in a diverse and heterogeneous society, which means that consensus on government action is unlikely. The primary hope for democratic legitimation therefore lies in identification with the *processes* of public opinion formation. If these processes do not offer a meaningful opportunity to shape the content of public opinion, persons may cease to identify with a government that will inevitably take actions to which they strongly object. The premise of First Amendment jurisprudence is that identification with the processes of public opinion formation requires that persons be given freedom to contribute to these processes in a manner of their choosing.

That is why First Amendment rights protect the opportunity of persons to participate in public discourse in a manner they regard as meaningful, which is to say in a manner adequate to their own convictions. If persons believe passionately about a particular public issue, they can express that passion in the intensity, substance, and length of their speech. They can expound their own views as they see fit.[29] Because different persons will be more or less passionate about their beliefs, because they will be differently persuasive, they will exercise disparate influences on the development of public opinion.

At their core, First Amendment rights are about meaningful participation, not about equal participation. There may be circumstances in which participation is so unequal that those on the short end of the draw experience their participation as meaningless. In such cases, it is the lack of meaningful participation that is constitutionally determinative, not the lack of equal participation. Conversely, if rights of participation in public discourse are equally distributed but structured in a manner that persons do not find meaningful—for example if each person is entitled to only five minutes of participation on some boring public access cable channel—persons are unlikely to experience public discourse as a medium in which government may be rendered accountable. Democratic legitimation will be lost, and First Amendment rights will lose their point.[30]

The upshot is that the First Amendment guarantees persons the right to determine for themselves how they will participate in public discourse.[31] The state cannot choose their vocabulary or medium or genre. The state cannot put words in their mouths. The First Amendment stakes the possibility of democratic legitimation on the freedom to make such choices. First Amendment doctrine is structured on the premise that the value of self-governance is most likely to be realized if persons are free to participate in public discourse in the manner they believe will be most effective.

Preventing persons from participating in public discourse on the mere ground that their participation is unequal to others is for this reason constitutionally suspect.[32] It would be unthinkable to enact legislation limiting each person to publishing no more than one book a year, or contributing annually no more than 200 column inches to a newspaper, even though such legislation might serve the goal of equality. The Court in *Buckley* was thus correct to hold that the principle of equality cannot mechanically be transposed from the logic of representation to the logic of discursive democracy.

B.

A second justification that has been advanced in support of campaign finance reform is what has become known as the "antidistortion interest."[33] The antidistortion interest first made its appearance in 1990 in *Austin v. Michigan Chamber of Commerce*,[34] in which the Court upheld a Michigan statute prohibiting corporations from using general treasury funds for independent expenditures in connection with elections for state office. The Court ruled that the legislation was justified by the state's interest in controlling "the corrosive and distorting effects of immense aggregations of wealth that are accumulated with the help of the corporate form and that have little or no correlation to the public's support for the corporation's political ideas."[35] The Court emphasized that this interest was distinct from the effort "to equalize the relative influence of speakers on elections."[36]

The antidistortion interest does not hold that each person should possess an equal right to influence the outcome of an election. It affirms instead that the outcome of an election should "reflect actual public support."[37] Because corporate expenditures can affect the outcome of elections, and because such expenditures are unrelated to actual public support, *Austin* held that the state possesses a constitutional interest in eliminating "the distortion caused by corporate spending."[38] Section

441b of BCRA was enacted in reliance on the Court's decision in *Austin*.

The antidistortion interest expresses a fundamental principle of representation. Elections should represent public sentiments in a manner that transparently reflects the actual opinions of the public. "[A] republic in the modern sense of the word is a government in which the real judgment and opinion of the body of the people are supposed to control the selection of the public officers."[39] Whatever disrupts the pure expression of that judgment and opinion undermines the function of an election.

In an election campaign, persons spend time and resources to convince public opinion about their view of the decision at hand. The Court in *Austin* adopted the plausible view that corporate expenditures are not correlated with the judgment and opinion of actual people. "'The resources in the treasury of a business corporation . . . are not an indication of popular support for the corporation's political ideas. They reflect instead the economically motivated decisions of investors and customers. The availability of these resources may make a corporation a formidable political presence, even though the power of the corporation may be no reflection of the power of its ideas.'"[40] Something like this judgment has been operational in the American polity since the first decades of the twentieth century; it was the rationale for Progressive regulation of corporate campaign expenditures that we discussed yesterday.

Because the antidistortion principle expresses a basic norm of representative government, there have been many versions of the principle advanced in support of campaign finance reform. To mention only the most prominent, Lawrence Lessig in *Republic, Lost* has recently argued that elections should function to make government "dependent upon the People alone."[41] Lessig explains that elections are about exercising "control" over the actions of elected officials.[42] If elections are properly designed, elected officials will be controlled by the opinions of the people, as collected and tabulated in the election itself. The republican principle of representation[43] requires that elected officials be *"dependent"* upon, "meaning answerable to, relying upon, controlled by" the opinions of the people *"alone*—meaning dependent upon nothing or no one else."[44] Departure from this "constitutional baseline"[45] is a "distortion"[46] of foundational republican values. Campaign expenditures must therefore be regulated so that elected officials will not be dependent upon "the funders" instead of "the People."[47] Because we have every reason to expect "a gap between 'the funders' and 'the People,'"[48] unregulated campaign expenditures will fundamentally undermine republican principles.

Antidistortion arguments of this kind follow directly from the logic of representation. Once it is assumed that "the real judgment and opinion of the body of the people" can be represented, whatever causes deviation from this representation may be condemned as a distortion. Lessig's version of the antidistortion argument follows from the premise that the opinion of "the people" can be known and that it can therefore be distinguished from that of the "funders." The distortion caused by the funders can be constitutionally excised from the formation of public opinion.

From the perspective of the First Amendment, however, the antidistortion interest is suspect. The discursive democracy established by the First Amendment conceptualizes public opinion as a continuous process. Within discursive democracy, public opinion does not make decisions, so the "true" identity of the people is never revealed. "The real judgment and opinion of the body of the people" is never definitively represented. There is thus no "baseline" from which "distortion" can be assessed. That is why it would be constitutionally unthinkable to prevent someone from speaking on the ground that their speech would distort public opinion. Public opinion is whatever persons choose to make it by speaking how they choose to speak in public discourse.[49] The First Amendment would undoubtedly prohibit legislation capping the budgets of feature films to prevent runaway blockbusters from "distorting" public opinion.

Lessig's distinction between "the People" and "the funders" presupposes that we can accurately represent the people in order to distinguish them from the funders. But within discursive democracy the people can be recognized only through the public opinion they produce, and that public opinion, as I suggested in yesterday's lecture, is "always in the making" and always subject to interpretation. Direct democracy may invite the people to appear and to register an unmediated expression of their will,[50] and within such a context it may be intelligible to claim that the appearance of the people has been distorted. But the communicative rights that undergird discursive democracy reject any such claim to transparent popular intelligibility. They instead privilege *processes* of public opinion formation. That is why, in discursive democracy, "sovereignty" is said to be "found" in the "subjectless forms of communication that regulate the flow of discursive opinion- and will-formation."[51]

The French political theorist Claude Lefort vividly expressed this thought by insisting that in a democracy the place of the people must be "an empty place,"[52] by which he meant that no group, institution, or party can claim fully to represent or embody the people. Lefort's famous metaphor captures the idea that in discursive democracy "the identity of the people" can never definitely be known and is always "subject to an ongoing contestation."[53] Discursive democracy substitutes the impersonal processes that form public opinion for a distinct portrait of the people.[54] Communicative rights establish "a process that has no endpoint, an argument that has no definitive conclusion. In democratic politics, all destinations are temporary. No citizen can ever claim to have persuaded his fellows once and for all. There are always new citizens, for one thing; and old citizens are always entitled to reopen the argument."[55]

Within the framework of discursive democracy, therefore, limiting speech to prevent distortion is equivalent to freezing public opinion and preventing it from changing in response to new ideas and new convictions. Because in discursive democracy "the real judgment and opinion of the body of the people" can never be decisively known or fixed, there can never be an "authentic" point at which to stop the unending unfolding of public opinion. There can be no "baseline," no Archimedean point, from which to normalize the content of public opinion. The criterion of "distortion" is thus inapplicable. Instead the legitimacy of public opinion depends upon the integrity of the processes by which public opinion is formed.

In discursive democracy, the integrity of these processes should be assessed in terms of their capacity to realize the value of self-government. First Amendment rights guarantee that persons can participate in public discourse in ways that facilitate their identification with the processes by which public opinion is formed. To this end First Amendment rights protect the liberty of speakers to communicate in a manner they deem adequate to their own convictions. First Amendment rights defined in this way will inevitably create circumstances in which speakers who care intensely about particular issues will devote more resources to crafting and disseminating their views than those who are apathetic about these issues. It follows that the processes that form public opinion are not "distorted" merely because some persons devote more resources to crafting and disseminating their views on specific issues than do others. Within public discourse there can be no clear constitutional distinction between "the People" and "the funders."

For these reasons, the antidistortion principle does not translate to the context of contemporary First Amendment doctrine. Although the principle makes good sense within the context of representation, it contradicts the essential logic of discursive democracy. The antidistortion principle, like the equal influence principle, expresses a government interest that is incompatible with the structure of First Amendment rights.

C.

The third and doctrinally most important state interest that the Court has discussed in the context of campaign finance reform is the need to prevent "corruption and the appearance of corruption."[56] The Court has even gone so far as to assert that "preventing corruption or the appearance of corruption are the only legitimate and compelling government interests thus far identified for restricting campaign finances."[57]

The Court has never been precise about the meaning of either corruption or the appearance of corruption.[58] It has "not always spoken about corruption in a clear or consistent voice."[59] All agree that the paradigm case of corruption is the quid pro quo contribution, the contribution given in return for official action.[60] The paradigm case of appearance of corruption is the appearance of representatives accepting quid pro quo contributions.[61]

In *Buckley v. Valeo*, the Court explained that "[t]he increasing importance of the communications media and sophisticated mass-mailing and polling operations to effective campaigning make the raising of large sums of money an ever more essential ingredient of an effective candidacy. To the extent that large contributions are given to secure a political quid pro quo from current and potential office holders, the integrity of our system of representative democracy is undermined."[62] A decade later the Court elaborated: "Corruption is a subversion of the political process. Elected officials are influenced to act contrary to their obligations of office by the prospect of financial gain to themselves or infusions of money into their campaigns. The hallmark of corruption is the financial quid pro quo: dollars for political favors."[63]

To speak roughly and schematically, the Court has conceptualized the state's interest in preventing corruption as the state's interest in preserving the integrity of representative government. Corruption occurs when "elected officials are influenced to act contrary to their obligations of office" by making "improper commitments."[64] The nature of the state's interest in regulating corruption thus depends upon how we understand the official obligations (or role morality) of elected representatives.[65]

The state's interest in eliminating corruption does not arise from the First Amendment but instead must be balanced *against* the state's interest in maintaining First Amendment rights.

The fundamental doctrinal structure of *Buckley*, which has shaped our entire jurisprudence of campaign finance reform, turns precisely on a compromise between the needs of representative government and the values of the First Amendment. In effect, the Court in *Buckley* held that because the state possesses a compelling interest in preventing the risk of corruption inherent in direct campaign contributions, the First Amendment values at stake in contributions can be overridden in order to preserve the integrity of representative government. But because independent expenditures create no such immediate danger to representative government, restrictions on independent expenditures must be sharply limited by First Amendment rights.

In crafting this compromise, *Buckley* badly underestimated the dangers to representative government posed by independent expenditures,[66] and it unduly minimized the First Amendment values inherent in contributions.[67] Nevertheless, the *Buckley* compromise has served since 1976 as the foundation for the constitutional law of campaign finance reform. Although the *Buckley* compromise has proved long-lived, it has been doctrinally sterile. This is because the Court cannot explain the concept of corruption on which it is based.

Funds deposited into a candidate's personal bank account may be in tension with the official obligations of a representative, no matter how we define these obligations. No one contends that bribery is not corrupt. But campaign contributions do not increase the personal wealth of candidates. They instead support electoral campaigns, and it is presumably in the public interest that electoral campaigns be supported.[68] For the concept of corruption to be theoretically generative, we must understand the official obligations of representatives in a manner that will help us to determine *when* commitments made in return for support are "improper."

It turns out that it is very difficult to construct such an understanding. Representatives, as distinct from judges or administrators, are officially expected to be responsive to the support of constituents. As the Court observed two decades ago, "Serving constituents and supporting legislation that will benefit the district and individuals and groups therein is the everyday business of a legislator."[69] The Court in *Citizens United* affirmed, quite plausibly, that "Favoritism and influence are not . . .

avoidable in representative politics. It is in the nature of an elected representative to favor certain policies, and, by necessary corollary, to favor the voters and contributors who support those policies. It is well understood that a substantial and legitimate reason, if not the only reason, to cast a vote for, or to make a contribution to, one candidate over another is that the candidate will respond by producing those political outcomes the supporter favors. Democracy is premised on responsiveness."[70]

The contemporary constitutional law of campaign finance reform holds that it is improper for a representative to promise to undertake official action in return for a campaign contribution. Although this conclusion is robust, it is not clear *why* Americans condemn such quid pro quo contributions.[71] There are many different possible explanations, which lead to very different accounts of the role morality of representatives.[72] Because we lack agreement about why we prohibit quid pro quo contributions, the concept of corruption has not proved theoretically generative.[73] It has not inspired a convincing account of representative role morality to balance against the concrete First Amendment concerns raised by campaign finance reform.

This may explain why the Court's efforts to expand the concept of corruption beyond the context of quid pro quo contributions have not been based upon an account of the official obligations of representatives. Instead the Court announced in *McConnell v. FEC*:

> Just as troubling to a functioning democracy as classic *quid pro quo* corruption is the danger that officeholders will decide issues not on the merits or the desires of their constituencies, but according to the wishes of those who have made large financial contributions valued by the officeholder. Even if it occurs only occasionally, the potential for such undue influence is manifest. And unlike straight cash-for-votes transactions, such corruption is neither easily detected nor practical to criminalize. The best means of prevention is to identify and to remove the temptation.[74]

In *McConnell* the Court defined "the appearance of corruption" as "the appearance of undue influence."[75]

It is noteworthy that neither "undue influence" nor the "appearance of undue influence" specifies what it is improper or proper for representatives to do. Because the Court accepts that representatives should be responsive to "the desires of their constituencies," and because the Court also accepts that constituents can express their desires through financial donations,[76] representatives cannot look to the concept of "undue influence" in order to understand the difference between appropriate and inappropriate action. From the point of view of representatives, the criterion of "undue influence" does not distinguish between support that should be influential and support that should not be.[77]

Instead the criterion of "undue influence," and its correlative expansion into "the appearance of undue influence," affirms a value that derives from the structural integrity of our *system* of representation. Influence is "undue" when it either "distorts" the behavior of representatives by making them unduly responsive to wealthy contributors, or when it promotes "inequality" by giving wealthy contributors undue influence with regard to the behavior of representatives.[78] This suggests that the state's interest in curtailing "undue influence" essentially depends upon its interest in implementing the "equality of influence" principle or the "antidistortion" principle.[79]

For the reasons that I have previously explored, these principles are deeply in tension with fundamental First Amendment values. That is why justices who privilege First Amendment rights over campaign finance reform also seek to limit the concept of corruption to quid pro quo transactions. In *Citizens United,* for example, the Court flatly ruled that "[w]hen *Buckley* identified a sufficiently important governmental interest in preventing corruption or the appearance of corruption, that interest was limited to quid pro quo corruption."[80] Building on the *Buckley* compromise, the Court in *Citizens United* held that the independent expenditures regulated by § 441b cannot pose a sufficient danger of quid pro quo corruption to justify regulation under the First Amendment.[81]

The legacy of *Buckley* is evident in the way that *Citizens United* conceptualizes the state's interest in preventing corruption. Because *Citizens United* conceives this interest as distinct from the values protected by the First Amendment, it imagines campaign finance reform as intrinsically in conflict with First Amendment jurisprudence. The conflict can be resolved only through unstable and arbitrary compromises of the kind advanced in *Buckley.*

Conceptualizing campaign finance reform in terms of the state's interests in preventing corruption leads down a constitutional blind alley. It not only stunts the impulse toward a comprehensive constitutional theory of campaign finance reform, it also deprives us of the jurisprudential resources necessary to craft a more durable and theoretically satisfying connection between basic First Amendment principles and the needs of representative government.

III.

To understand how the First Amendment ought to be applied in the context of campaign finance reform, we must theorize the relationship between discursive democracy, which the First Amendment protects, and representative government, which campaign finance reform seeks to preserve. Discursive democracy and representative government each strive for the good of self-government. Each seeks to empower the people to claim "ownership" of their government. Yet each functions according to a different logic.

Representative government requires constant and recurring episodes of decision making, whereas discursive democracy depends upon uninterrupted and continuous processes of communication. In representative government, the people must become visible so that their will can be represented; in discursive democracy, the people must disappear into impersonal processes of communication. This divergence means that although principles of "equality of influence" and "antidistortion" are required within representative government, they are forbidden within discursive democracy.

This does not imply, however, that discursive democracy and representative government are incapable of being theorized within a common constitutional framework. Discursive democracy requires not only free participation in public discourse but also a structure of government that connects official decision making to public opinion. We have historically and constitutionally embraced institutions of representative government in order to serve this purpose. Like the Framers, we believe that "frequency of elections" is "the great bulwark of our liberty."[82] We use elections to guarantee that government will be responsive to public opinion. Jürgen Habermas formulates the point in this way: "The flow of communication between public opinion-formation, institutionalized elections, and legislative decisions is meant to guarantee that influence and communicative power are transformed through legislation into administrative power."[83]

Elections underwrite discursive democracy by focusing and prompting public opinion. Participants in public discourse debate what to do in the next election and whether officials already elected remain sufficiently attentive to public opinion. Public opinion continuously evolves in the course of this debate.[84] Although elections provide momentary glimpses of public opinion, they do not displace ongoing processes of public opinion formation, and in fact elections promote these processes. Elections give citizens good reason to participate in public discourse and hence to fashion an "effective democracy." Elections are essential to discursive democracy because they inspire public trust that representatives will be responsive to public opinion.[85]

First Amendment rights protect the possibility of participating in the formation of public opinion. The hope is that government will be responsive to public opinion and thus to the communicative efforts of citizens. Elections are essential to the First Amendment because they are the principal mechanism by which government is made responsive to public opinion. If the public does not believe that elections choose officials who attend to public opinion, the link between public discourse and self-government is broken.[86] Unless there is public trust that elections select officials who are responsive to public opinion, the First Amendment rights so vigorously affirmed in *Citizens United* cannot produce democratic legitimation. They cannot connect communication to self-government.[87]

This strongly suggests that First Amendment rights presuppose that elections must be structured to select for persons who possess the "communion of interests and sympathy of sentiments" to remain responsive to public opinion.[88] I shall henceforth use the term *electoral integrity* exclusively to denominate elections that have the property of choosing candidates whom the people trust to possess this sympathy and connection. Without electoral integrity, First Amendment rights necessarily fail to achieve their constitutional purpose. If the people do not believe that elected officials listen to public opinion, participation in public discourse, no matter how free, cannot create the experience of self-government.

It is perhaps because discursive democracy requires its own form of electoral integrity that the Court has taken to characterizing the United States as a "representative democracy."[89] If we analyze campaign finance reform from the perspective of this kind of electoral integrity, we are not, as with principles like "equality of influence" and "antidistortion," attempting to force a procrustean marriage between discursive democracy and representative government. We are instead seeking to make First Amendment rights, and the discursive democracy for which they stand, more efficacious.

Electoral integrity does not require that representatives be delegates, as distinct from trustees. It does not require that representatives "take instruction" from public opinion. It presupposes only public trust in the responsiveness of representatives to public opinion. Within the framework of discursive democracy, public opinion cannot be a source of instruction because public opinion is incapable of definitive representation. The influence of public opinion is always indirect, because the substance of public opinion is intrinsically subject to interpretation and judgment, and because the substance of public opinion is constantly evolving and changing. Electoral integrity thus requires that representatives be responsive to a public opinion whose contents they must in part construct and affect.

As Hanna Pitkin rightly explains, "None of the analogies of acting for others on the individual level seems satisfactory for explaining the relationship between a political representative and his constituents. He is neither agent nor trustee or deputy nor commissioner."[90] Electoral integrity is not a concept that can be applied to the particular decisions of particular representatives. It is instead a property of a *system* of representation, in which the public trusts that representatives will be attentive to public opinion. In Pitkin's words, "the representing done by an individual legislator must be seen . . . as embodied in a whole political system. . . . What makes it representation is not any single action by any one participant, but the over-all structure and functioning of the system."[91]

The democratic structure and legitimacy of our government depend on electoral integrity. Yet the Court in its campaign finance opinions has not considered the state's interest in promoting the electoral integrity required by the First Amendment. The Court has instead been preoccupied by the attempt to balance First Amendment rights against the need to prevent corruption. The upshot has been a series of unstable constitutional compromises that have left the jurisprudence of campaign finance reform vulnerable to wildly inconsistent holdings.

If we instead reformulate our campaign finance jurisprudence upon the principle of electoral integrity, on which all sides can potentially agree, we may create a more enduring foundation for the contested area of campaign finance reform. Those who treasure First Amendment rights should support the electoral integrity necessary for First Amendment rights to achieve their constitutional purpose. Those who embrace campaign finance reform should affirm the electoral integrity required for contemporary representation to exemplify the value of self-government.

Once the bitter dust of the current controversy settles, the principle of electoral integrity offers the possibility of reconstructing on firm *common* ground the constitutional jurisprudence of campaign finance reform.

This ground is not utterly foreign to the Court. *Buckley* itself emphasized the state's compelling interest in maintaining "'confidence in the system of representative Government,'"[92] noting that in previous decisions the Court had held this interest sufficient to justify restrictions on the First Amendment rights of government employees to engage in partisan political activities. But *Buckley* linked this interest to a concern with preventing "the appearance of corruption,"[93] and thus severed the interest from any internal connection to First Amendment values. Understood as a specifically First Amendment principle, electoral integrity must focus carefully on public confidence that elections are structured to produce officials who are attentive to public opinion.

As I discussed in yesterday's lecture, the Progressive era experienced a crisis of representation because of the widespread belief that elected officials were beholden to political parties, which in turn were answerable to corporate wealth rather than to public opinion. The solution to the crisis was to create institutional structures that Progressives hoped would make representatives more directly dependent upon public opinion. Contemporary campaign finance reform proposals may best be understood as analogously seeking to ameliorate the widespread perception that elected representatives are responsive to personal and corporate wealth, but not to public opinion.[94]

In 1914 Harvard president A. Lawrence Lowell wrote that if "reëlection depends upon a boss whose good will in the matter is . . . contrary to the real sentiment of the electorate, then this mode of expressing public opinion is vitiated at its source."[95] Americans responded by seeking to minimize the influence of the boss in determining the outcome of elections. They acted to ensure that elections would hold candidates accountable to public opinion. Contemporary campaign finance reform has exactly the same ambition. It seeks to assure Americans that elections will select candidates who are responsive to public opinion, not merely to the views of the wealthy.[96]

This formulation of the issue does not require us to impose a strict grid of equality on the formation of public opinion; nor to preserve public opinion from distortion by hypostasizing the true nature of "the People"; nor to balance First Amendment rights against the potential corruption of the representative process. It requires us merely to affirm what is undeniably true—that Americans cannot maintain the blessing of self-government unless they believe that elections produce representatives who are responsive to public opinion. "Public opinion" should in this context be defined as the meanings thrown off by communicative processes conducted in compliance with First Amendment rights designed to facilitate democratic legitimation.

Electoral integrity is a compelling government interest because without it Americans have no reason to exercise the communicative rights guaranteed by the First Amendment. The closest the Court has come to expressing this constitutional principle is in *Nixon v. Shrink Missouri Government PAC,* where the Court observed that "the cynical assumption that large donors call the tune could jeopardize the willingness of voters to take part in democratic governance. Democracy works 'only if the people have faith in those who govern. . . .' "[97]

The Court in *Shrink* properly understood that the achievement of electoral integrity was empirically contingent. At times in our history elections have possessed electoral integrity, and at other times they have not. Electoral integrity can be lost, and it can be gained. To the extent that the Court in *Citizens United* glimpsed the profound constitutional significance of electoral integrity, it seemed to imagine electoral integrity as a matter of law, rather than of fact. The Court impatiently swatted away the suggestion that corporate expenditures might cause corruption or the appearance of corruption:

> The appearance of influence or access, furthermore, will not cause the electorate to lose faith in our democracy. By definition, an independent expenditure is political speech presented to the electorate that is not coordinated with a candidate. The fact that a corporation, or any other speaker, is willing to spend money to try to persuade voters presupposes that the people have the ultimate influence over elected officials. This is inconsistent with any suggestion that the electorate will refuse "to take part in democratic governance" because of additional political speech made by a corporation or any other speaker.[98]

The American people have worried since the Progressive era that unlimited corporate expenditures might make elected officials responsive to corporate wealth rather than to public opinion. They have been apprehensive that unlimited corporate political spending might endanger electoral integrity. This concern has been expressed in the long-standing, democratically endorsed legislative judgments of the American people. It is the height of hubris for the Court, by a vote of five justices on a bench of nine, simply to dismiss concerns for electoral integrity on the ground that electoral integrity is a question of law rather than of social fact.[99]

Since the beginning of our nation, since the debate between Madison and Brutus, Americans have agreed that electoral integrity depends on questions of institutional design. It is certain that if the design of contemporary elections has caused Americans to lose faith in the electoral integrity of their representative system, that faith will not be restored by the professional legal assertions of the Supreme Court, particularly in the context of a divisive, politically controversial opinion.

Electoral integrity depends upon how Americans believe their elections actually work. In 2012 the Supreme Court was presented with a petition for certiorari to review a decision of the Montana Supreme Court upholding the state's prohibition on corporate campaign expenditures in order to preserve "the integrity of its electoral process."[100] The state prohibition was first enacted in 1912 in response to a manifest loss of faith in electoral integrity caused by massive expenditures by mining corporations, which virtually owned the state. The history is vividly and convincingly recounted by the Montana Supreme Court. As one Montana newspaper said at the time, "If the copper trust must rule Montana, why not cut out all pretense of representative government and haul down the flag of a free state? Why not abolish the legislature and dispense with a state government?"[101] It could not plausibly be denied that electoral integrity had been seriously impaired.

In a shocking result, the United States Supreme Court, by a vote of five to four, granted the petition for certiorari summarily to reverse the Montana decision on the basis of the legal principle announced in *Citizens United*.[102] In effect the Supreme Court held that the loss of electoral integrity could never under any circumstances justify limitations on independent corporate campaign finance expenditures. It is beyond my comprehension how a responsible Court might regard electoral integrity as irrelevant to the protection of First Amendment rights, and how it might regard history as irrelevant to the precious resource of electoral integrity.

Electoral integrity is a foundational value for American democracy. Not only is electoral integrity consistent with received First Amendment jurisprudence, it is *required* by that jurisprudence. And there are good reasons to worry that electoral integrity is today under threat. Americans' trust and confidence in their representative institutions has fallen to record lows; we are once again experiencing what most regard as a crisis of representation.[103] In such circumstances it is especially disappointing that the Court seems unwilling to recognize even the existence of the constitutional principle of electoral integrity, much less to think through the doctrinal implications of how threats to electoral integrity might constitutionally be established.

In these lectures I shall not explore whether electoral integrity is in fact at risk, or whether campaign finance reform will in fact ameliorate that risk. I argue only that the protection of electoral integrity constitutes a compelling state interest, and that the need for such protection depends upon the relevant facts of the matter. Anyone who reads the undisputed facts of the Montana case must acknowledge that there have been times in our history when electoral integrity has been threatened.[104] The example of the Montana Corrupt Practices Act suffices to illustrate that dangers to electoral integrity can be real and potentially catastrophic, and that they can be addressed by changes in institutional design. It is the height of folly to allow arid legalisms to blind us to these essential lessons. Formalism in this context is especially dangerous because virtually all existing First Amendment doctrine, including the strict scrutiny test applied by the Court in *Citizens United,* presupposes the existence of electoral integrity.

When government acts to preserve electoral integrity, it acts for the right reasons. Tailoring state action to the maintenance of electoral integrity is thus unlikely to produce counterintuitive results. Consider that *Citizens United* had originally come to the Court as a narrow, technical case,[105] and that it escalated into a major constitutional controversy only after a government lawyer conceded during initial argument that corporations could be prohibited from using treasury funds to publish books of express advocacy during a campaign.[106] The concession produced shock that campaign finance reform could reach so surprisingly far. No doubt the shock prompted the Court's determination to author an equally broad repudiation of efforts to regulate campaign finance expenditures.[107]

Under the present constitutional framework of campaign finance reform, the government's concession follows directly from the broad and ill-defined nature of the state's interest in preventing corruption and the appearance of corruption, which can justify a seemingly endless series of overreaching prohibitions. Providing practically anything of substantial value to a candidate to support her election can easily be categorized as a bid for "undue influence" or reciprocal favors.[108]

If the government were instead required to justify legislation in terms of preserving electoral integrity, I very much doubt that books (or pamphlets,[109] or even movies) would be seen as responsible for Americans' fear that elected representatives are not responsive to public opinion. If electoral integrity is presently at risk because of substantial expenditures, it is almost certainly because of the relentless tide of campaign advertisements on broadcast and cable television.

My best guess is that justifying campaign finance regulation on the basis of actual threats to electoral integrity would suggest natural and intuitively obvious constitutional limits to the regulation of campaign speech. Regulation should be confined to the kinds of expenditures that actually undermine faith in democratic responsiveness. It would of course require empirical study to identify such expenditures. I claim only that we ask the right constitutional question when we inquire about the relationship between campaign expenditures and electoral integrity.

IV.

Electoral integrity depends upon popular trust that representatives are responsive to public opinion. Public opinion, in turn, must be defined in terms of the communicative rights guaranteed by the First Amendment. The holding of Citizens United is that § 441b unconstitutionally curtails these rights. To assess this holding we must carefully parse the nature of First Amendment rights.

Although its exact logic is obscure, the reasoning of Citizens United draws importantly on First Amendment doctrine that prohibits discrimination among speakers. The Court is quite categorical about the unconstitutionality of such discrimination:

> Premised on mistrust of governmental power, the First Amendment stands against attempts to disfavor certain subjects or viewpoints. Prohibited, too, are restrictions distinguishing among different speakers, allowing speech by some but not others. As instruments to censor, these categories are interrelated: Speech restrictions based on the identity of the speaker are all too often simply a means to control content.

Quite apart from the purpose or effect of regulating content, moreover, the Government may commit a constitutional wrong when by law it identifies certain preferred speakers. By taking the right to speak from some and giving it to others, the Government deprives the disadvantaged person or class of the right to use speech to strive to establish worth, standing, and respect for the speaker's voice. The Government may not by these means deprive the public of the right and privilege to determine for itself what speech and speakers are worthy of consideration. The First Amendment protects speech and speaker, and the ideas that flow from each.[110]

The Court views § 441b as presumptively unconstitutional because it violates a First Amendment "rule" against speaker discrimination. Although it is true that § 441b treats the speech of corporations differently than it treats the speech of natural persons, the Court's reasoning fundamentally misunderstands the First Amendment rights the Court seeks to protect.

It is easy to recognize the paradigm case from which the Court derives its "rule" against discriminating "among different speakers." If a liberal and a conservative are each vying for public support, the state may not suppress the speech of the conservative because it supports the views of the liberal. The conservative and the liberal each possess the independent right "to strive to establish worth, standing, and respect" for their own voice, and so to influence the development of public opinion. This conclusion is clear.

The question is whether this paradigm case supports a general and abstract rule forbidding discrimination among speakers. In point of fact, the paradigm case illustrates that all persons are entitled to an equal opportunity to participate in public discourse. The paradigm case is mute about discrimination among persons who are not participating in public discourse. Such discrimination is actually quite ordinary and necessary.

A simple example might be the unauthorized practice of law. Assume A and B each communicate the same legal advice to the same client, but that A is a licensed lawyer and that B is not. Contrary to the dicta of *Citizens United,* the law will treat the speech of B differently than the speech of A. B will be sanctioned for the unauthorized practice of law, but A will not. This difference in treatment between A and B will not receive any First Amendment scrutiny at all. This is because the speech of A and B forms no part of public discourse, but instead concerns professional speech between lawyers and clients. The state typically regulates the professional communications of professional speakers in ways that would be flagrantly unconstitutional in the context of public discourse.[111]

The example illustrates that First Amendment "rules" of the kind invoked by *Citizens United* are of little value unless we know the purpose that such rules are designed to serve.[112] Many First Amendment rules exist to protect the value of democratic legitimation, and it is all too easy to leap to the mistaken conclusion that these rules should apply to all regulations of speech. But the constitutional value of democratic legitimation inheres in public discourse, and public discourse is a very distinct and limited kind of speech.

Citizens United is correct that the First Amendment does not allow government to discourage persons within public discourse from using "speech to strive to establish worth, standing, and respect" for their own voice.[113] Within public discourse, persons strive to shape the substance of public opinion by making it responsive to their views. Because each person has an equal right to establish the worth, standing, and influence of his own views, the First Amendment forbids government from discriminating within public discourse among speakers based on identity or viewpoint.

But not all speech is public discourse. The advice of a lawyer to a client does not form any part of public discourse. At stake in lawyer-client communications is the provision of sound and reliable legal advice, not the "worth, standing, and respect" due to a lawyer or to a client. For this reason the First Amendment does not interfere with state regulations of lawyer-client communications that discriminate on the basis of speakers and viewpoint in order to prevent legal malpractice or the unauthorized practice of law.[114]

The scope of public discourse is defined by the constitutional value of democratic legitimation. When democratic legitimation is not at issue in speech, the speech is not constitutionally classified as public discourse. The value of democratic legitimation applies to persons, not to things. If there were a self-perpetuating viral communication on the Internet, it would not possess First Amendment rights. This is because computer programs cannot experience the value of democratic legitimation. That is why the speech of robots does not form part of public discourse.

At issue in *Citizens United* are the First Amendment rights of corporations. Corporations are not persons; they cannot experience the value of democratic legitimation. The good of self-government does not apply to corporations. That is why we do not permit corporations to vote in elections or to hold seats in a legislature. The corporation, qua corporation, is a legal entity, nothing more. Because a corporation cannot experience the value of democratic legitimation, it does not possess an equal right to participate in public discourse.

A corporation can, however, serve as a proxy for the First Amendment rights of natural persons.[115] We can authorize corporations to assert the rights of persons who make up the corporation, or to assert the rights of persons who are strangers to the corporation. With regard to the former, the question is how and when the rights of persons employed by a corporation should be attributed to the corporation itself.

First Amendment doctrine contains a well-worked-out theory of when organizations can exercise the First Amendment rights of their members. Although there is no independent First Amendment right to associate, there is an independent First Amendment right to associate to exercise First Amendment rights more effectively. As Chief Justice Roberts has written for the Court:

> We have recognized a First Amendment right to associate for the purpose of speaking. . . . The reason we have extended First Amendment protection in this way is clear: The right to speak is often exercised most effectively by combining one's voice with the voices of others. If the government were free to restrict individuals' ability to join together and speak, it could essentially silence views that the First Amendment is intended to protect.[116]

First Amendment rights of association protect the "ability and the opportunity to combine with others to advance one's views."[117] "The Court has recognized a right to associate for the purpose of engaging in those activities protected by the First Amendment—speech, assembly, petition for the redress of grievances, and the exercise of religion."[118]

If persons form an association for the purpose of engaging in First Amendment activities, the association may claim to act in the name of the First Amendment rights of its individual members.[119] First Amendment doctrine characterizes such associations as "expressive associations."[120] In *FEC v. Massachusetts Citizens for Life, Inc.,*[121] the Court explicitly held that even if an expressive association assumes the form of a corporation, it may nevertheless assert the First Amendment rights of those who have associated together to form the corporation. It is thus possible for corporations to be expressive associations. If speech by a natural person would constitutionally be classified as public discourse, First Amendment doctrine treats as public discourse the same speech by an expressive association, even if it happens to be a corporation.

Most corporations are not formed for the purpose of engaging in First Amendment activities. Ordinary commercial corporations are not expressive associations, and for this reason they may not assert the First Amendment rights of persons who make up ordinary commercial corporations. As Justice Scalia has written, "The robust First Amendment freedom to associate belongs only to groups 'engage[d] in "expressive association . ."'. The Campbell Soup Company does not exist to promote a message, and 'there is only minimal constitutional protection of the freedom of *commercial* association.'"[122]

Justice Scalia's point is fundamental to our constitutional understanding of ordinary commercial regulations. State corporate laws pervasively regulate how persons may join together to form a corporation and how they must act together once they are members of a corporation. If there were a First Amendment right to associate to form ordinary commercial corporations, if Justice Scalia were not correct, every aspect of state corporate law would be subject to strict First Amendment scrutiny.[123] This is not now the case, and it should not become the case.

If ordinary commercial corporations possess First Amendment rights, therefore, it must be as proxies for the rights of persons who are strangers to the corporation. This is in fact the explicit holding of the Court in *First National Bank of Boston v. Bellotti*,[124] the Court's seminal decision on the First Amendment rights of commercial corporations, and the decision most heavily relied upon by the Court in *Citizens United*. In *Bellotti*, the Court stated, quite carefully:

> The court below framed the principal question in this case as whether and to what extent corporations have First Amendment rights. We believe that the court posed the wrong question. The Constitution often protects interests broader than those of the party seeking their vindication. The First Amendment, in particular, serves significant societal interests. The proper question therefore is not whether corporations "have" First Amendment rights and, if so, whether they are coextensive with those of natural persons.

Instead, the question must be whether [the statute at issue in this case] abridges expression that the First Amendment was meant to protect.[125]

At issue in *Bellotti* was a Massachusetts statute prohibiting ordinary business corporations from making independent expenditures to influence the result of election referenda. Reasoning according to logic first systematically explored by Alexander Meiklejohn, the Court in *Bellotti* held that the First Amendment protects the flow of information to voters in an election, because such information is "indispensable to decisionmaking in a democracy."[126] The Court concluded that the "inherent worth of the speech in terms of its capacity for informing the public does not depend upon the identity of its source, whether corporation, association, union, or individual."[127]

Because ordinary commercial corporations are not natural persons who can experience the subjective value of democratic legitimation, they do not possess original First Amendment rights to participate in public discourse as speakers.* *Bellotti* holds that ordinary commercial corporations

---

* First Amendment rights safeguard the constitutional values we attribute to expression. The most important such value is that of democratic legitimation. *Bellotti* is best interpreted as holding that the dissemination of information also contains constitutional value, regardless of whether the speaker is a corporation. It is important to recognize that expression can embody constitutional values in addition to those of democratic legitimation and the dissemination of information. Religious speech, for example, frequently involves the distinct constitutional value associated with the free exercise of religion.

The First Amendment explicitly recognizes the constitutional value of a free press. When this constitutional value is at stake, the corporate form *vel non* of a speaker is not decisive, just as it is not decisive in the context of expressive associations or of the dissemination of information. The Court in *Citizens United* intimates that if corporations were not entitled to the same speech rights as individual persons, the state would be free to suppress the speech of "media corporations." 558 U.S. at 351–354. *See* Martin Redish & Peter B. Siegal, *Constitutional Adjudication, Free Expression, and the Fashionable Art of Corporation Bashing*, 91 Tex. L. Rev. 1447, 1459–1460 (2013). I find this suggestion fanciful and baffling.

The Court mistakenly asserts, "'We have consistently rejected the proposition that the institutional press has any constitutional privilege beyond that of other speakers.'" 558 U.S. at 905 (quoting Scalia, J., dissenting in *Austin*, 494 U.S. at 691). This is manifestly incorrect. In *Minneapolis Star v. Minn. Comm'r*, 460 U.S. 575 (1983), for example, the Court held that the First Amendment prohibits the imposition of unique taxes on the press. States can impose unique taxes on virtually every kind of

instead possess the derivative First Amendment right to speak in ways that inform auditors who are strangers to the corporation.[128]

There are obvious and important distinctions between these two different kinds of First Amendment rights. Those who possess an original right to participate in public discourse cannot be compelled to speak in public discourse.[129] First Amendment rights include "both the right to speak freely and the right to refrain from speaking at all."[130] By contrast commercial corporations are routinely required to make factual public disclosures, and these requirements do not trigger any First Amendment

---

business, including non-press communicative businesses like film distributors, but they are constitutionally prohibited from imposing a singular tax on the press. In *Minneapolis Star,* the Court explained that this is because a unique tax on the press would be inconsistent with the distinct constitutional function of the press, which is to "serve as an important restraint on government." Ibid., 585.

The constitutional value of the press articulated in *Minneapolis Star* has been theorized as the "checking value," and it is well established in law and history. *See, e.g.,* David A. Anderson, *The Origins of the Press Clause,* 30 UCLA L. Rev. 455, 491 (1983) ("[A] press clause was necessary, not to induce the press to provide a check on governmental power, but because it was universally assumed that the press would indeed provide such a check and that government therefore would seek to suppress it."); Potter Stewart, *Or of the Press,* 26 Hastings L.J. 631, 633 (1979) ("The primary purpose of the constitutional guarantee of a free press was . . . to create a fourth institution outside the Government as an additional check on the three official branches."); Vincent Blasi, *The Checking Value in First Amendment Theory,* 1977 Am. B. Found. Res. J. 521, 538 ("[O]ne of the most important values attributed to a free press by eighteenth-century political thinkers was that of checking the inherent tendency of government officials to abuse the power entrusted to them."). The distinct constitutional value of the press justifies the distinct constitutional treatment of the press. *See, e.g.,* C. Edwin Baker, *The Independent Significance of the Press Clause Under Existing Law,* 35 Hofstra L. Rev. 955 (2007); Randall P. Bezanson, *The Developing Law of Editorial Judgment,* 78 Neb. L. Rev. 754 (1999); Randall P. Bezanson, *No Middle Ground? Reflections on the* Citizens United *Decision,* 96 Iowa L. Rev. 649 (2011).

Corporations that serve the checking value should receive constitutional protections appropriate to that value. Corporations that do not serve the checking value should not receive these constitutional protections. What is constitutionally decisive is the relationship between a speaker and the checking value; the corporate form of the speaker is irrelevant. Corporations that serve the checking value are *for this very reason* constitutionally distinct from both expressive associations and ordinary commercial corporations. No doubt it may be difficult to distinguish corporate speakers that serve the checking value from those that are ordinary commercial corporations, but analogous difficulties afflict much constitutional law.

scrutiny at all. This is because the First Amendment rights of commercial corporations derive from the rights of auditors to be informed, not from the rights of speakers to experience democratic legitimation.[131]

The Court in *Citizens United* is oblivious to this fundamental distinction, misinterpreting *Bellotti* as rejecting "the argument that political speech of corporations or other associations should be treated differently under the First Amendment simply because such associations are not 'natural persons.' "[132] *Bellotti* was at pains to explain that it was holding no such thing. *Bellotti* explicitly signaled that in theory and practice the First Amendment rights possessed by commercial corporations differ from those possessed by natural persons.

At its core, First Amendment doctrine is designed to restrict government regulation of public discourse. By *public discourse* I refer to the participation of natural persons or their expressive associations in the formation of public opinion. Only natural persons can experience the good of democratic legitimation. First Amendment doctrine holds that participation in public discourse is "delicate and vulnerable, as well as supremely precious in our society. The threat of sanctions may deter [its] exercise almost as potently as the actual application of sanctions. Because First Amendment freedoms need breathing space to survive, government may regulate in the area only with narrow specificity."[133] This reasoning supports the application of strict scrutiny to restrictions on public discourse.

Participation in public discourse is "supremely precious" because such participation makes democratic legitimation possible. Democratic legitimation is necessary for self-government. As Brandeis wrote almost a century ago, the "full and free exercise" of First Amendment rights is a "political duty" essential to the nation; the "greatest menace to freedom is an inert people."[134] Only active participation can produce the democratic legitimation that underwrites self-government. When the state chills public discourse, it chills the possibility of self-determination.

The derivate right of an ordinary commercial corporation to contribute to informed decision making does not involve the "supremely precious" value of democratic legitimation. Ordinary commercial corporations have no "political duty" to participate in public discussion. It is not a menace to freedom if commercial corporations are inert. Ordinary commercial corporations are not vehicles of self-governance. The First Amendment is not concerned with protecting the "worth, standing, and respect"[135] accorded to the voice of ordinary commercial corporations.

If public opinion is constitutionally understood as the "resultant of the struggle between contending forces,"[136] ordinary commercial corporations have neither the right nor the responsibility to contribute their views to public opinion. Instead ordinary commercial corporations have the right only to publish such information as may be useful to natural persons who seek to participate in public discourse.

Important constitutional distinctions follow from this difference. Because government restrictions on public discourse potentially impair democratic legitimation, courts may properly prevent the state from restricting public discourse unless in the service of the most compelling interests. Because restrictions on the speech of ordinary commercial corporations potentially impair only the circulation of possibly valuable information, courts should allow the state to regulate such speech on the basis of less pressing interests.[137] The Court has explicitly embraced this conclusion in the closely analogous context of commercial speech, which, like the corporate speech we are considering, triggers First Amendment scrutiny *only* because it provides potentially valuable information to auditors.[138]

Government cannot prohibit participation in public discourse on the ground that it fails to promote informed public decision making.[139] This is because participation in public discourse is not protected because it promotes informed public decision making, but instead because it creates democratic legitimation. By contrast, if the speech of an ordinary commercial corporation fails to inform public decision making, the speech may be regulated. This is because the speech is protected only because it promotes informed public decision making. There is once again a strong analogy to the doctrinal category of commercial speech.[140] It is a contingent, empirical question whether independent campaign expenditures by commercial corporations promote informed public decision making.[141]

The Court's opinion in *Citizens United* is pervasively confused by its failure to appreciate these basic constitutional distinctions. Section 441b of BCRA does not absolutely prohibit ordinary commercial corporations from express advocacy or electioneering communications. It instead provides that expenditures for such purposes must be made from separately segregated funds called PACs,[142] funds especially created for this purpose by corporations and supported by donations from stockholders and employees of the corporation. The Court held that § 441b was nevertheless the constitutional equivalent of an absolute prohibition:

Section 441b is a ban on corporate speech notwithstanding the fact that a PAC created by a corporation can still speak. A PAC is a separate association from the corporation. So the PAC exemption from § 441b's expenditure ban, § 441b(b)(2), does not allow corporations to speak. Even if a PAC could somehow allow a corporation to speak—and it does not—the option to form PACs does not alleviate the First Amendment problems with § 441b. PACs are burdensome alternatives; they are expensive to administer and subject to extensive regulations. . . .

. . . .

Section 441b's prohibition on corporate independent expenditures is thus a ban on speech. . . . If § 441b applied to individuals, no one would believe that it is merely a time, place, or manner restriction on speech.[143]

This passage flatly equates the First Amendment rights of ordinary commercial corporations with those of natural persons. It thus basically misunderstands the constitutional status of ordinary commercial corporations. The First Amendment has nothing to say about the kinds of commercial associations a state can authorize. It is open to a state to create forms of commercial associations that are forbidden from participating in politics, either through express advocacy or electioneering communications. Individuals may have a First Amendment right to form expressive associations, but they have no First Amendment right to form ordinary commercial associations. An ordinary commercial corporation has no original First Amendment right to speak in its own voice.

Because the speech of an ordinary commercial corporation possesses constitutional value only because it provides information to auditors, it is of no constitutional significance whether this information is communicated in the voice of a distinct commercial corporate entity or in the voice of a PAC created by the corporation. The only constitutional question presented by BCRA is whether prohibiting ordinary commercial corporations from speaking through the corporate form, as distinct from speaking through a PAC, undermines informed public decision making.

The Court's opinion in *Citizens United* repeatedly appropriates the form of First Amendment doctrine that is associated with "chilling effect" analysis.[144] It argues that because it is more burdensome to speak through a PAC than to speak directly without a PAC, BCRA might discourage protected speech that would otherwise be produced. Chilling effect analysis turns on the premise that First Amendment rights are "delicate and vulnerable, as well as supremely precious." Yet the speech of ordinary commercial corporations is not supremely precious, because ordinary commercial corporations do not promote the good of democratic legitimation.

Although the value of a politically active citizenry is incalculable, it is always easiest for citizens to retreat to private life and to refuse the challenge of public participation.[145] The First Amendment has therefore been interpreted to prohibit state regulations that chill the creation of democratic legitimation. Because the speech of ordinary commercial corporations is by law required to promote its corporate financial interests, there is no reason to regard such corporate speech as vulnerable and delicate. That is why chilling effect analysis typically does not apply in the analogous arena of commercial speech.[146]

Even if we assume that the regulation of PACs might be burdensome if applied to the speech of natural persons, therefore, it does not follow that the regulation is constitutionally disfavored in the context of ordinary commercial corporations. The relevant question, which the Court neither asks nor answers, is whether prohibiting direct corporate speech, but allowing the speech of PACs, promotes or undermines informed public decision making.[147]

V.

The First Amendment theorist who has thought most deeply about how First Amendment rights might be structured so as to promote informed public decision making is Alexander Meiklejohn. Meiklejohn famously argued that the whole point of First Amendment rights is to ensure that "a self-governing community," committed to "the method of voting," can "gain wisdom in action."[148] "The point of ultimate interest," Meiklejohn observed, "is not the words of the speakers, but the minds of the hearers. The final aim . . . is the voting of wise decisions."[149] After careful analysis, Meiklejohn concluded that this aim could be achieved only if First Amendment rights were structured to permit, and sometimes even to require, discrimination among speakers.

Citing the protocols of "the traditional American town meeting,"[150] Meiklejohn observed that if our goal is to allow "all facts and interests relevant to the problem [to] be fully and fairly presented," we must adopt procedures that enable "facts and interests" to be presented "in such a way that all the alternative lines of action can be wisely measured in relation to one another."[151] In constructing such procedures, "what is essential is not that everyone shall speak, but that everything worth saying shall be said. To this end, for example, it may be arranged that each of the known conflicting points of view shall have, and shall be limited to, an assigned share of the time available."[152]

We adopt procedures like those described by Meiklejohn whenever informed decision making is our primary goal. Meiklejohn himself regarded the orderly procedures of American town meetings as paradigmatic. These procedures discriminate among speakers based upon whether they are "in order" or "out of order"; whether they intend to speak about relevant or irrelevant matters; whether they are disruptive or orderly; whether they are repetitive or original; and so on. It is only by making such distinctions that a town meeting can effectively and cogently promote informed decision making by townspeople.

Analogous rules obtain in legislative proceedings and hearings, which are designed to promote the informed deliberations of lawmakers. During hearings or debates, Congress does not permit speakers to talk about whatever subject at whatever length they wish. It routinely discriminates among speakers to promote the orderly presentation of information and debate. Analogous rules govern courtroom proceedings, which are designed to inform the verdicts of judges and juries. Imagine the chaos that would transpire if persons could speak in a courtroom according to their resources and desires. Analogous rules apply in educational settings like universities and schools, which aim to effectively and efficiently inform students. Teachers who truly wish to inform their students do not permit class time to be taken up by the indiscriminate chatter of anyone who has the capacity or desire to talk.

The Court itself has applied Meiklejohnian principles to regulations of speech not involving the original right to participate in public discourse. In *Red Lion Broadcasting Co. v. FCC*,[153] the Court considered a constitutional challenge to the fairness doctrine, as well as to subsidiary FCC rules requiring that those personally attacked be given a right to reply. These rules discriminated among speakers based upon the content of their speech. Yet the Court, assuming that broadcast frequencies were a scarce commodity and that it was therefore "idle to posit an unabridgeable First Amendment right to broadcast comparable to the right of every individual to speak, write, or publish,"[154] declared that "it is the right of viewers and listeners, not the right of the broadcasters, which is paramount."[155] The Court based its reasoning on the conclusion that broadcasters were not independent speakers but were instead proxies or fiduciaries "with obligations to present those views and voices which are representative of his community and which would otherwise, by necessity, be barred from the airwaves."[156]

The Court interpreted the First Amendment rights of the public in light of the constitutional imperative of informed public decision making. It declared that "the people as a whole retain their interest in free speech by radio and their collective right to have the medium function consistently with the ends and purposes of the First Amendment."[157] It stressed that "the right of the public to receive suitable access to social, political, esthetic, moral, and other ideas and experiences . . . may not constitutionally be abridged either by Congress or by the FCC."[158] It approved the fairness doctrine and the right of reply regulations because they created procedures that advanced "the First Amendment goal of producing an informed public capable of conducting its own affairs."[159] The Court concluded as a matter of constitutional law that such orderly procedures would produce a more informed public than unregulated communicative laissez-faire.

In the opening decades of the twentieth century, when public opinion became the foundation for self-government, the authority of public opinion emerged simultaneously with a profound critique of public opinion. Many feared that public opinion was vulnerable to "the manufacture of consent" based upon "propaganda" and "censorship."[160] Deeply moved by the perversions of public sentiment during World War I, Walter Lippmann in his 1922 masterpiece *Public Opinion* spelled out modern techniques for the manipulation of popular thought, stressing the incapacity of ordinary citizens to assimilate and understand the information necessary for self-governance. Lippmann's insights have since given birth to a cottage industry dedicated to illustrating the limitations and inadequacies of public opinion.

Taken to their logical conclusion, Lippmann's insights undercut the very aspiration to self-determination. Like most Americans, however, Lippmann was unprepared to accept a government controlled by Platonic (expert) Guardians.[161] He was therefore moved to stress the need for "a procedure" by which popular intelligence could be educated.[162] He imagined fora of discussion, like those elaborated by Meiklejohn or *Red Lion,* in which there would be a "chairman or mediator, who forces the discussion to deal with the analyses supplied by experts," a procedure analogous to "the essential organization of any representative body dealing with distant matters."[163] The insight that public opinion might require orderly educational procedures in order to become more informed arose in our history at about the same time as the insight that public opinion requires a framework of judicially enforceable First Amendment rights.

Meiklejohn teaches that if we take seriously the constitutional value of informed public decision making, it makes little sense to commit ourselves to a flat and invariant rule that forbids discrimination among speakers. *Citizens United* thus has it exactly backward. Informed public decision making is best facilitated by scrupulous rules of procedure, like those we employ in courtrooms, legislative hearings, or classrooms. All such procedures discriminate among speakers. This insight underlies the conclusion of the Canadian Supreme Court that election expenditures ought to be carefully regulated in ways that differentiate between speakers:

> The question, then, is what promotes an informed voter? For voters to be able to hear all points of view, the information disseminated by third parties, candidates and political parties cannot be unlimited. In the absence of spending limits, it is possible for the affluent or a number of persons or groups pooling their resources and acting in concert to dominate the political discourse. The respondent's factum illustrates that political advertising is a costly endeavour. If a few groups are able to flood the electoral discourse with their message, it is possible, indeed likely, that the voices of some will be drowned out.... Where those having access to the most resources monopolize the election discourse, their opponents will be deprived of a reasonable opportunity to speak and be heard. This unequal dissemination of points of view undermines the voter's ability to be adequately informed of all views.[164]

Our constitutional structure differs from that of Canada because we classify election speech as public discourse. We protect public discourse to serve the constitutional value of democratic legitimation rather than that of informed public decision making.[165] But the essential point, as I have observed, is that democratic legitimation is not at stake in the speech of ordinary commercial corporations. With regard to such speech, *Bellotti* holds that the correct First Amendment value to adopt is that of informed public decision making.

Government ought therefore to be free to regulate the speech of ordinary commercial corporations in order to promote informed public decision making. This freedom should not be compromised by inapplicable "rules" that forbid speaker discrimination. Such rules chiefly apply to public discourse, in which ordinary commercial corporations do not participate.

VI.

First Amendment jurisprudence routinely distinguishes public discourse from speech that may be regulated in order to facilitate the achievement of specific governmental purposes, like the promotion of informed public decision making. In *Citizens United,* the Court thoughtfully observes:

> The Court has upheld a narrow class of speech restrictions that operate to the disadvantage of certain persons, but these rulings were based on an interest in allowing governmental entities to perform their functions. *See, e.g., Bethel School Dist. No. 403 v. Fraser,* 478 U.S. 675, 683 (1986) (protecting the "function of public school education"); *Jones v. North Carolina Prisoners' Labor Union, Inc.,* 433 U.S. 119, 129 (1977) (furthering "the legitimate penological objectives of the corrections system"); *Parker v. Levy,* 417 U.S. 733, 759 (1974) (ensuring "the capacity of the Government to discharge its [military] responsibilities"); *Civil Service Comm'n v. Letter Carriers,* 413 U.S. 548, 557 (1973) ("[F]ederal service should depend upon meritorious performance rather than political service"). The corporate independent expenditures at issue in this case, however, would not interfere with governmental functions, so these cases are inapposite. These precedents stand only for the proposition that there are certain governmental functions that cannot operate without some restrictions on particular kinds of speech. By contrast, it is inherent in the nature of the political process that voters must be free to obtain information from diverse sources in order to determine how to cast their votes. At least before *Austin,* the Court had not allowed the exclusion of a class of speakers from the general public dialogue.[166]

The cases cited by the Court stand for a simple proposition. When government creates institutions in order to accomplish specific ends, it must organize persons within these institutions to accomplish relevant "governmental functions." The state must manage the behavior of such persons, and so it must also manage their speech.[167] Managing persons inevitably entails discriminating between persons and viewpoints. Within public schools, the First Amendment does not prevent teachers from allowing some students to speak but not others; within courtrooms, the

First Amendment does not prevent judges from allowing some witnesses to testify but not others; within government bureaucracies, the First Amendment does not prohibit supervisors from allowing some employees to speak but not others.

We might generalize these observations by saying that within state institutions the government possesses what I shall call *managerial authority* to regulate speech in ways that would be impermissible within public discourse. Managerial authority rests on the necessity of supervising speech in order to accomplish the "governmental functions" of specific state institutions. Within schools, speech must be regulated to achieve the task of education; within courtrooms to realize the value of justice; within bureaucracies to attain the distinct goals for which the different bureaucracies have been created.

Managerial authority is typically exercised upon a showing of functional need. The scope of managerial authority is circumscribed by the boundaries of the organization within which it is exercised. These boundaries define what for First Amendment purposes we might designate as a *managerial domain*. Managerial domains are inevitable in modern states because they are required to achieve goals that have been democratically determined. Speech within managerial domains is constitutionally distinct from speech within public discourse. Within managerial domains, speech may be regulated in order to achieve the instrumental goals of the domain; within public discourse, speech must be kept free in order democratically to determine what these goals should be.

The Court in *Citizens United* is incorrect to claim that elections are not institutions that serve "governmental functions." Elections are government institutions designed to accomplish a specific purpose, in just the same way that schools, courtrooms, or bureaucracies are organizations designed to accomplish particular objectives. The purpose of elections is to transform public opinion into legitimate public will. They are "the means through which a free society democratically translates political speech into concrete governmental action."[168] There are many ways in which elections can work this transformation,[169] but elections, like all government institutions, must be organized and managed in order to accomplish their distinctive mission.

"Elections and related democratic processes are pervasively regulated (far more so than the general realm of public debate). In the more visible foreground, states print ballots, determine the conditions under which candidates and parties attain ballot access, and organize and structure the process of voting. In the background, prior decisions have been made about the underlying structure of elections and representative institutions."[170] Like every government institution, elections must manage speech as well as behavior. In holding that Hawaii's ban on write-in voting did not violate the First Amendment rights of voters, the Court affirmed that "Common sense, as well as constitutional law, compels the conclusion that government must play an active role in structuring elections; 'as a practical matter, there must be a substantial regulation of elections if they are to be fair and honest and if some sort of order, rather than chaos, is to accompany the democratic processes.'"[171]

The Court has held that "'A State indisputably has a compelling interest in preserving the integrity of its election process.' Confidence in the integrity of our electoral processes is essential to the functioning of our participatory democracy."[172] To the end of preserving electoral integrity, the state can and must restrict speech in ways that would be unconstitutional if applied to public discourse. It is well recognized that "election laws invariably 'affec[t]—at least to some degree—the individual's right . . . to associate with others for political ends.'"[173]

From a historical perspective, the state has not hesitated to exercise the managerial authority necessary to ensure that elections serve their "governmental functions." Throughout much of the nineteenth century, for example, voters expressed their preferences by using ballots privately printed by political parties. Because voters' preferences were revealed by the color and shape of their ballots, bribery and coercion thrived, and elections lost integrity. The state responded by adopting the Australian ballot, which was formulated and printed by the state and which was cast in secret.[174] The constitutionality of the Australian ballot is now unquestionable, yet the Australian ballot restricts the preexisting rights of political parties to express themselves through privately printed ballots.

In the early twentieth century, when distrust of private political parties threatened to undermine the purpose of elections, the state moved to assert "public control and regulation of the machinery of party nominations," most especially through direct primaries.[175] The direct primary constricted the associational rights of private political parties, which previously had been free to nominate candidates as they wished, but which after the direct primary were obliged to follow government rules to access the state-organized Australian ballot. When it was later perceived that the function of elections was threatened because racial discrimination made primaries responsive to white public opinion rather than to public opinion, the Court itself chose to intervene in the White Primary Cases to regulate the private political speech of private political parties.[176]

The Court has "'repeatedly upheld reasonable, politically neutral regulations that have the effect of channeling expressive activit[ies] at the polls.'"[177] The managerial authority of the state in organizing elections is obvious at polling places, where the state is explicitly given wide latitude to regulate speech in order to ensure the legitimacy of the electoral process.[178] Within the polling place, the state can authorize the speech of some persons (election workers), but deny the speech of others (partisan advocates). What justifies such regulation is the need for elections to fulfill their "governmental function" of freely and fairly choosing candidates.

It is sometimes controversial whether speech occurs inside or outside the managerial domain of a state institution. Institutional boundaries are not marked with signposts. Organization theory regards "organizations as open systems," whose "boundaries must necessarily be sieves, not shells, admitting the desirable flows and excluding the inappropriate or deleterious elements."[179] Boundaries are therefore "very difficult to delineate in social systems, such as organizations."[180] Because all organizations are dependent on their environment, they have strong incentives to reach out and extend their "control" over important external resources,[181] pushing their already open boundaries into a state of constant motion.

The porous quality of organizational boundaries is visible in the decisions of the Court that establish managerial authority. The Court has held that a police department can punish a police officer who made a raunchy video on private time and in a private location, in private dress and privately distributed through eBay, on the mere ground that the video was "detrimental to the mission and functions of the employer."[182] The Court has held that a privately funded and maintained mailbox can be regulated as if it were Postal Service property, on the ground that mailboxes are "an essential part of the Postal Service's nationwide system for the delivery and receipt of mail,"[183] and must be "under the direction and control of the Postal Service"[184] if the Service is "to operate as efficiently as possible a system for the delivery of mail."[185] The Second Circuit has held that a public school can punish a student for speech distributed through an independent blog posting made from a private computer at home during nonschool hours, so long as punishment is required to maintain institutional discipline within the school.[186]

These decisions illustrate that when exercising managerial authority, the state can regulate speech upon a showing of mere functional need, in contrast to the "compelling" interests that must be demonstrated to justify restrictions on public discourse.[187] They also illustrate that the managerial domain of a state institution can extend far beyond its ordinary physical geography. State institutions exercise managerial authority over speech that does not occur on state property; that does not occur during regular working hours; that is not clothed with the accoutrements of official uniforms or other indicia of official control or direction. Courts seem to locate the institutional boundaries of managerial authority on the basis of their perception of an institution's functional needs.

Courts have in the past located the institutional boundaries of elections in this same way. Before the Australian ballot, political parties expressed themselves by printing and organizing private ballots. Because the state needed to maintain the effectiveness of elections, the state preempted this heretofore private speech and converted ballots into a "public expense."[188] Before the state created the direct primary, nominations for public office were decided by the voluntary procedures of private political parties. When these procedures caused the public to lose confidence in elections, the state expanded the managerial domain of elections to preempt the associative rules used by private expressive associations to qualify candidates for the state-produced Australian ballot.[189]

We may conclude that speech within the managerial domain of an election can be regulated to achieve the purpose of the election, and that the boundaries of the domain should be determined in a manner that is sensitive to the functional requirements of the election. These conclusions were recently confirmed by the Court itself when it summarily affirmed the constitutionality of a federal statute prohibiting foreign nationals from making independent expenditures or contributions in connection with any national, state, or local election.[190]

Although the federal statute plainly discriminates among speakers, the Court upheld its constitutionality without even bothering to write an opinion. In the judgment of the three-judge district court that decided the case below, the prohibition was self-evidently required to serve the basic governmental function of elections—the "democratic self-government" of the American people.[191] The court reasoned that this function could be achieved *only* if the contributions and independent expenditures of foreign nationals could be regulated within the managerial domain of an

American election.[192] The court held that the objective of "democratic self-government" rendered it immaterial whether the independent expenditures of foreign nationals might also contribute to informed public decision making.[†]

The campaign advertisements and advocacy that accompany elections are usually classified as public discourse. Courts are reluctant to subject such speech to managerial control because they properly seek to enlarge the scope of public discourse. Courts wish to maximize the "precious" resource of democratic legitimation. But the speech of ordinary commercial corporations, as I have emphasized, does not form part of public discourse. The holding of *Bellotti* is that the speech of ordinary commercial corporations is constitutionally valuable only because it facilitates informed public decision making.

[†] The logic of the three-judge district court diverged in important ways from that of *Citizens United*. The three-judge district court reasoned that "[i]t is fundamental to the definition of our national political community that foreign citizens do not have a constitutional right to participate in, and thus may be excluded from, activities of democratic self-government. It follows, therefore, that the United States has a compelling interest for purposes of First Amendment analysis in limiting the participation of foreign citizens in activities of American democratic self-government, and in thereby preventing foreign influence over the U.S. political process." Bluman v. FEC, 800 F. Supp. 2d 281, 288 (D.D.C. 2011), *aff'd mem.,* 132 S. Ct. 1087 (2012).

Commercial corporations "do not have a constitutional right to participate in, and thus may be excluded from," elections, in the sense that they cannot vote or run for office. Yet it did not follow for *Citizens United* that the federal government *therefore* had a compelling interest in limiting their independent expenditures. *Citizens United* instead insisted that because corporate independent expenditures could promote informed public decision making, the regulation of these expenditures should receive strict judicial scrutiny.

Evidently the three-judge district court believed that the "governmental function" of enabling democratic self-government should displace the function of promoting informed public decision making. The court sustained regulations it deemed necessary to preserve electoral integrity, regardless of whether these regulations might diminish the possibility of informed public decision making. In an opinion summarily affirmed by the Supreme Court, the three-judge district court effectively held that electoral integrity trumps informed public decision making as a governmental function of elections. By contrast *Citizens United* did not even consider the relationship between § 441b and electoral integrity. *Citizens United* focused *only* on the goal of promoting informed public decision making and failed entirely to analyze any other governmental function elections might serve.

There should thus be no First Amendment objection to establishing a managerial domain within which government may regulate the expenditures and contributions of ordinary commercial corporations in order to promote the purposes of an election. From a constitutional point of view, these purposes include both the maintenance of electoral integrity and the promotion of informed decision making.[193] The boundaries of the managerial domain associated with an election should be determined by the requirements of achieving these "governmental functions."

How corporate speech might be organized to serve these functions can be determined only on the basis of a working knowledge of the material facts. It cannot be ascertained on the basis of abstract doctrinal rules. The ordinary regulation of speech within institutions like courts, legislatures, schools, or town meetings strongly suggests that a presumptive constitutional prohibition against speaker discrimination should have no place within the managerial domain of an election. Instead, judicial review should focus on whether government regulation advances the goals of electoral integrity or the promotion of informed government decision making.

VII.

The Court in *Citizens United* writes as if First Amendment analysis ends with the observation that § 441b of the BCRA prohibits public discourse and must therefore receive the strictest form of First Amendment scrutiny. The Court finds § 441b without compelling justification and consequently unconstitutional.

If the arguments I have thus far advanced are correct, the Court's entire framework of analysis is flawed. First, and most importantly, the Court fails to acknowledge the fundamental significance of electoral integrity as a justification for state regulation of campaign expenditures. Electoral integrity is required for the very First Amendment rights the Court seeks to protect. It is far more fundamental than any merely "compelling" interest the Court might seek to plug into a formula for "strict scrutiny." Such interests must be weighed *against* First Amendment rights; electoral integrity, by contrast, is a precondition *for* such rights.

Second, to the extent that the Court glimpses the possibility of a state interest in electoral integrity, it falsely imagines that electoral integrity is a matter of law, rather than of fact. Electoral integrity is contingent on the design of government institutions. Governments in the United States have continuously altered the structure of elections in order to maintain the supremely precious resource of electoral integrity.

Third, the Court writes as if § 441b of BCRA regulates public discourse. But § 441b does not control the speech of natural persons. Section 441b does not create an inert people. As applied to ordinary commercial corporations (as distinct from expressive associations that happen to be corporations), § 441b regulates entities that merely provide constitutionally valuable information to the public. As in the context of commercial speech, strict scrutiny is an inappropriate standard of review.

Fourth, it is an empirical question whether § 441b actually diminishes the flow of useful information to the public. Section 441b permits the distribution of information by corporate PACs. *Citizens United* presumes the public will be better informed after it strikes down § 441b than in the decades before the *Citizens United* decision. But this is far from obvious.[194]

Fifth, the Court ignores the possibility that the speech of ordinary commercial corporations might constitutionally be organized into a managerial domain dedicated to achieving the purpose of elections. Because the speech of ordinary commercial corporations does not form part of public discourse, the First Amendment should allow government to create such a domain so long as it is governed by the First Amendment goals of maintaining electoral integrity and promoting informed public decision making. Within such a domain, the state will inevitably distinguish among speakers. It is therefore inappropriate for the Court to invoke a strong constitutional presumption against speaker-discrimination.

Sixth, assuming that § 441b actually produces a less informed public, this loss must be set against whatever gains in electoral integrity § 441b may promote. Since the beginning of the twentieth century, the American public has associated unrestricted corporate electoral expenditures with the loss of electoral integrity. In *Citizens United* five members of the Court brush this history aside without so much as noticing the constitutional stakes. The constitutionality of § 441b cannot be assessed unless the potential informational losses caused by § 441b are somehow balanced against potential gains to electoral integrity.

Electoral integrity consists of public confidence that elected officials attend to public opinion. It has rightly been observed that the state's "interest in protecting public confidence 'in the integrity and legitimacy of representative government'" is of the highest order, because "public confidence in the integrity of the electoral process . . . encourages citizen participation in the democratic process."[195] Electoral integrity is in this regard a unique kind of constitutional value, for it depends upon what people actually believe.[196] Electoral integrity should be contrasted to constitutional values like the "equally effective voice"[197] principle, which guarantees to each citizen the right to cast an equal vote. The "equally effective voice" principle should be applied on the basis of the actual facts relevant to equality, rather than on the basis of subjective beliefs about equality.

When I have discussed the thesis of these lectures with friends and colleagues, the subjective foundations of electoral integrity have been a frequent source of concern and misgiving. This is understandable. Binding a constitutional value to the caprice of public opinion is deeply unsettling. For good reason the Framers' fear of the "fury of democracy" has never entirely dissipated.

Concern is compounded because electoral integrity can be known only by interpreting the substance of public opinion. Whether the public trusts elections to select representatives who attend to public opinion cannot be ascertained merely through voting statistics or opinion polls, which are at best static, partial, and schematic representations of public opinion.[198] The question of electoral integrity ultimately involves judgment about the contents of public opinion. Because any such judgment will always be controversial, recognizing a constitutionally compelling interest in electoral integrity will inevitably authorize restrictions on the political process that courts will have difficulty scrutinizing.

There is merit to these objections, but they must be evaluated in light of alternative possible conclusions. It does not seem plausible within our political tradition to repudiate the premise that democratic legitimacy depends upon actual beliefs about the responsiveness of elected officials to public opinion. To deny this premise in the twenty-first century is to repudiate self-government itself, for a people cannot experience the value of self-government unless they believe themselves to be self-governing. Yet if the premise is true, it would seem perverse to prohibit courts from incorporating the premise into their reasoning. Any such prohibition would blind constitutional law to the foundational facts of our political life, facts no less real because they resist precise measurement and can be discerned only through the lens of judgment.

Courts have reason to be wary of efforts to regulate the political process. Legislatures are populated by politicians who possess a common interest in preserving their own positions. In reviewing campaign finance legislation, therefore, courts should be alert to the risk that statutes are designed to protect incumbents rather than to sustain electoral integrity. But the chance that legislation might be self-serving does not rule out, either logically or practically, the possibility that legislation might also be required to enhance electoral integrity.

It is the job of courts to distinguish self-serving legislation that corrupts the political process from wholesome legislation that nourishes democratic legitimacy. In making this distinction, courts would do well to keep in mind that discerning electoral integrity ultimately requires political judgment of a kind that judges are not well positioned to exercise. Ascertaining the basic legitimacy of our democratic state is not the sort of legal question that courts are accustomed to deciding. Courts do not ordinarily determine constitutional questions by interpreting public opinion. These tasks require skills that we expect from our popularly elected branches when they are acting at their best.[199]

The fundamentally political nature of electoral integrity does not justify courts in ruling out electoral integrity as a compelling government interest. Electoral integrity is indispensable for constitutional self-government. American legislatures have in the past repeatedly regulated elections in ways designed to preserve electoral integrity. We now acknowledge and applaud the necessity and wisdom of many of these interventions. That *courts* may find it difficult to assess electoral integrity is thus no reason to prevent *legislatures* from pursuing their historic mission of conserving electoral integrity. Were courts to deny legislatures the constitutional authority required to safeguard electoral integrity, they would undermine the very constitutional value of self-government that underlies judicial efforts to protect First Amendment rights.

In reviewing campaign finance legislation aimed at enhancing electoral integrity, therefore, courts should temper their natural suspicion of political self-dealing with a margin of judicial appreciation for the necessarily *political* judgment involved in evaluations of electoral integrity.[200] Such evaluations must necessarily underlie any attempt to balance the informational losses inflicted by § 441b's restrictions on independent corporate campaign expenditures against potential gains in public confidence achieved by these restrictions. It may not be easy for courts to maintain this precarious balance, but surely no one ever seriously believed that the practice of constitutional law could be mechanical or simple.[201]

VIII.

I have so far been exceedingly conservative in my constitutional analysis. I have attempted to explicate how the democratic principles of the First Amendment and the representative principles of elections might be reconciled in the narrow context of the precise restrictions contained in § 441b. But I shall conclude this lecture by observing that the constitutional issues posed by *Citizens United* might be considered from a somewhat broader perspective. Instead of analyzing the specific constitutionality of § 441b, we might briefly consider how the larger question of independent electoral expenditures, whether corporate or otherwise, might be theorized under the First Amendment. The most useful conceptual tool for this analysis is that of the managerial domain.

The compromise struck by *Buckley* has proved unstable and unsettling. Some would say that it has produced a disastrous electoral environment. Because *Buckley* prohibited government from regulating independent expenditures while allowing it to regulate contributions, it "produced a system in which candidates face an unlimited demand for campaign funds (because expenditures generally cannot be capped) but a constricted supply (because there is often a ceiling on the amount each contributor can give). . . . [T]he result is an unceasing preoccupation with fundraising."[202]

Forty years ago a majority of Americans believed that the dependence of elections on private funding held great dangers for the American Republic.[203] In succeeding years American political campaigns have grown exponentially more expensive, and concomitant dangers have accordingly multiplied. The public cannot help but worry that he who pays the piper will call the tune. In a recent decision the Court has even gone so far as to hold that it would violate the appearance of impartiality required by the Due Process Clause for a judge to decide the case of someone who had made significant independent expenditures in support of the judge's own reelection campaign.[204] It is not difficult to understand why the *Buckley* compromise has put public confidence intrinsically and perennially at risk.

A truly systemic risk to electoral integrity might require a comprehensive constitutional response. We might kick aside the rotten floorboards of *Buckley* and begin our analysis from the premise that electoral integrity remains fundamentally threatened so long as campaign expenditures remain unregulated. The threat does not derive from corporate expenditures alone, but from all campaign expenditures, including those of wealthy candidates and supercharged PACs. Because election speech is public discourse, we ordinarily guarantee persons the right to participate in the manner of their choice. We do not permit expenditure limitations because we wish to promote democratic legitimation.

Citizens United should have been a relatively easy case, because democratic legitimation is not at stake in the restrictions on corporate speech imposed by § 441b. When we consider the regulation of individual independent expenditures, by contrast, the potential loss of democratic legitimation is unavoidable. Yet if it is indeed true that uncontrolled expenditures threaten to undermine the electoral integrity of our representative system, we also face a potential loss of democratic legitimation if we choose to do nothing.

We thus face a deep paradox. If we prevent government control over independent expenditures, we diminish the very democratic legitimation that uncontrolled independent expenditures are meant to enable. But if we permit government control over independent expenditures, if we prohibit persons from expressing themselves in the manner they believe best, we also circumscribe the possibility of democratic legitimation.

A paradox like this does not disappear because we ignore it. Sooner or later it must be faced down. How we resolve this paradox should ultimately depend upon the relevant facts of the matter. My point in this lecture is a limited one: If circumstances warrant deciding that the "governmental function" of elections requires the regulation of independent expenditures, we have the doctrinal tools necessary constitutionally to express this conclusion. We can explain that the managerial domain associated with elections must be enlarged to authorize control of independent expenditures that threaten electoral integrity.

A properly designed managerial domain would require government regulations to advance the goal of sustaining public confidence that elections select officials who are attentive to public opinion. It would permit judicial review to ensure that government requirements are necessary and adapted to this end. Courts should be authorized to review government regulations to ensure that they also promote the First Amendment value of informed public decision making.[205] Whether to encase elections in such a managerial domain ought to depend upon whether the dangers to electoral integrity of government inaction outweigh the risks to democratic legitimation of potential government regulation. This is a difficult, fraught, empirically based calculus.

Although managerial authority in the context of electoral speech may at first sound quite alien and strange, because it would displace the public discourse that we normally expect to accompany electoral contests, it is in fact practiced by many democracies in the world. These democracies conceive elections as discrete temporal periods that are bounded by sharp beginnings and ends. They authorize managerial public control of electioneering within these designated electoral periods.[206] The state regulates to assure that the public receives a fair and comprehensive education,[207] in much the same way that courts presently control the flow of information to juries so that they can reach informed and fair decisions.[208]

Creating a distinct managerial domain for elections requires "drawing a line between elections and politics."[209] The "crucial issue" is to establish a "boundary between [an] institutionalized electoral realm and general civic or public life."[210] Our present law already tentatively draws such lines. We impose disclosure requirements that apply to campaign-related expenditures but not to expenditures for public discourse generally.[211] We impose disclosure obligations on speakers that are triggered only during an "election."[212] We impose obligations on media that are triggered only during an "election."[213]

BCRA uses the definition of an "electioneering communication" to establish a boundary between politics and elections. The statute defines an "electioneering communication" to be any broadcast, cable, or satellite communication that refers to a candidate for federal office and that is aired within thirty days of a federal primary election or sixty days of a federal general election in the jurisdiction in which that candidate is running for office.[214] BCRA seeks to impose obligations on electioneering communications that government cannot impose on speech generally.[215]

BCRA's ungainly definition of an electioneering communication should be understood as a rough attempt to distinguish communications within an election from political speech generally. It is an early, halting effort to define a distinct managerial domain for American elections. BCRA's efforts in this regard were blasted by the Court in an important 2007 decision holding that because BCRA's definition of an electioneering communication "burdens political speech, it is subject to strict scrutiny."[216] In essence the Court held that public discourse could not be preempted by any distinct managerial domain for elections. Apparently the Court believed that systematic threats to electoral integrity were insufficient to warrant expanding the managerial domain of elections to include electioneering communications.

Sadly, the court reached this conclusion without ever explaining its reasons. Restrictions on public discourse are subject to strict scrutiny to protect the precious value of democratic legitimation. But electoral integrity is also essential to democratic legitimation. First Amendment rights are meaningless without electoral integrity. It follows that the First Amendment itself cannot answer the question of where constitutional boundaries for election domains ought to lie to protect electoral integrity. This question cannot be resolved by any doctrinal test. It can be settled only by the relevant facts of the matter. And these were never considered by the Court. Instead, as in *Citizens United,* the Court chose to rest its decision entirely on formal and abstract First Amendment doctrine.

In these Tanner Lectures I do not argue that the facts lead inevitably to any particular conclusion about where we should draw the boundaries of the managerial domain of elections. I am not now engaged in the serious historical and empirical inquiry that would be necessary to address this issue. I do not even argue that the much simpler question presented in *Citizens United* must necessarily be settled in one way or another. I do not contend that gains in electoral integrity from restricting independent corporate campaign expenditures constitutionally outweigh any informational costs that § 441b may create.

As I confessed at the outset, it is not my business to point the way forward to specific measures of reform. My own personal inclination is to establish effective public support for electoral campaigns, rather than to impose limits on campaign spending.[217] My untutored intuition is that it might be best to require TV and radio stations to provide free time for electioneering communication as a condition of receiving broadcast licenses. But in the past Congress has chosen to pursue a different policy, and in these lectures I am concerned only with how this policy ought constitutionally to be evaluated.

My conclusion is that the Court in its recent campaign finance cases has posed the wrong constitutional questions and has failed to consider the material constitutional facts. The Court has focused far too narrowly on the opaque question of corruption and has never squarely addressed the First Amendment necessity of electoral integrity. It has never articulated doctrine adequate to recognize the constitutional requirement of restoring public confidence and trust in representational government. Barricaded behind formidable formal First Amendment rules like strict scrutiny or antidiscrimination, the Court has failed to appreciate, much less to consider, the true First Amendment stakes that underlie contemporary campaign finance legislation.

A line of cases this misguided about matters of such fundamental importance to American politics is a frightful thing. In the long run, self-government will not be denied. It does not require a prophet to foresee a constitutional impasse of potentially tragic proportions.

II

COMMENTARY

3

OUT-POSTING POST

Lawrence Lessig

Among the many issues that the Framers struggled over was the question of how to select a president. The idea of a national popular vote was both fanciful and terrifying, so quickly the convention fixed upon the device of an Electoral College.

But what if the College were tied? Who should resolve the deadlock?

Some suggested the Senate. But that idea was quickly rejected, and it is the argument for that rejection I focus upon here. As summarized by Zachary Brugman:

> "Referring the appointment to the Senate lays a certain foundation for corruption & aristocracy," noted Hu Williamson from North Carolina. "The aristocratic complexion proceeds from the change in the mode of appointing the President which makes him dependent on the Senate." George Mason similarly asserted that this dependence on the Senate—while there was simultaneous (indirect) dependence on the People—would "subvert the Constitution." He would, "prefer the Government of Prussia to one which will put all power into the hands of seven or eight men, and fix an Aristocracy worse than absolute monarchy." James Wilson agreed, because of his "dependence on them," the Senate, "the President will not be the man of the people as he ought to be," he would be a "Minion of the Senate." The dependent relationship posed, "a dangerous tendency to aristocracy."[1]

To a modern, like most of us, this use of the word "corruption" is strange. The tendency toward aristocracy is clear enough. But wherein is the "corruption"? As we use that term, our minds are likely to race to the idea that a candidate for president might be tempted to buy off a few senators.

But that is not the sense in which the Framers meant the word. It is rather Wilson's usage that is most salient here—this "dependence on them," the Senate, will mean that "the President will not be the man of the people as he ought to be." The "corruption," in other words, follows from an "improper dependence"—or more precisely, from the mere chance of an improper dependence, if indeed the Electoral College were to tie.

As a longtime student of the work of Robert Post, I am quite certain that he has cracked the question of "campaign finance reform." I'm just not certain he has done so in these Tanner Lectures, or at least not completely. That is, I am certain that his method and approach to the First Amendment give us the tools to see just how the Supreme Court has gone wrong in its campaign finance jurisprudence. But I fear that in these lectures, because of a confusion about this word "corruption," a key Postean move has been left on the cutting-room floor. And in this response, I would like to reedit Post's argument a bit, to include this critical outtake and thus restore pride of place to an idea that should be central to any understanding of campaign finance in America today—institutional corruption.

Where Post Goes Wrong

Dean Post describes my work as an example of work criticizing the system of campaign finance for the "distortion" it produces within our political system. But mine is not a distortion theory of campaign finance. Mine is a corruption theory. No doubt I believe that corruption produces distortion. But a consequence is not a cause. Just as alcoholism is distinct from the liver disease it may produce, so too is "corruption" distinct from any distortion that it might cause.

Instead, in my view, it is not "distortion" that would justify campaign finance regulations. It is "corruption"—at least if we understood that term properly. The aim of my work then is to sketch a proper understanding of the word, and why, given that understanding, Congress would have the power to regulate even speech to remedy that corruption.

Yet Post ignores the possibility that "corruption" might justify campaign finance regulation, because he has given up on the concept of "corruption" within First Amendment jurisprudence. In his longest footnote in an incredibly well-documented lecture, Post summarizes the scholarship struggling to understand the Supreme Court's conception of "corruption." The upshot of that work, as Post delicately suggests, is that the Court's conception of "corruption" is confused.

But rather than resolving that confusion, Post gives up on the concept. That in turn forces him to construct a new idea of "representative integrity" to justify regulation designed to address the failings of the current campaign finance system.

As a conceptual matter, I fully embrace Post's notion of "representative integrity," and more importantly, the function he means it to have within our democracy. But as a question of rhetorical (or litigation) strategy, I do not believe it is necessary. It is easier to get clear about a conception of "corruption" that offers a clear path to a remedy than it is to convince at least the Court to open up a new branch of jurisprudence under the name of "representative integrity" designed to do essentially the same thing. Of course, we could pursue both strategies—both a better conception of "corruption" and the establishment of a richer concept of "representative integrity." But my aim in this short essay is to argue that the smaller step is worth taking too, and is strongly supported by the approach Post takes to the question of constitutional interpretation.[2]

To see how, or why, begin with the obvious: the emperor indeed is wearing no clothes. The conception of "corruption" that the Supreme Court has used has no solid theoretical grounding.

For why is it that Congress has the power to ban quid pro quo corruption, let alone the appearance of quid pro quo corruption? After the Court affirmed that power in *Buckley v. Valeo*,[3] it did not take long for scholars to tease apart the incompleteness in that conception. David Strauss did it most effectively and most clearly.[4] As we could summarize Strauss's argument, there are two types of quid pro quo that might constitute "quid pro quo corruption"—one to benefit a member personally, and the other to benefit a member politically. The former we call bribery. The latter we, or at least Chicagoans such as David Strauss and Rod Blagojevich, call politics.

Put aside bribery and compare two hypothetical statements, one by Drew Faust, Harvard's president, and one by Bill Jaeger, Harvard's director of the almost-5,000-person Clerical and Technical Union.

Imagine Faust said to a member of Congress, "If you promise to secure an earmark for Harvard, I promise to contribute $5,000 to your campaign."

And then imagine Jaeger said to the same member of Congress, "If you promise to secure an earmark for Harvard, I promise to secure 5,000 votes in your election."

Under current American law, a member of Congress who agreed with the plan Faust hypothetically proposed would have committed a felony.[5] But under current American law, a member of Congress who agreed with the plan Jaeger hypothetically proposed would have been engaging in simple politics.

Why the difference? For, after all, as Strauss and others have noted, the only purpose of the $5,000 contribution is to fund speech designed to persuade people to vote. So why is doing something in two steps a crime, when doing it in one step is not?

This is indeed a puzzle—but it is a puzzle for the Court. Because the implications of this one clear paradigmatic case are in tension with the Court's most recent First Amendment commitments. That was Strauss's point. In *Arizona Free Enterprise*,[6] for example, the Court seemed to embrace as foundational the idea that any reform designed to "level the playing field" violates the First Amendment. But obviously, to ban quid pro quo corruption is to "level the playing field"—in a kleptocracy, the rich have more power than the poor; to ban bribes or quid pro quo corruptions in a kleptocracy is thus to level the playing field between the rich and the poor. So why is that leveling permitted, but the leveling of Arizona's public funding system is not?

I'm not arguing that the Court could not offer a response. My point instead is just that any such response would be contestable; it would hang upon a particular theory of representative government, and as these Tanner Lectures demonstrate well, such theories change. They evolve. They are therefore contingent. And what that contingency should do is to drive us to ask whether there is not—for an originalist, at least—a more stable or historically solid conception of "corruption" that might more reliably guide the Court in its protection of what Post calls "representative integrity."

And here we turn back to the corruption of the presidency with which I opened this essay. For what Wilson and Mason and Madison were doing in that passage in particular, and in their language more generally, was evincing a conception of "corruption" different from the conception we moderns use; a conception that predicates corruption of institutions, or societies, or whole peoples—a collective conception—as well as individuals, and that thinks about the corruption of an institution in a specific way. As Lisa Hill describes,

> Until the end of the eighteenth century, "corruption" had a much broader meaning than it does today; it referred "less to the actions of individuals" than to the general moral health of the body politic. . . . [7]

The usage of the Framers confirms Hill's account. I asked two research assistants to collect every instance of the term "corruption" being used in the standard framing texts.[8] Of the 325 usages they identified, in 56 percent of the cases "corruption" was predicated of institutions, not individuals. "Quid pro quo" corruption was rare in this sample—only 6 instances, all of them predicated of individuals. Thus, there is no doubt the Framers used the term "corruption" to refer to quid pro quo corruption. Just not usually, or ordinarily, or even primarily.

More interestingly, the Framers offered at least one important definition of corruption particularly relevant to the corruption of an institution: improper dependence. According to this definition, an individual or institution would be corrupt if it developed an improper dependence. In at least 29 cases, the Framers spoke of corruption in just this way—five times the frequency of quid pro quo corruption. And in 69 percent of those cases, the corruption spoken of was predicated of an institution.

Thus, for the Framers, while the idea of quid pro quo corruption was present and used, a much more familiar conception of corruption was an institution that had developed an "improper dependence." That conception, of course, depends upon there being a "proper dependence" for that institution. But assuming that there is, this conception offers a simple way to identify corruption for that institution.

For example: one could conceive of an "independent judiciary" as one that is to be "dependent upon the law." Corruption for such an institution could then be constituted by its developing a different and conflicting dependence—a dependence, for example, upon the government that provided it the resources it needed if and only if the judiciary did not decide cases against it.

Likewise, the Framers meant the president to be "independent," which for them meant dependent upon the people, and not upon the courts, or, as the initial passage emphasizes, dependent upon the Senate. A conflicting dependency, as the opening passage by Brugman suggests, would corrupt the presidency. Or more precisely, a conflicting dependency would be one of the ways in which the presidency might be corrupted.

This conception of corruption—what I call "dependence corruption"[9]—has an obvious application when applied to Congress.[10] Congress was to be independent, which, as Madison described, meant "dependent upon the People," and not, for example, upon the president (as Parliament had been dependent upon the king). And not just "dependent upon the people," but as *Federalist 52* put it, "dependent upon the People alone."[11] An exclusive dependence, which would be corrupted if another inconsistent dependency were allowed to evolve within the economy of influence that is Congress.

Yet that is precisely what has happened with our Congress. Members of Congress have permitted another inconsistent dependence to evolve within the economy of influence that drives Congress: a dependence upon the funders of political campaigns. There is no doubt of that dependence: without their money, elections could not be won. There is no doubt "the funders" are not "the People": the relevant funders of campaigns are less than .05 percent of America.[12] And therefore there should be no doubt that an improper dependence now corrupts the institution of Congress.

But how does this help Post, who is not himself an "originalist"?

This conception of corruption first complements Post's idea of "representative integrity." Indeed, the corruption is a corruption of intended integrity, for however the concept of representative might have evolved, there is no way to see this current dependence as consistent with any plausible conception of "representative integrity."

This conception of corruption also suggests an obvious distinction that I was certain would be at the center of these Tanner Lectures, given everything Post has written to date: a distinction between (1) regulating speech intended for "public discourse," as Post would call it, or as I will call it, the "Public Domain," and (2) regulating speech intended to influence government officials. These two different constitutional domains should admit, at least for Posteans, of two different standards of First Amendment review. On this view, the First Amendment properly forbids the government from managing speech intended for the Public Domain but would differently limit the government in its management of speech affecting its own constitutional domain.

This is the difference, for example, between regulating corruption (à la *Buckley*) and regulating independent expenditures (à la *Buckley* and *Cit-*

izens United). An independent expenditure is speech meant for the Public Domain. Its purpose is to affect us, the citizens, and it is not the government's job to protect us citizens from the effect of such speech, whether the government likes it or not, or whether the government thinks its effect is properly earned or not.

But speech manifesting corruption is speech targeted at government officials, not ordinary citizens. The offer of a bribe is not intended for *60 Minutes*. And the intercourse between candidates and their funders is not speech meant to facilitate "democratic deliberation." (Just ask Mitt Romney whether he intended his 47 percent comment to be sprayed across the YouTube domain.) Such speech is instead speech intended to affect the "chain of representation" between candidate and funder. But from the Framers' perspective, and I suggest our own too, that means it is speech intended to corrupt the chain of representation if it manifests a dependence different from a "dependence upon the People alone."

Let's call the domain targeted by corruption regulation the Republic Domain. Within it are all the regulations necessary to preserve the "representative integrity" of a republic. And so understood, following Fred Schauer, while the First Amendment certainly "covers" speech within the Republic Domain, it does not "protect it" in the same way it protects speech within the Public Domain.[13]

If we distinguish between this Public Domain and the Republic Domain, then it is clear why Professor Kagan was right that *Austin v. Michigan Chamber of Commerce* was wrong.[14] In that case, the Court upheld a regulation on corporate speech, but corporate speech intended for the Public Domain. The government should not have that power, Kagan believed, to protect us from disfavored speech, regardless of its source. That is why independent expenditures are protected—at least from individuals, as *Buckley* holds, and possibly also from corporations, as *Citizens United* holds.

But that conclusion says nothing about the regulations that should be permitted within the Republic Domain. We can ban speech within that domain by regulating secrets.[15] We can prohibit speech on the basis of content by regulating bribes, or quid pro quo campaign contributions.[16] And we should also be able to regulate dependencies of corruption within that domain—or again, dependencies that manifest improper dependence. All of these regulations must pass through a First Amendment filter, of course. But the scrutiny is not strict, as it should be for regulations of speech meant for the Public Domain.

So how would such a move matter to the current state of campaign finance jurisprudence?

Well, again, the precise "independent expenditure" holding of *Citizens United* would stand—as would the same point in *Buckley*. The government cannot regulate speech meant for the Public Domain without clearing a strict scrutiny bar.

Likewise would the limits on contributions in *Buckley* stand—those are regulations of speech within the Republic Domain, speech targeting government officials, or official wannabes, by regulating quid pro quo corruption of them, or the appearance of quid pro quo corruption by them.

But *Buckley* likely cannot justify aggregate limits on campaign contributions—the issue the Court is now considering in a case called *McCutcheon v. FEC*.[17] It is difficult (to say the least) to see how aggregation of non-quid-pro-quo corrupting contributions are quid pro quo corruption if the individual contributions alone are not. Yet dependence corruption could well justify those aggregate limits, since once you remove aggregate contribution limits, you shrink even further the likely number of funders of elections and exacerbate even more the gap between "the funders" and "the People."

Buckley likely also could not justify limits on contributions to independent political action committees—the issue that the DC Circuit decided in *SpeechNow.org v. FEC*,[18] which was the trigger that created super PACs. But again, dependence corruption could justify limits on contributions to super PACs, since the focus is upon the attention of government officials, as they get distracted by this growing dependence on well-funded super PACs.[19]

Finally, *Buckley*'s focus on quid pro quo corruption does not make clear the compelling interest in publicly funded elections. But dependence corruption certainly does: Only publicly funded elections, whether the top-down sort upheld in *Buckley* or the bottom-up sort increasingly popular among reformers, could produce an election cycle where members were not dependent upon a tiny slice of us who are not "the People."

In short, it is Robert Post who has most helped us recognize the constitutional domains within our constitutional and First Amendment traditions. Those different domains invite a recognition of the different purposes regulation within each might have. Such a distinction in this context would show us why "corruption" properly understood should be regulable. And such regulations could also strongly reenforce the "representative integrity" Post seems to advance.

As powerfully illuminating as his characterization of that tradition has been in these lectures—in the battle between what he calls RR and DD, Republican Representation and Democratic Deliberation, with the ironic twist that the Left is RR and the Right is DD—it is perhaps a more properly Postean approach that could bridge the gap between RR and DD a bit more artistically with RD, the Republic Domain, within which representative integrity is protected, and for which both Rs and Ds have important ideological loyalty. The First Amendment should yield to regulations of speech within the Republic Domain designed to limit corruption, whether quid pro quo corruption or dependence corruption. Within that domain, in other words, the restriction of the First Amendment is different from its restrictions on regulations of speech meant for the Public Domain.

This is a foundation a Post can stand upon, and one the Court should be able to recognize as well.

4

LEGITIMACY, STRICT SCRUTINY, AND THE CASE AGAINST THE SUPREME COURT

Frank Michelman

I. Introduction

A. Error of Law

A great treasure of Robert Post's Tanner Lectures is the tale they tell of an American national historical adventure of the mind, wish fathering thought in the pursuit of the possibility of government by the people. Dean Post takes us through a succession of imaginative recastings of that possibility, right down to a currently prevailing, modernistically extenuated construction of it that Post names as "discursive democracy." Superbly, Post stands before us as chronicler of an American political wisdom and as prophet of an American constitutional faith.

But of course that is not all there is to it. Our friend speaks also, and sharply, in the name of the law. The Supreme Court stands charged by him, to be sure, with a default of political vision, but that is only a step on the way to a complaint of failure to get *the law* right. Now, *that* complaint proceeds (as of course it would have to do) from the proposition of a one best way to explain—and accordingly a one right way, a one judicially responsible way, to construe and apply—the overall course and content of the free-speech law, the "First Amendment doctrine," that our political and legal history has bequeathed to us.

In Post's rendition, the preemptively best explanatory account of our received First Amendment doctrine—at least as it applies to the regulation of campaign finance—has at its core a proposition about how, in these times, we can hope to approximate a realization by citizens of the "value" or "good" of self-government. At the crux of it stands an idea of the force of public opinion. As Post explains: "By participating in the ongoing and never-ending formation of public opinion, and by establishing institutions designed to make government continuously responsive to public opinion, the people might come to develop a 'sense of ownership' of 'their' government and so enjoy the benefit of self-government." On that resulting sense of ownership depends the "democratic legitimation" of the American political and legal order. That fact of contemporary political understanding gives the state strong reason to take measures, as needed, to prevent disruptions of the visionary scheme—"discursive democracy"—for producing and sustaining the sense of ownership. The answer to the puzzle of self-government in modern conditions thus lies in the cultivation and protection of a certain state of the public imagination (I explain below my use of that odd phrase): to wit, the public's belief in the responsiveness of state actions to a public opinion whose formation is freely open to all persons and all views.

That all reads like a proposition of academic social theory, and so it is.[1] In the view of Dean Post, though, it is more: a proposition that certifiably has been received into the normative fabric of American constitutional law, whence it can potentially figure in a charge of legal error against the Supreme Court.[2] Let us accept it as such. The question remains of how to articulate Post's lesson on American constitutional *wisdom* with the extant, doctrinal housing of American constitutional *law*, so as to produce the kinds of adjudicative approaches and results that Post, contradicting the Supreme Court, says the law of this land demands.

B. A Fixture of Doctrine: "Strict Scrutiny"

The problem, to be clear, is not with scriptural judicial expressions of substantive First Amendment values composing what we lawyers like to call our First Amendment tradition;[3] those expressions are already, Post says, on his side, and on that point we can trust him to hold his own against whoever may think not. The difficulty—as I think—lies rather with the entrenched doctrinal status of an adjudicative protocol known as "strict scrutiny." Post's legal case against *Citizens United* and its ilk incorporates elements, both conceptual and normative, that would seem to carry us well past a finding of a specific miscarriage, in the targeted set of cases, of an otherwise benign and welcome practice by our courts of strict scrutiny of election regulations for compliance with the First Amendment. They push us on toward a sweeping retrenchment of judicial oversight from the entire field of statutory election controls. Nor would the overkill stop there. The elements I have in mind seem poised not only to make a shambles of strict scrutiny in the field of election controls but to attack more broadly strict scrutiny's supportive institutional logic of a nondelegable, buck-stops-here *judicial* responsibility to ensure fulfillment of the Constitution (save for—a point to which we shall return—a very few matters that the Constitution itself "demonstrably" commits for decision to another branch of government).[4]

C. A Problem for Post?

I have called "overkill" these effects of Post's argument, implying they pose a difficulty for him. But why not rather take him to be contending for the retirement of strict scrutiny or, more broadly, judicial supremacy— either across the board or from the field of campaign finance regulation? I write as I do with the thought of collaborating in Post's own ambitions for the lectures. His plan, it appears, has been to advance both a more and a less "conservative" doctrinal path to correction of the catastrophe of *Citizens United*. On the conservative side, he would avoid having his case against *Citizens United* be weighted down by the burden of any such radical implications as those I have just now been suggesting. His posture would be to support and defend strict scrutiny of restrictions of election-related speech, while arguing "only" a point about something— the pursuit of "electoral integrity," treated as a matter of social fact— that should count as a "compelling interest" within the terms of that protocol.

I am not sure that is a tenable option. But neither, it appears, is Dean Post. Toward the end of the lectures, he suggests the possibility of more radical doctrinal cures for *Citizens United*, in case the conservative treatment turns out not to work. Toward the end of my comment, I will address these proposals. My main effort, however, goes toward explaining, in some detail, why the conservative treatment indeed may fail and the more radical cures be needed. I hope thus to contribute to critical understandings both of Dean Post's stance against *Citizens United* and of the doctrine of strict scrutiny, with a view to exposing in the stance a potentially deeper subversion of the doctrine than Post's own text proclaims. My working hypothesis will be this: As it stands under currently established doctrine, the model of strict scrutiny simply cannot accept, either as a superprotected constitutional concern that sets strict scrutiny going or as a state's "compelling interest" rejoinder, the redemption of a good conceived strictly in terms of the occurrent, subjective experience of the people. By building his castigation of the Supreme Court around exactly such a conception of the constitutionally compelling good of democratic legitimation, Post would appear to be pulling the plug on strict scrutiny.

II. A Summary of the Argument

A. The Protocol of Strict Scrutiny

Cases come to court that may or may not require, for their disposition according to law, a determination of the compatibility of some regulatory enactment with what we may broadly call the rights-protective parts of the Constitution. Among cases that do so require, some but not all will engage strict scrutiny "all the way through" (as we might say); that question itself falls just at the edge of the established doctrinal protocol of strict scrutiny. Disposition of the case according to that protocol will require answers for at least the first of the following questions and then possibly for some or all of the succeeding ones:

(i) whether the complaining party has successfully named a super-protected constitutional value (as I will call it) on which the regulation in question allegedly encroaches; *if "no," then strict scrutiny is off and the regulation is very likely constitutional, but if yes, then on to*

(ii) whether the regulation really does encroach as alleged; *if "no," then strict scrutiny is off and the regulation is very likely constitutional, but if yes, then on to*

(iii) whether the defending party has successfully named an admissibly "compelling" competing value allegedly served by the regulation; *if "no," then the regulation is unconstitutional, but if yes, then on to*

(iv) whether the statute really serves the competing value; *if "no," then the regulation is unconstitutional, but if yes, then on to*

(v) whether the infringement wrought by the regulation on the protected value is "necessary to" an adequate servicing of the competing value, is "narrowly tailored" to the service of that value, and is the "least restrictive" way that could feasibly have been devised to serve that value adequately.

B. A Test Case

Now let us try out an exemplary case. Suppose that an American state's electorate, by ballot measure, under conditions of unrestricted public debate, enacts a law with roughly the following content: (1) a broad definition of paid political advertising; (2) a prohibition on paid political advertising during defined election periods; along with (3) a reasonably generous provision for state-financed TV slots for candidates during election periods. Applying strict scrutiny in the manner of *Citizens United*, the Supreme Court would have that law for lunch, as the saying goes. That does not settle, though, that the law cannot pass a properly organized strict-scrutiny test. Dean Post urges, to the contrary, that laws like that one would have a fair chance to survive, if the Court would just *apply* strict scrutiny according to the established protocol for doing so, only treating the pursuit of social-factual "electoral integrity" as a compelling interest.[5]

On Post's account, the people of the American here-and-now achieve (if and insofar as they do) their sense of ownership of their government— "democratic legitimation"—through their engagement in a form of democratic practice called "discursive." Discursive democracy in turn is constituted by the coordinated fulfillment of two political-structural requirements: the integrity of elections, by which they instill confidence in the responsiveness of state action to public opinion, and the guaranteed freedom of access ("integrity") of the structure of communication— "public discourse"—by which public opinion is produced. Accordingly (since democratic legitimation is the point of the First Amendment), a judicial test of the constitutionality of our exemplary law must take account, somehow, of urgent concerns for both the integrity of elections and the integrity of public discourse. Post easily suggests how the strict-scrutiny protocol might accommodate that need. The concern for the integrity of public discourse would dictate strict scrutiny of our statute as a content-based restriction on contributions to public discourse,[6] while the concern for the integrity of elections would fit into place as a compelling interest of the state.

Now let us take a closer look at the concern for electoral integrity. As Post insists, democratic legitimation is ultimately subjective. "Democratic legitimation occurs when persons believe that government is potentially responsive to their views." It follows that the corresponding "First Amendment necessity" is that of sustaining the people's confidence *in fact* that elections are geared to the selection of officials who will "attend to public opinion." And then, you see, "it is the height of hubris for the [Supreme] Court, by a vote of five justices on a bench of nine, simply to dismiss concerns for electoral integrity on the ground that electoral integrity is a question of law rather than of social fact."

Thus reasons Post with regard to a court's due concern for the integrity of elections. Although Post does not say so, the same would seem to hold in regard to the court's due concern for the other requisite integrity, the integrity of public discourse. By the terms of our exemplary law, there will occur, within the space of the election but not beyond it, a temporary, partial suspension of the rules of unrestricted public discourse. But so what? As Post explains, while election-focused politicking may incidentally provide "momentary glimpses" of public opinion, that effect is no part of the constitutional function of elections, nor is it of any particular constitutional value. That is because, in the pursuit of democratic legitimation through discursive democracy, it is not and cannot be the function of public opinion to decide anything, an election or anything else. Being "always in the making," public opinion cannot ever act decisively. Discursive-democratic legitimation is served when and insofar as the people believe they can be confident that the officials who do make decisions do so responsively to a public opinion, about which they can, in turn, be confident that it is constantly forming itself in the background, through a public-discursive process that elections do not displace and are not meant to replicate. Underwriting public belief in official responsiveness to that ceaseless process of opinion formation is, on Post's account, the prime democratic function of elections.

It seems that, in order to reap the value of self-government on these terms, the people would on some level have to grasp or understand these terms as the terms of their self-government. "A people cannot experience the value of self-government unless they believe themselves to be self-governing." Thus presumably believing, the state's voters have chosen to enact our hypothetical law with its time-limited incursion on the freedom of public discourse. And why should they not? Knowing as they are, they take public-opinion formation to be the kind of sociological, "subjectless," behind-our-backs process that Postean discursive democracy postulates—the river flowing night and day relentlessly on, into which you cannot step twice in the same place. The people see that observance of their campaign spending law will result in some alteration of the flow of public-opinion formation during the election period from what it otherwise would have been; just as, say, a major extended power outage would have done. They understand that the alteration will be unmeasurable, unfathomable, literally indescribable. From their point of view it will be hard to see how an occasional partial suspension of the public-discourse rules, for a month or two, could palpably affect any given citizen's ability to identify, then or later, with the river's onward flow, around the island of the election period, by reason of his or her autonomous inputs to it.[7] There surely can be no certainty on anyone's part (including any reviewing court's) that there will or could be much of any such effect, let alone an effect that is decisively adverse to democratic legitimation. But to whom, in any event, does such a judgment properly belong? Why, again, should the Supreme Court be stipulating such a consequence as a matter of law, rather than treating it as a contingency of social fact to be found on the evidence?

If I am correct in these musings, then it does not only seem that the question of the endangerment *of electoral integrity* lies beyond a court's capacity to decide, as a matter of law, against the credible contrary testimony of the people themselves. The same must also be said of the question of the endangerment of the integrity *of public discourse* by reason of any given instance of regulation of elections. Such would seem to be the consequence of treating democratic legitimation as a "subjective" matter of the actual, occurrent beliefs of citizens, rather than as an objective matter of the conformity of the regime's political practice to standards that a judge finds sufficient in reason to sustain such beliefs. It is not immediately clear what can remain of First Amendment strict scrutiny of duly enacted regulations of campaign finance.

III. Strict Scrutiny as Strict Judicial Control

Recall our outline of strict scrutiny.[8] Within the extant American doctrine of the distribution of governmental powers—in which it is "emphatically the province and duty of the judicial department to say what the law is"[9]—steps (i) and (iii) in that outline pose pure questions of constitutional law, which the judge must decide independently of the opinion of any party to the case (but of course after hearing the legal contentions of the parties). With respect to other steps in the protocol, and depending on contexts, it might be more or less plausibly maintained that the legal "rule" to be directly applied by the judge ought to be only a second-order rule, something like this: The judge upholds the regulation if and only if satisfied that the duly authorized issuing body has applied its mind responsibly and competently to the questions in the protocol and has decided them, reasonably, in favor of constitutionality. In line with the terminology of current debates over such matters in comparative constitutional studies, we might name such a doctrine as "weak-form" strict scrutiny.[10] A retreat from strong-form to weak-form strict scrutiny may seem hardest to resist—again, depending on contexts—with regard to step (v), where deciders on the scene may have knowledge and know-how that cannot easily be conveyed to a nonexpert, remotely situated judicial officer.

Notice that, under weak-form strict scrutiny, the case is still decided under a legal rule and the judge still decides the case as a matter of law. The ultimately decisive legal "rule" in the case is the law's demand on the issuing body to apply its mind up to the standard set by the rule. The judge decides *that* question of law, yes or no, independently of the opinion *on that point* of the issuing body. The effect is to create a sharply hedged "zone of discretion" for the issuing body, with the court policing the borders.[11]

Especially in the wake of the Supreme Court's very recent decision in *Fisher v. University of Texas at Austin*,[12] we can say with confidence that *our* strict-scrutiny protocol is "strong-form," not "weak-form," all the way through and regardless of context. For us, "strict" simply *means* strong-form. In *Fisher*, the Supreme Court reversed two lower-court decisions, precisely on the ground that the lower courts had impermissibly retreated from strong-form to weak-form strict scrutiny of the University's use of a racial criterion as a part of its admissions process. Our constitutional law of strict scrutiny, the Supreme Court insisted, requires that judges in such cases decide independently, as a matter of law, whether a university's particular use of a racial criterion does or does not satisfy the "narrowly tailored" and "least restrictive" branches of step (v).[13] The Supreme Court's intransigence on this point is all the more striking because the Court quite readily acknowledged the University's special "experience and expertise in adopting or rejecting admissions processes."[14]

The broader thought behind the Court's strong-form stance appears to be that these are, after all, requirements of constitutional *law,* for the satisfaction of which, in the American scheme of government, the judicial branch holds a responsibility so sensitive and special that no iota of an abdication of it to others can be tolerated.

In cases such as *Fisher,* the protected value for step (i) is the avoidance of special harms and costs attributed to racial classifications,[15] and the competing value for step (iii) is educational diversity. A part of Post's legal contention is that, in cases such as *Citizens United,* the integrity of public discourse must obviously count as a superprotected value, and the integrity of elections should equally plainly count as a "compelling" competing value—understanding both of those integrities as contributory toward an overarching aim of democratic legitimacy. It is time, now, to take a harder look at those values as developed by Post.

IV. Post's Compelling Interest

A. Discursive Democracy, Democratic Legitimacy, and Constitutional Law

In Post's presentation, the best explanatory account of our received First Amendment doctrine has at its core a proposition about the institutional preconditions for the realization by individual citizens, in modern times, of the value of self-government. Those preconditions, to repeat, are two in number. They are, first, the protection of the electoral integrity by which elections credibly serve, in the eyes of the public, as a guarantor of the responsiveness of state action to public opinion; and, second, the protection of the discursive integrity (so to name it) of the structure of communication—public discourse—by which public opinion is produced. Operating together, these two integrities compose the attainable approximation to individual and collective self-government that Post names "discursive democracy."

Let us (as I do) accept that account as both morally and sociologically compelling. How does that make it into *law,* make it into the legally sovereign account of the First Amendment? Well, consider first that there can be no more urgent political value, and certainly none higher in the eyes of a country's courts, than the legitimacy of that country's system and practice of government and legal ordering. It is wrong, and in America foolhardy, to try to subject citizens to the legal force of a regime with whose edicts they cannot or do not connect their own self-government. In our modern conditions, fulfillment of the stipulations of discursive democracy is one way, if it is not the only way, in which the possibility of such a connection can be sustained. So we have going here a sociological thesis on democratic legitimacy, regarding the conditions of the possibility of an identification by citizens of the state's acts with their own self-government; and that very thesis can be shown—this is Post's claim—to be reflected by the course of the American history of political ideas and of our First Amendment doctrine.[16] It follows that fidelity to law by American judges means following faithfully the lead of that thesis when judging the constitutionality of campaign regulations. "Those who treasure First Amendment rights," writes Post, "should support the electoral integrity necessary for First Amendment rights to achieve their constitutional purpose." "Not only is electoral integrity consistent with received First Amendment jurisprudence, it is *required* by that jurisprudence." The argument chimes neatly with Ronald Dworkin's conception of law as the outcome of a conversation between reason and history, between "justification" and "fit," between the felt demands of right-minded political wisdom and the legal-historical-doctrinal facts as they stand.[17]

B. Legitimacy as Logic and as Experience

So there we are. The dominant, guiding purpose of the First Amendment (at least in the context of campaign finance regulation—Post's theory of campaign finance need not be read as a theory of everything) is democratic legitimation; and democratic legitimation comes and goes, rises and falls, along with the appearance on the scene or disappearance from it of the two integrities, of elections and of public discourse. Translated to constitutional-legal doctrine-talk, a due concern for the integrity of public discourse has quite rightly dictated strict scrutiny of content-based restrictions on speech (of course including speech related to elections),[18] while a due concern for the integrity of elections ought to have dictated—but to date has not—the law's recognition of the protection of that integrity as a "compelling interest" of the state. But in which medium—"objective" reason or "subjective" experience—do we scan for the presence of these integrities, or reckon the gravity of threats to them?

It may seem that the answer should turn on exactly what you want to mean by the "legitimacy" of a state regime. That term typically connotes a regulative standard of "rightful rule."[19] Legitimacy is a measure of the regime's exhibition (in actual practice, not just on paper) of commitments to major structural features that are deemed to suffice, in combination, to make morally supportable the regime's demands on citizens for a regularity of submission to its outputs of political acts, regardless of who does or does not agree with the policy, or even the justice, of this act or that one.[20] Post's lectures present material to fit that usage. Construed as normative political theory, the Postean conception says that a state cannot rightly demand from citizens a disposition to comply with its political acts (just because they *are* its political acts), *unless* the larger shape of its practice is such as to supply citizens with sufficient grounds for an identification of the regime's political acts with their own self-government—specifically by its dedicated pursuit of the two integrities, of public discourse and of elections. Such would be the Postean account of normative legitimacy.

Alternatively, though, "legitimacy" may be used in what is called an "empirical" or "sociological" sense, to mean a population's acceptance in fact—whether or not with philosophically certified good reason—of the regime's claim to merited political authority.[21] Now, Post's lectures are primarily cast as normative argument; you cannot nominate X as a "compelling" state interest in our law while professing a strictly value-neutral, social-scientific interest in X. Yet the lectures also look straight in the direction of a sociological, experiential account of legitimacy. Post is over and over insistent that the legitimacy he is concerned with resides not in some judge's opinion, or philosopher's theory, about the right way for the state to behave, but rather in the "subjective" experience of the people, in *their* (not some judge's) "beliefs" and "imaginings" regarding the fulfillment of the integrities and a resulting sense on their part of identification with, or ownership of, the governmental acts of their state. "[I]f persons are persuaded to forfeit confidence in their government, their government will *pro tanto* lose democratic legitimacy, even if impartial reason might suggest a different conclusion."[22] It is the pursuit of that "subjective" legitimacy that Post wants the Court to recognize as a compelling interest for strict-scrutiny purposes.

We should be clear that Post's inquiry is still normative, not merely "sociological." His claim is that subjective democratic legitimacy is, just in itself, an urgent interest of the state and of the society whose peace and order the state is there to help sustain. "It is certain," he writes, "that if the design of contemporary elections has caused Americans to lose faith in the electoral integrity of their representative system, that faith will not be restored by the professional legal assertions of the Supreme Court. . . ." It is evidently on that basis that Post speaks of the "hubris" in the Supreme Court's insistence on treating electoral integrity as "a question of law rather than of social fact." Post thereby separates "fact" (of a certain kind, the subjective experiential kind) from reason, from logic, from "law." He is not, however, severing fact *from value*. To the contrary, he is insisting that some facts *are* values—or rather, to speak more precisely, that some constitutionally urgent values reside quite immediately in facts of subjective experience that no one, on the basis of philosophical or legal expertise or authority, should pretend or presume to know better than the subjects themselves.

C. Intersubjectivity?

If you put to a judge the question of whether a challenged statutory reform of election campaigning is really "necessary" to provide the people *with sufficient reason for* confidence in electoral integrity, the judge might feel uneasy or discomfited. She might feel that others have better access than she to relevant information. (Compare the responses of the lower courts in the *Fisher* case.) At least, though, she will know what the question is. If one person has a sufficiency of reason, then so do all; if one lacks it, then so do all. Sufficiency of reason is an *impersonal* question. It is a question of, well, *reason*—logic, principle, "law"—about which a judge supposedly knows as much or more than the average Joe or Josie.

If you ask the judge a question about the difference made by the challenged law to the actual, occurrent, state of belief or experience of "the people"—as opposed, say, to what a normatively reasonable people would feel—she is likely to object that the question is not well formed. *Some* people experience *E* and some do not, but how is a judge to answer for "the" people? It could be that an intuition of a difficulty of that kind helps to drive the Supreme Court toward its stance of framing as a question of law—of reason, logic, or principle—what Post so persuasively insists makes best sense as a question of social fact.

The difficulty is perhaps not insoluble; or at least it may not appear so to the social-theoretically instructed. Its possible solution is what caused me to speak, near the beginning, of "a state of the public imagination." Post could be thinking—I expect he *is* thinking—that the achievement, or not, of the fact/value of subjective democratic legitimation, by any given regime at any time, is an experiential fact of a type that some social theorists might call "intersubjective":[23] My experience of E is in part a reflection of my experience of your experience, and vice versa, and so on. The people, more or less self-consciously, are sharers, through their communicative exchanges, in a reciprocating, reflexive process of the production of a kind of background knowledge or understanding that constitutes a part of everyone's belief.

Post does not expressly offer this account of the matter of "the people's" beliefs and imaginings. I am bolstered in my attribution of it to him by its plain kinship with a comparably sociologized notion of public opinion as "subjectless," "always in the making," "enveloping," neither susceptible of punctual description nor capable of decisive expression. Indeed, it seems we can simply say (as Post himself does say) that the "fact" of the people's confidence (or not) in the current fulfillment of the two requisite integrities of discursive democracy—a confidence on which democratic legitimation depends—*is* a state of public opinion, to be "judged" or "interpreted" as such.

That would strike me as an acute and persuasive bit of sociological analysis. But the question, again, is about how possibly to fit it within the constitutional-legal protocol of strict scrutiny.

V. Rebuttal of Post or Wreck of Strict Scrutiny?

A. Rebuttal of Post?

Let us say there is value in a state's conducting itself rightly, meaning as a good state ought to do. Call that a value of reason ("objective"). There also is value in a person's having and enjoying a certain kind of self-confirming apprehension of the world and her place within it (say, an apprehension of democratic legitimation). Call that a value of experience ("subjective"). Suppose a good state objectively ought to conduct itself (a value of reason) so as to enable the subjective enjoyment by persons of democratic legitimation (a value of experience). These particular values of reason and of experience would in that way be practically connected, but that would not make them into one and the same value; as values, they would remain different and distinct: one of reason, the other of experience.

Construed as a value of experience, democratic legitimation is a matter of the subjective beliefs and imaginings of citizens; it comes and goes as belief in it comes and goes. We take it that democratic legitimation, thus construed, is a true and important value. It follows that a good state is one that conducts itself—other things being equal—so as to assist the belief in coming and not going. The door, then, is open to a claim from the state of a legally cognizable "compelling" interest in doing just that. The state shows up in court as an actor possessed of a constitutionally compelling interest in doing what it must always be supremely right for any American state to do—that is, act as required to secure to the people their enjoyment of the subjective good of democratic legitimation, and thereby also, in consequence, to secure to them the very great, objective goods of political stability. The state claims constitutional permission to do so.

Such a view of the case would seemingly be one that Post cannot reject. But such a view of it also contains what may look like a rebuttal to his excoriation of the Supreme Court for confusing a question of fact with a question of law.

In the view of American constitutional law, on Post's own showing, for the state to act rightly in this setting is for it to tailor its regulatory pursuit of electoral integrity to a due regard for public-discourse integrity and vice versa, all in the larger pursuit of democratic legitimacy (all three construed as "subjectively" as you like). A comparison with the *Fisher* case leaps to mind: For UT Austin to have acted rightly in that case would have been for it to tailor its pursuit of the value of educational diversity to a due regard for the social harms and costs of racial classifications. Maybe it did, maybe it didn't. The answer depends on the application of a standard of due regard, called by the doctrinal name of "necessary to" (see step (v) in the strict-scrutiny protocol). That standard is "law," not "fact," and "strict scrutiny" means, in our constitutional-legal practice as it currently stands, that the judicial branch carries a nondelegable responsibility for an independent-minded application of it to the case at hand.

It seems the same must hold for *Citizens United* and all its ilk including the truly stunning *Bullock* decision.[24] We can charge the Court, in those cases, with an erroneous failure to recognize electoral integrity as a compelling interest; we can charge it with an egregiously blind-to-reality application of the legal standard of necessity; we can charge it with weighting excessively a distrust of the purity of the motives or the clarity of the vision of the state's lawmakers. But still—and I mean granting every other claim Post makes about the sovereign value of subjective democratic legitimacy and that value's commanding status in our law—you cannot charge the Court with a prideful, arrogant, usurpative confusion of fact with law; not while—or if, or insofar as—strong judicial reviewability of campaign finance law stands as the accepted law of the land.

B. Wreck of Strict Scrutiny?

Take all of the following as settled:

1. In our time and place, democratic legitimation depends on the state's satisfactory observance of the two constitutive integrities of discursive democracy.
2. A hard ("fraught") challenge results for every American state, including the federal state: to keep its pursuits of the two integrities in equipoise, reciprocally adjusting the pursuit of each in such a way that the inevitable dents to each from the pursuit of the other do not, in combination, place democratic legitimation at risk.
3. American constitutional law, rightly read, demands recognition, as a compelling interest of the state, of its achievement of success in meeting this challenge. (These first three points are settled, says Post, by a combination of history and general political intelligence.)
4. Democratic legitimation occurs, if at all, in the actual, subjective responses of the public to what goes on in the state—meaning those responses as they are in fact, regardless of what anyone finds they reasonably could be or ought to be. (That point is settled, says Post, simply by a recognition of what legitimation ineluctably is.)

The question before us is whether the legal protocol of strict scrutiny can accommodate those four propositions in combination.

It is not hard to get a "yes" answer partway home. The challenge of mutually adjusted pursuits of the two integrities is the necessity question—step (v) of the protocol—in light disguise, and "necessary to" is a legal standard that the court is responsible to apply independently of anyone else's opinion. The seeming stumper, though, is that the goal-state that the state's challenged practice is to be judged "necessary to" (or not) is a state of public opinion.

It follows that a court purporting to operate the strict-scrutiny protocol on a case like *Bullock* or *Citizens United* would have to make an application of the legal standard of necessity to facts of public opinion.

But it seems that may be impossible because, as explained by Post, the punctual content of public opinion—"always in the making" in the back rooms of consciousness—is nonobservable, defying description. On that ground, having come this far, one might feel tempted to conclude that a proper application of American constitutional law to these cases requires a conclusion that they are nonjusticiable, depending as they do on a question—the state or content of public opinion—that defies resolution by any "judicially manageable standard."[25]

Let us pass, for now, that somewhat extremist-looking suggestion. (We will come back to it later.) Let us treat the state of public opinion as a matter of social fact determinable, in principle, by social-scientific observation and report. The trial court will have access to the testimony and other evidence at the legislative hearings, if there were any. It can hold its own hearing of scientific experts, analyzing whatever their science will regard as evidence of the relevant state of the public mind, and then decide for itself, on the evidence, whether "necessary to" has or has not been proved.

It feels queer. The judge will hear social-scientific experts and weigh their conflicting claims as if she were the lawmaker. She either will or will not stop her ears and her intelligence to any and all indications of the "feel" and the "sense" of the politicians on the scene—experts, one might say, in their own right. If she does do that, she provokes a rebellion of common sense, almost certainly including her own; it seems to verge on the psychologically impossible. (Witness the lower courts in *Fisher*.) But conversely, the more her defenses break down and she lets leak into her judgment the express and implicit opinions of the responsible politicians about the state of public opinion, the further she slides from strong-form to weak-form "zone-of-discretion" strict scrutiny—or, in other words, into scrutiny that is not strictly strict in our currently prevailing legal-doctrinal sense of that term. That looks as if it might be the beginning of a seriously strong critique of the doctrine of strict scrutiny in toto.

VI. Ship of Doctrine, Ship of Fools?

A. "Political Question?"

Thus, the conservative cure for *Citizens United*, consisting of a corrected application to that case and others like it of the protocol of strict scrutiny, may fail. Post knows it. A maximally radical alternative would be to come up with a workable definition of a class of "political-campaign" cases that would be roped entirely out of court. We could call that an extension of the extant piece of our constitutional law known as the doctrine of political question. We would have to extend to fit the case either or both of those branches of the doctrine that proscribe judicial intervention where "judicially discoverable and manageable standards" are lacking, or where the matter is covered by the Constitution's "textually demonstrable commitment" of it for decision by "a coordinate political department."[26]

That project is not on. Engineering a judicial evacuation of the field of campaign finance, by any means short of express constitutional amendment, would be an impossibly hard sell to American constitutional culture.[27] We can nevertheless use the idea as a Plimsoll line for gauging how close Post may come to tipping over the ship of doctrine as he works through his roster of alternative cures, which basically are two in number.

B. Weak-Form Strict Scrutiny

Post writes:

> Ascertaining the basic legitimacy of our democratic state is not the sort of legal question that courts are accustomed to deciding. Courts do not ordinarily determine constitutional questions by interpreting public opinion. These tasks require skills that we expect from our popularly elected branches when they are acting at their best. . . . In reviewing campaign finance legislation aimed at enhancing electoral integrity, therefore, courts should temper their natural suspicion of political self-dealing with a margin of judicial appreciation for the necessarily *political* judgment involved in evaluations of electoral integrity.

That is a proposal, in effect, for weak-form strict scrutiny. Post does not name it so, or classify it—as I have done—as a disruptive deviation from current doctrinal orthodoxy. He rather treats it as an application of strict scrutiny, with a modest adaptation to fit the circumstances of the case, and that is about the extent of any difference between us on this point.

C. "Managerial Domain"

Failing less radical doctrinal cures, we might consider a treatment of elections as a "managerial domain," within the metaphorical space of which a government is allowed to proceed upon a showing of any kind of workaday "functional need" for its restriction on speech. A typical managerial domain would be a governmental workplace; a typical functional need—falling far short of a compelling interest that could normally justify a restriction on political speech—would be workplace decorum or efficiency.

Managerial domains are closely akin to the zones of discretion allowed by weak-form strict scrutiny. Given a basal commitment to strong-form strict scrutiny for restrictions of freedom of public discourse, the definition of their boundaries thus becomes a matter of deep constitutional concern. It would, for example, be highly problematic for a state to proclaim its flagship university as a managerial domain where racist speech can be suppressed for the sake of a functional need for stress-free relations on campus.[28] It would be likewise problematic—or, as Post says, paradoxical—to allow the state to proclaim as "managerial" the "domain" of "elections" and thereby insulate from strict scrutiny its restrictions on election-related speech. Seeing this, but driven by the felt urgency of the need to find a remedy for the disaster of *Citizens United,* Post does permit himself to speculate on such a possible doctrinal deployment.[29] However close you may think that comes to the political-question Plimsoll line, the Tanner Lectures are not yet at the point of yelling a plague on all our doctrines.

In a notable pair of sentences, though, very near the end, Post does let loose with connections he sees among "formalism," "legalism," "danger," and "folly." Can the folly, if such it be, be confined to the field of campaign finance? Post suggests it is exceptional for a case to turn on findings of facts of public opinion, but need or ought it to be so? Take the *Fisher* case, our paragon of strict scrutiny. Is the very strongly presumptive intolerability of any and every racial classification a fixture in the heaven of legal concepts, as the Supreme Court (hubristically?) insists, or do we deal here with a contingent, contextually variable matter of intersubjective social fact? What about the weights of the competing educational values at stake in the case to be decided; are those weights to be assigned as a matter of law, or are they to be gauged as a matter of intersubjective social fact? The answers to such questions are not fixed in logic, they are rather to be found out by institutional prudence. The answers we live with will be, from case type to case type, as the Supreme Court's prudence may decide.

The point is not that these choices—question of law versus question of social fact—are easy, for in fact they can be genuinely hard.[30] The point is that the set of case types in which such questions may at any time flare up and demand answers cannot ever be treated as closed. Perhaps, then, a grateful and appreciative reader may be excused for wondering whether a measured critique of doctrinism—of legal formality in general—might be counted among the manifold beauties of *Citizens Divided*.

5

FREE SPEECH AS THE CITIZEN'S RIGHT

Nadia Urbinati

Robert Post delivered two extraordinarily important lectures, which will certainly have an impact on the constitutional and political debate concerning the quality of actual democracy in the United States. My task is very demanding because I am asked to comment on a work in relation to which I have no reasons for disagreement whatsoever and actually sympathize deeply with Post's goal (to defend the reason for campaign finance reform) and with his method (to prove that this reform is consistent with the purpose of the basic of First Amendment principles, which is "to make possible the value of self-government").

The issue of campaign finance reform is one of the most contested in the United States, a *vexata quaestio* of difficult solution for constitutionalists. Disagreement is not of course something exceptional or avoidable in democracy. Democratic societies have written and write constitutions and bills of rights because they foresee the possibility of dissent; democracy's procedures are representative of a collective that takes dissent as the main feature of its public and social relations, and it expects politics meaningfully to reflect such dissent. Because politics concerns interpretations rather than unquestionable truths, disagreement and discord are the flesh and blood of democracy. Not only do conflicting interpretations exist among supposedly biased ordinary citizens and partisan politicians, but they also afflict competent scholars and experts like judges. The *Citizens United v. Federal Election Commission* decision was not unanimous, and its reception by the public was still more controversial. The split between the voice of the Court and the general opinion could not be more profound: 65 percent of a poll's respondents affirmed that they "strongly" opposed the Supreme Court decision, which allowed corporations freely to spend on political campaigns and which extended to corporations the same political rights enjoyed by individual citizens. Although corporations have no suffrage rights, the court gave them the right to a strong voice in the public sphere, and this conclusion aroused fierce opposition.

Disagreement here points directly to the meaning and functioning of representative democracy as a system that I propose to conceive as a *diarchy* of "will" and of "opinion"; which is to say, of the power of the vote (and the decision-making procedures that derive their authority from this power) and of the power of forming and expressing opinions, which is protected by the right to free speech and association. Democracy's diarchy holds that voice is the organ that citizens use when they perform at the ballot box and when they develop the opinions that guide their vote. Even more than direct democracy, representative democracy is characterized by speech and by the opinion of the people, for the obvious reason that the will (the authorized decision) is the outcome of a process of open interaction and communication that unites and separates representatives and represented. Speech is simultaneously the matter and the medium of this form of government, the core of political activity as a combination of thinking, speaking, and expressing. These performing activities make for the political identity of what we call self-governing citizens in a democracy. This will be the theoretical framework for my comment on Post's argument.

But let me proceed gradually and start precisely with disagreement inside of the Court on the interpretation of the First Amendment, which Robert Post reconstructs so effectively, between Justice Anthony Kennedy and Justice John Paul Stevens. Justice Kennedy identifies private and corporate money in political campaigns with free speech and concludes that state regulation would imply making "political speech a crime." By contrast, Justice Stevens concludes that without regulation private and corporate money in politics would undermine "the integrity of elected institutions." The division could not be deeper, because both opinions are justified in the name of the same fundamental principles of freedom of speech and invoke the same jurisprudential and political tradition. The *Citizens United* decision, Post argues, exemplifies a polarization between two equally basic goods for representative democracy: "free speech" and the "integrity of elected institutions." Post depicts this polarization as a "horrifying disjunction." Why is this disjunction "horrifying"? Because, Post explains, both opinions seek to reason from constitutional doctrine. Justice Kennedy's opinion suffers from doctrinal and rhetorical abstraction; it is disassociated from the specific political context from which it emerged. Justice Stevens's opinion is justified by general concepts like "distortion" or "equality" of the electoral system, which are themselves the object of disputation and disagreement. "It is surprisingly difficult," Post argues, "to express the fundamental republican value of 'the integrity of elected institutions' in a manner that can be reconciled with the structure of received First Amendment thought." The "horrifying disjunction" thus derives from two interpretative problems which Post devotes these lectures to solving: first, "the Court lacks a disciplined and coherent explanation of its own First Amendment jurisprudence"; and second, "proponents of campaign finance reform have failed to advance justifications for regulation that can be inosculated with basic First Amendment principles."

To amend these faulty approaches, Post suggests the following theoretical reasoning: "state interests in campaign finance reform may be reconciled with traditional constitutional commitments" if we show that the "purpose of First Amendment rights is to make possible the value of self-government, and that this purpose requires public trust that elections select officials who are responsive to public opinion." On the one hand, free speech must be seen as both a civil right and a political right; and, on the other, the goal of political free speech is self-government itself, not merely the integrity of the electoral system.

To reach his goal, Post thinks it is paramount to redirect First Amendment jurisprudence by taking it away from abstract (I would say Cartesian) doctrine and instead to base that jurisprudence on the political and historical experience of the American republic. He proposes that we move from metaphysics to historiography in the hope of finding a common denominator. Post embraces a pragmatic methodology that operates in the domain of political and constitutional history that is putatively common to all participants in the debate. We may have different ideas about the meaning of electoral integrity or political equality, but we surely possess a common historical background to which we can refer when we discuss these important principles. This is the meaning of what I call Post's pragmatic methodology. It might seem that reference to principles diminishes when the focus shifts to historiography. Yet this does not mean that we do not refer to principles when we seek to solve our disagreements. It means instead that these principles are not to be found in the metaphysical sky of pure ideas, but in our shared political history. De-ideologizing the jurisprudential debate on the First Amendment is possible, Post suggests, if we reposition the debate from the doctrinal purity of first principles to the pragmatic impurity of political and constitutional experience, our historical experience. This seems to be an excellent point of departure, methodologically more in tune with the democratic spirit, which depends upon opinions and judgments more than upon abstract truths and dogmatic definitions.

The problem is that despite Post's certainty, there is no guarantee whatsoever that history is less a controversial terrain than theory or metaphysics, or that it is a more reliable domain for solving disagreements about the interpretation of the First Amendment in the context of campaign finance reform. This is the kernel of my comment, which aims to translate Post's historical strategy into an interpretation of representative democracy as diarchy. We cannot avoid principles, although historiography can be of some help when we interrogate it from a theoretical perspective that is consistent with the democratic principles sustaining the form of government that the First Amendment is designed to protect. In a word, in order to tackle the *vexata quaestio* of campaign finance reform in a way that is less controversial, we must return to principles, the principles of representative democracy, although they are not disembodied or written in the sky of abstract ideas but emerge gradually and by trial and error in the specific narrative of a country's progress toward democratization. Theory is back, although not as the application of an abstract blueprint but instead as immanent in the process of representative democracy itself, as developed through the history of the American republic.

In the debates on the First Amendment and the unsatisfactory solutions proposed by the Supreme Court, I see the urgency of rethinking the meaning of representative democracy, until now and for many theorists still second-best in relation to direct democracy. Only if we overcome this second-best perspective can we achieve an understanding of our form of government that, among other things, can offer us a more secure path toward the resolution of this *vexata quaestio*. The debates concerning campaign finance reform reveal how we conceive democracy at a time when crucial innovations are changing the nature of democracy, especially in the domain of opinion formation and communication.

Robert Post offers us a majestic historical picture of the steps that brought us here. He reconstructs the trajectory of the American polis from "republican representation" to democratic deliberation or discursive democracy, or from the founding ambitions of creating a republic of a selected/elected wise few, who were supposed to contain the passion, interests, and irrationality of the many, to the expansion of democracy through the growth of public opinion in an electoral republic. Post writes that the fundamental principle upon which the American republic was built was self-determination or self-government. Yet, he explains, this principle was pursued in two different manners: as "republican representation" and as "discursive" democracy. This dualism, he argues, is the ancestry of the *vexata quaestio* we now face. As the value of communicative rights became clear to American society, free speech became a necessary political right.

In the first stage of this political history, the value of self-government was located in the act of elections, when citizens selected the few and renounced their own direct presence in government. In the second stage, self-government was thought to be realized "when the people actively participate in the formation of public opinion." Only in this second stage did the democratic transformation of the representative republic take place and communicative rights come to be seen as fundamental and political. Hence, Post writes, the Court in *Citizens United* explains that "speech is an essential mechanism of democracy, for it is the means to hold officials accountable to the people." Yet, if this is true, citizens must have an equal chance to acquire information and to participate in the channels of communication.

The central part of Post's lecture is devoted to proving this argument through the reconstruction of the growth of the American republic from the eighteenth-century classical arguments in favor of free mandate representation, to the Jacksonian expansion of popular democracy and the strengthening of political parties as intermediary bodies between citizens and the elected, to the post–World War I democratization of the public sphere itself, with the growth of public opinion as the medium through which citizens reappropriated a direct link with government institutions. The consequence of this last development was the view that democracy could exist without political parties and in fact did not consist in elections but in popular participation through the press and ideas. From representation to a new kind of direct democracy, one that operates through information and communication: this is the historical narrative that Post reconstructs to strengthen his argument in favor of a political interpretation of the right to free speech. Opinion takes here the role of direct participation as a connecting power that keeps citizens and government institutions always in contact. Opinion thus diminishes the power of the intermediary body that suffrage creates (e.g., the representative assembly). Consistent with American pragmatism, Post acknowledges public opinion to be a form of participation in its own right. Based on this recovery of participation through voice, Post advances his reformist interpretation of the First Amendment and depicts the political history of the American republic as a trajectory from representative government to a discursive (deliberative) democracy.

The growth of the role of opinion in American history, Posts explains, was associated with a decline of trust in political parties and elected institutions. Moreover it was associated with the transformation of political parties from institutions that connected the electorate to elected officials to institutions that served their own ends by capturing public patronage for their own officers. Political parties, as became clear during the twentieth century, increased the distance between citizens and their government and occulted state power from inspection rather than unveiling it. They were supposed to discipline representatives, whom free mandate made totally independent from the voters, but instead they used party discipline to create a new oligarchy. As Bernard Manin has shown in his book on the conceptual history of representative government, in relation to party democracy, democracy of opinion seems to have played a transparency function.[1] American history exemplifies the same trajectory that was followed by representative governments in all European countries during the last two and a half centuries. Europe has witnessed a transition from party-based democracy to opinion-based democracy. Positions on the role of public opinion have never been unanimous among liberal scholars. Authors like John Stuart Mill and Alexis de Tocqueville (and Walter Lippmann as their most original interpreter in the twentieth century) were extremely worried about the tyrannical potential of public opinion on individual freedom (and freedom of speech, among others). They did not share the optimistic view of James Bryce and American pragmatists like Herbert Croly and John Dewey, from whom Post draws inspiration, who attributed to public opinion a quasi-sovereign role that prized participation in and by itself.

The debate on the meaning of the First Amendment thus started along with the transformation of democracy from merely electoral to party and finally to opinion democracy. It started when Jacksonian democracy (party democracy that amended the representative republic) was supplanted by opinion democracy. Free speech became relevant in proportion as the public also became relevant in the making of the American republic. This historical process, Post explains, was exemplified by two aims in the domain of free speech: (1) regulating private businesses when they operated in the domain of politics; and (2) restructuring politics by containing the role of political parties and expanding that of public opinion. This dualism induced reformers to oppose not only private money in politics but also the role of parties in representation. Reformers sought to facilitate a direct relationship between electors and representatives; they sought to make citizens active sovereigns, not merely electors. The goal of the reformers was that of installing a direct mandate democracy in which identification between electors and elected would be central. Public opinion without parties seemed to achieve this goal. This was Croly's position, who theorized direct democracy as a system of consent that "involved a direct relationship between each citizen and the state, a relationship unmediated by elected officials." This is the frame of mind that shaped the constitutional history of the First Amendment, the ancestry of *Citizens United.*

Today's equivalent of Croly's direct democracy (democracy via petition and recall) would be what Post calls "discursive democracy," a process of democratic legitimation via opinion formation in the tradition of Jürgen Habermas. Building on the intuition of Croly and the American pragmatists who inspired the early reformers, Post devises his pivotal argument. Like them, and like Croly in particular, Post thinks that the representation of public opinion is necessary to self-government: it occurs through institutions like initiatives or referenda or polling, not only electoral representation. Yet Post also thinks that Croly's intuition on direct as discursive democracy versus representative democracy is partial and unable to show the whole picture, because it fails to recognize that public opinion must remain "continually in process." Communicative rights must be protected because popular opinion is temporary; public opinion cannot be captured by any group in society, no matter how large. Post rejects the dualism between representative republic and discursive democracy and deems Habermas's contribution to deliberative democracy essential to amend the dualistic approach of early reformism.

First Amendment jurisprudence began with the emerging consciousness that public opinion could be subordinated to the ends of government leaders and so become an organ of propaganda. Not by chance, First Amendment jurisprudence emerged in the years after World War I, when freedom of speech came to be seen as essential for liberty of thought, discussion, and dissent so as to contain the building of a nationalist opinion; in a word, when free speech acquired a quite explicit and direct political meaning. After World War I, Brandeis translated the doctrine of free speech into a pathway to self-government that would make possible discursive democracy: "public discussion is a political duty." The structure of the doctrine of the First Amendment was built in the 1930s on Brandeis's conception, and for the last eighty years constitutional jurisprudence has been founded on the premise that the right to free speech is a political right because it allows democracy to work and public officers to be held accountable to their electors. First Amendment doctrine mirrors a permanent effort of the Court to protect discursive democracy or, in other words, democratic legitimacy. The First Amendment should be seen as a guardian of democracy insofar as it "promotes" the value of self-determination, not of direct democracy; it promotes discursive democracy or democracy as it operates within the institutional frame of representation. This is the historical reconstruction within which Post situates the possible overcoming of the theoretical division within First Amendment jurisprudence.

I have no historiographical competence in American history to validate or question Post's reconstruction, to decide, that is, if it is capable of putting an end to the existing dogmatic approaches. Yet I think that Post's historical reconstruction contains an important theoretical argument, which interests me the most, and that pertains to the identity of representative democracy itself, not only American political history. Post's reading of the meaning of the First Amendment in relation to campaign finance regulation is consistent with what I propose to call, as I have mentioned, democracy's diarchy. Representative democracy is not simple or mono-archic but has a diarchic identity: this is the premise in relation to which we should appreciate the political meaning of free speech and thus welcome campaign finance reform. In his second lecture, Post himself advances a kind of diarchic argument when he writes: "Regulations of the 'franchise' must comply with the logic of representation, whereas regulations of 'political expression' must comply with the logic of discursive democracy." The First Amendment pertains to the latter and is essential to the performance of the former. This is precisely the meaning of what I propose to call diarchy, a reference point that is primed to have a formidable impact on First Amendment jurisprudence.

Let me say briefly something on democracy's diarchy. Since its ancient experience in Athens, we agree that democracy pertains to the opportunity all citizens ought to have to both sit in the assembly (franchise) and to speak freely in the assembly (free speech and toleration of dissent). Ancient Athens gave three different names to these freedoms: *isonomia, isegoria,* and *parrhesia.*[2] Equal by law and before the law in order to enjoy their liberty as persons, Athenian citizens understood they could preserve that isonomic liberty by giving themselves the chance, if they so wanted, to participate in the political life of the city (making the laws) and be certain that their participation would not reflect their economic and social inequality (equal voting power in the assembly). They made clear that procedures had to be autonomous from the evaluation of the outcome: having an equal opportunity to participate in the *ekklesia* was good in and by itself because it gave each citizen the chance to make his contribution valuable (regardless of the fact that they made de facto a valuable contribution).[3]

We have here schematized the first normative definition of democracy as a process of participation in decision making: we do not need to prove that political rights allow us to achieve any particular good in order to conclude that political rights are valuable. Political rights are essential in principle, not for what we can do with them. Good outcomes, if and when they occur, are a reward for procedures; they do not endow procedures with normative value. The Athenians enjoyed and praised their political right to talk freely and frankly in the assembly even if they only rarely used it, and even if only some used it, or even if only fewer used it effectively. According to Hans Mogens Hansen, in that old city, democratic politics was like an athletic competition in which it was essential that all begin at the same starting line. The political order could not be recognized as democratic unless conditions allowed citizens to start as equals.[4] Political liberty thus requires an equal distribution among individuals who are not necessarily equal economically. This is the founding principle of democracy's diarchy, the fact that this form of government is based on *equal power to vote and talk* in the domain of decision. It is also the normative starting point for the regulation of private resources that are employed in politics.

Contemporary societies are democratic not only because they have free elections and multiple political parties, but also because they allow effective political competition and debate among diverse and competing views. In contemporary societies, elections transform the elected into objects of control and scrutiny.[5] Manin has connected representative government's foundation on opinion to its egalitarian premises, because its procedures require that disagreement not be ended "through the intervention of one will that is superior to the others," but through a majority decision that is open to revision.[6]

Clearly, institutions and procedures are exposed to distortion; in a democratic society distortions come from the violation of political equality or the increase of inequality in the conditions that determine a fair use of those institutions and procedures. Charles Beitz wrote some years ago: "One could hardly take seriously one's status as an equal citizen, for example, if owing to a lack of resources one was precluded from advancing one's views effectively in the public forum."[7] Working democratic procedures require that the overall political system take care not only of its formal conditions (franchise) but also of the perception citizens have of its effectiveness and value. Democratic procedures require continuous maintenance. This maintenance should block the translation of socioeconomic inequalities into political power.[8] This task—the self-governing task—is challenging because the insulation of the political system from economic power should be achieved without blocking the communication between civil society and political institutions, which is one of the most important features of representative democracy, which makes it a diarchy.

Diarchy of will and opinion (namely the process of authoritative decision making and the process of opinion formation) or of franchise and political expression (*isonomia* and *isegoria* and *parrhesia*), applies to representative democracy, a system in which an elected assembly is endowed with the ordinary function of making laws. The representative assembly, which is the core institution of a democracy based on elections, presumes and requires a constant relationship with citizens, as single persons or political groups and movements. Public opinion is the means through which this relationship develops. The conceptualization of modern democracy as diarchy makes two claims: that "will" and "opinion" are the two powers of the democratic sovereign; and that they are different and should remain distinct, although in need of constant communication.

The terminology I use derives from the language of sovereignty, which in its modern codification renders the power of the state as a "will" capable of making authoritative decisions that obligate all subjects equally. For Jean Bodin, Thomas Hobbes, Jean-Jacques Rousseau, and the theorists of constitutional government in the nineteenth and early twentieth centuries, the will stood for institutions, rules, and procedures, that is to say, the normativized set of public behaviors that give birth to and implement the law. Suffrage is the starting power of will, the source of authorization of democratic decisions.

Yet the classical theory of sovereignty, which was coined before representative democracy started its journey, did not contemplate judgment or the opinion of the subjects as a function of the sovereign.[9] But democracy, above all when it is implemented through elections, cannot ignore what citizens opine or say when they act as citizens (political actors in the general sense), not electors. Thus in representative democracy, the sovereign is not simply the authorized will (franchise), but is instead a dual entity in which the will or decision is one component, the other being the opinion of those who obey the law and participate only indirectly in ruling.

Moreover, unlike direct democracy, representative democracy compels citizens to be always more than electors, to transcend the act of suffrage (or will) in the effort to reassess the relationship between the weight of their ideas and the weight of their votes through the time between elections. Only in direct democracy are opinions identical with the will because they translate immediately into decisions.[10] In direct democracy, sovereignty is *mono-archic*. But representative democracy breaks that sovereign unity, because opinions acquire a power that is independent from the voting act or the will.

Opinion partakes of sovereignty although it does *not* have any authoritative power; its force is external to the institutions and its authority is informal (it is neither translatable into law nor endowed with the signs of command). The representative democratic system is "one in which supreme power (supreme insofar as it alone is authorized to use force as a last resort) is exerted in the name of and on behalf of the people by virtue of the procedures of elections."[11]

The challenge awaiting representative democracy is thus that, although the will and opinion cannot be truly separated, they need to operate separately and remain different in the outcomes and the form of actualization. Of course we are here talking of normative separation: we do not want the opinion of the majority to become one and the same thing with the will of the sovereign or the law; and we do not want our opinions to be interpreted as passive reactions to the spectacle leaders put on stage. That representative democracy is government by means of opinion entails that the public forum keeps state power public and under scrutiny, both because the law imposes what is performed under the people's eyes and because it is not owned by anybody (in agreement with appointment by elections, which stipulates that political power does not belong in the category of property). The criterion deriving from the paradigm of diarchy may be rendered as follows: as a twin-power, the public forum requires being ruled according to the "same egalitarian value that is embodied in people's equal right to be self-governing."[12]

I need to make a further clarification. Democratic diarchy pertains essentially to representative government, in which will and opinion—or as Post writes, "franchise" and "political expression"—do not merge in the direct voting power that each citizen holds but remain two different modes of participation, so that only the latter is in the hands of all the citizens all the time. But diarchy is not only a descriptive concept. Most importantly, it designates a separation of functions and it extends the principle of equal opportunity to opinion formation and expression. Post does not want to endorse this political egalitarian principle, perhaps because he wants to avoid any a priori rigidity that would compromise the overcoming of the division within the jurisprudence on the First Amendment. Yet this political egalitarian principle is a fundamental achievement that a diarchic conception of representative democracy allows, an achievement that might have an impact in the constitutional jurisprudence on the First Amendment.

Indeed, diarchy consists in keeping decision and deliberation that occur inside of the institutions distinct from the informal world of opinion, without this distinction implying that only the former matters because it can be rendered in numerical certainty or, to the contrary, that only the latter matters because it is conceived as the genuine expression of the voice of the people above the strictures of the constituted power and representation. On this diarchic premise, political liberty acquires security not only in the legal system but also in the perception of the citizens. We may say that the world of opinion creates a buffer zone or a distance between citizens and political power, and that this distance opens the door to, on the one hand, citizens' opinion on power and, on the other, citizens' protection from power.[13]

One of the consequences of the diarchic perspective, in fact the one that interests us here, is that it makes the right to free speech and freedom of opinion an essential component of the political rights of the citizen, not only a civil right of the individual. The right to take part in the formation of public opinion is a right that produces power, not only a right that protects from power.[14]

The informal nature of political opinion requires some pondering and specification. It is true that by itself public deliberation among ordinary citizens decides nothing;[15] that preparing for and informing decisions with a broad process of discussion and communication offers no guarantee that voters will be influenced by good reasons. There can be no such guarantee because voting is arbitrary and unaccountable (as electors we are not accountable to anybody when we cast our ballot and this is the condition of our autonomy) and because the inequality between speakers and listeners is part of the political game of opinion formation. The formal equality that makes us citizens does not equalize the power that the right of free speech gives us to influence each other.[16] Representation does not change the opinion-based nature of democracy; if anything, it makes it even more pronounced (as Rousseau well understood when he opposed it).

In fact the representative system gives the forum a determinate role because it consists in putting politics in public as citizens are required to judge and choose politicians according to what they say and do, or to exercise their prospective and retrospective judgment on them. In this sense it makes the society outside government a large and articulated sphere of participation, democratic in all respects. Without this outside of government there would be no representative democracy. Hence, the dualism between representative republic and discursive democracy is unwarranted—it is based, one might say, on a mono-archic vision of democracy that gives preponderance to the will only, and sees opinion as only a counter power against it.

The idea of democracy as diarchy is thus equally distant from a pure electoralist conception of democracy (or what Post calls a "representative republic," in which voting is the only right that counts) and a conception that interprets government by opinion as a government in which sovereignty is in permanent mobilization and thus belongs, fatally, to those who are more active or vociferous and exercise it through acclamatory voice outside and above the voting procedures.

What makes the sphere of opinion share in sovereignty depends, therefore, on the form the sovereign takes. Voting for or electing a candidate is what makes the forum of public opinion share in sovereignty; it is the reference point in relation to which speech plays a political role. Democratic theorists have argued, rightly, that the centrality of decision to politics makes elections the only truly democratic institution.[17] Votes are the most reliable public data at our disposal, and voting is the only formal way citizens have to punish and threaten their rulers. "Voting is an imposition of a will over a will" and is that which counts as a decision beyond reasonable doubt.[18]

But the diarchic architecture can have tricky effects. Indeed, the circularity of giving authority/checking on authority is what makes the power of opinion so hard to define scientifically and to regulate normatively, yet so indispensable practically. This complexity and elusiveness brought David Hume to define "public opinion" as a "force" that makes the many easily governed by the few and the few unable to escape the control of the many.[19] After the casting of their ballot one by one, it is the circular movement of opinion that links citizens among themselves and bridges state institutions and society.[20] This makes sense of representative democracy as a diarchy and as a form of democracy that is not a second best. But it also makes sense of the risks this diarchic structure embodies.

Indeed, the interaction between the people and their candidates and representatives may induce some to think that the loudest citizens, or public debates on TV or lobbies of polls or powerful sponsors, are legitimate in vindicating a sovereign power. Populist and plebiscitarian phenomena are incubated within democracy's diarchy as a longing to overcome the distance between will and opinion and to merge them so as to achieve unanimity and homogeneity, an idealization that has characterized democratic communities since antiquity.[21]

On the other hand, because of its diarchic nature, representative democracy should be engaged in an extra effort to guard the opportunity of citizens to participate in the making of the democratic discursive sovereign. Since there is an unavoidable link between public opinion and political decision, concern about the disproportioned possibility that the wealthiest or the more socially powerful have to influence the electors and the government is sacrosanct. As Yasmin Dawood writes, empirical research proves this concern is well taken when it demonstrates how economic inequality and political inequality "are mutually enforcing with the result that wealth tends to entrench, rather than distribute, power over time."[22]

Theorists of democracy take this evidence as a justification to argue that in representative democracy citizens may suffer from a new kind of corruption, a "duplicitous corruption" that consists in excluding those who have equal citizenship from a meaningful presence in the forum and doing so in a way that the excluded cannot prove their exclusion because they retain the equal right to throw a "paper stone" in the ballot box, which is factual evidence of their equal citizenship.[23]

The crucial insight of the diarchic theory of representative democracy (an argument that meets magnificently with Post's lectures) is thus that when opinion is introduced in our understanding of democratic participation, political representation must attend to the question of the *circumstances of opinion formation,* an issue that pertains to political justice or the equal opportunity citizens should have meaningfully to enjoy their political rights.[24] Citizens' equal right to an equal share in determining the political will (one person, one vote) ought to go together with citizens' meaningful opportunities to be informed but also to form, express, and communicate their ideas and give them public weight and influence.

Although influence can hardly be equal and estimated with rigorous calculation, the opportunity to exercise it can and should be. Although we can hardly prove beyond any reasonable doubt that there is a causal relationship between media content, public opinion, and political results or decisions (no data can prove that Berlusconi won three electoral competitions because of his media television empire), the barriers to equal opportunity to participate in the formation of political opinions should be kept low and their level permanently monitored. This is the salient meaning of political equality as liberty protection; that is, the idea that the focus of democracy is on inclusion because its concern is "on the reasons for excluding individuals" and money is a powerful reason for exclusion even when exclusion does not take the radical form of suppressing franchise.[25] Thus the same reasoning that holds for voting also holds for opinion: although we can hardly prove that voting translates to some desirable outcome, we do not conclude that to distribute it equally is meaningless.

Let me conclude by recalling the words used in 2003 by Justices Stevens and O'Connor when the Supreme Court approved the campaign finance law passed by Congress, words that confirm the diarchic nature of representative democracy: although the secret ballot prevents us from producing "concrete evidence" that "money buys influence," the secret ballot is not a sufficient guarantee of democracy because, presumably, the secret ballot is not the only form that the people's voice takes. "Congress is not required to ignore historical evidence regarding a particular practice or to view conduct in isolation from its context." In a word, opinion is a power both when it is used to advance a political program or sponsor a candidate and when it is used by citizens to voice their dissent from the opinion of the majority or to ask for more complete information on the government's practices. This makes the equal opportunity to partake in the sovereignty of opinion a sensitive issue, although no evidence can prove that the influence of opinion translates into decisions. Yet as effectively argued by C. Edwin Baker, the "democratic distribution principle is an end in itself, not a means predicted to lead empirically to some desirable result," and it holds both for the function of making decisions (voting) and the function of forming and questioning them.[26]

Robert Post thus makes a seminal contribution to the solution of this *vexata quaestio* when he shows that the First Amendment is predisposed so as to protect the idea of representative democracy as diarchy, to acknowledge that political participation in representative democracy is complex and does not mean merely selecting lawmakers but also counting upon effective representatives as advocates both outside and inside state institutions; in a word, enjoying an equal opportunity to participate in the public forum as not only electors but also as citizens.[27] Through the reconstruction of American political history, Post proves that the First Amendment iterates the normative value of democratic procedures in their impeccable ability to reproduce self-government through time, and finally that a democratic government should feel the responsibility to regulate the forum of public opinion so as to ensure that all have always at last an equal opportunity to exercise some influence on the political system, even if not all intend to use that opportunity, those who have more material power to effect political influence abstain from using it, and elected politicians are virtuous enough to be deaf to the pressure of influential citizens.

6

CITIZENS DEFLECTED: ELECTORAL INTEGRITY AND POLITICAL REFORM

Pamela S. Karlan

Robert Post's ambition is "to provide a constitutional account of how . . . two distinct paths to self-governance"—on the one hand, "our republican tradition" of government through representative institutions and on the other, a more contemporary commitment to continuous democratic participation—"may be integrated, one with the other," particularly with respect to the question of campaign finance reform. Much of Post's first lecture is taken up with a rich and thoughtful history of how these two paths diverged. "[O]ur nation's initial commitment to republican self-government" was expressed through the Constitution's creation of "complicated and carefully balanced structures of representation." In this constitutional order elections were a central guarantor of liberty—not just because they ensured the consent of the governed, but because the representative government they produced "checked and channeled the unstable force of popular sentiment." In the twentieth century, however, our constitutional understanding evolved. Self-government now rested on ongoing popular engagement and discussion. The First Amendment came to take pride of place. The "discursive democracy" the amendment protected was "distinct from," and "more essential than, any particular or momentary representation of public opinion." Individuals' speech rights came to "tak[e] precedence over representation as a pathway for American self-government." As a result, assertions of free speech trumped arguments about the need to protect particular features of the election process itself.

141

But at the end of the day, democracy—as opposed to other practices—cannot be entirely discursive. Democracy is a form of government—"government of the people, by the people, for the people" as Lincoln put it—and government "requires constant and recurring episodes of decision making." To borrow the title of Jim Gardner's influential article, at some point we must just shut up and vote.[1] If the "uninhibited, robust, and wide-open" debate the First Amendment protects[2] does not ultimately produce "officials who attend to public opinion, the link between public discourse and self-government"—the motivating force behind modern First Amendment doctrine—"is broken."

The idea of "electoral integrity" captures the nature of this link. Elections have integrity, Post explains, when they "have the property of choosing candidates whom the people trust to possess" the "communion of interests and sympathy of sentiments . . . without which every government degenerates into tyranny."[3] Post hopes that this understanding—that electoral integrity is a value internal to the First Amendment rather than in tension with it—can provide common ground in the debate over campaign finance reform.

Somewhat surprisingly, although Post claims that "there are good reasons to worry that electoral integrity is today under threat," on the very same page of his lecture he expressly declines to "explore whether electoral integrity is in fact at risk, or whether campaign finance reform will in fact ameliorate that risk." All he wants to argue is that "the protection of electoral integrity constitutes a compelling state interest."

Where this leaves us is not entirely clear. Post rightly criticizes the Supreme Court in *Citizens United*[4] for "falsely imagin[ing] that electoral integrity is a matter of law, rather than of fact."[5] But unless some form of campaign-related spending actually *is* causing citizens to lose confidence that elected officials are responsive to public opinion, the principle of electoral integrity has little to contribute to the debate over campaign finance reform. And conversely, to the extent that electoral integrity is a bedrock of constitutional self-governance, we should be looking elsewhere to reinforce it. More fundamentally, "electoral integrity" is a phrase that, almost deliberately, can mean very different things to different people. Particularly in our contemporary society, with its deep political polarization,[6] there may be profound disagreement over whether a particular regulation promotes or undermines electoral integrity.

In what follows, I make three points. First, if we are concerned about the health of representative democracy, we should be looking at causes beyond corporate spending on candidate elections. Focusing on *Citizens United* deflects attention from a variety of structural features that may better explain why the link between the public and its representatives has frayed and why citizens have lost faith that elected officials conscientiously represent the public interest. Second, in the arena of political spending, Post's principle of electoral integrity may ultimately collapse back into the existing, and largely unsuccessful, rationales for regulation. This raises the question whether electoral integrity offers a distinctive justification for regulation of the political process or is, instead, only a reformulation of existing arguments. Third, precisely because electoral integrity is a subjective concept, it can be used to justify highly contestable electoral regulations. In the hands of the current Supreme Court, for example, invocations of electoral integrity may undermine, rather than further, democratic participation in the electoral domain.

I.

As Sam Issacharoff and I pointed out sometime last century, "[t]he First Amendment and political spending are only two of the many institutional structures within which our politics take place."[7] The pernicious kinds of political spending we now have are shaped not only by the law of campaign finance but also by a range of other factors. For example, the Constitution and federal law create fixed terms of office with predictable election dates. As a result, political campaigns last far longer in the United States than in many comparable democracies (thereby increasing the demand for funds), and the ability to raise money long before an election is important not only to funding a candidate's campaign but also in sending a signal to deter potential rivals from entering the race. Or consider our long-standing use of single-member territorial districts to elect the members of Congress.[8] Duverger's Law predicts that such elections will produce a two-party system with head-to-head contests between candidates. Such races may be particularly likely to see political spending concentrate on negative advertising.[9] So even if electoral integrity is in part a function of political spending, it may be that we should be focusing on other aspects of the electoral domain as the areas where reform might be more productive at changing the effects of political money.

More fundamentally, if we are concerned about electoral integrity, it is worth asking whether campaign finance reform is where we should be training our focus.

The empirical evidence on the extent to which citizen confidence is driven by campaign finance is somewhat equivocal. For at least the past half century, the American National Election Survey (ANES) has been asking voters two questions that map quite closely onto the concept of electoral integrity: "How much of the time do you think you can trust the government in Washington to do what is right—just about always, most of the time, or only some of the time?" and "Would you say the government is pretty much run by a few big interests looking out for themselves or that it is run for the benefit of all the people?"[10] While Post points to a significant rise between 2002 and 2008 in the percentage of respondents who gave skeptical answers to those two questions, the longer-term record shows a more complex pattern. For example, the level of distrust peaked (at least so far) in 1994, and by 2002 distrust had fallen back to roughly where it had stood in 1970.[11] More importantly, levels of trust and distrust appear to float independently of what is going on with respect to legal regulation of political spending: during the period Post identifies, distrust increased even as the Bipartisan Campaign Reform Act (the law at issue in *Citizens United*) ratcheted up the level of regulation, eliminating soft money and imposing new restrictions on electioneering communications.[12] It is also worth remembering that throughout this period, until the decision in *Citizens United*, corporate political spending in federal elections (and many state elections) was sharply limited. So if citizen confidence was decreasing, it was not because of the kind of spending the *Citizens United* decision unleashed or that current reform efforts target. Some other factor was presumably at work.

Nor is it clear that corporate spending is likely to be a major factor in public confidence going forward. Post does a wonderful job of devastating the Court's assertion in *Citizens United* that the First Amendment necessarily precludes the government from applying different rules to corporate political speech than to individual political speech. But our experience since the Court's decision at least raises the question whether corporate spending in candidate elections is a particularly serious threat to electoral integrity, or likely to become one.

First, when it comes to spending within the "distinct managerial domain" of elections, there are, as Post notes, several different types of corporations. Media corporations (however complex a category that is in a world of conglomerates that manufacture everything from home appliances to the nightly news) and ideological corporations whose funds come from individuals exercising their associational rights are distinctively situated: they operate at the center of democratic discourse.[13] Even under Post's formulation, their election-related spending would seem entitled to the highest constitutional protection. But "[o]rdinary commercial corporations" also come in at least two major flavors: closely held businesses, which really should be understood as the creature of their owners, and large publicly traded entities, where ownership and management are quite separate. For a variety of reasons, the primary political spenders in most candidate elections are likely to be wealthy individuals (and perhaps the companies they control directly), rather than large corporations.[14] Think Sheldon Adelson and Foster Friess and George Soros and the Koch brothers, rather than Apple or Wal-Mart. If the source of the confidence-destroying funds that slosh through the system is individuals, rather than corporations, then the trade-off between discursive democracy and electoral integrity becomes starker.

Second, we may be looking at the wrong event. I am not saying that large corporations don't engage in massive spending to influence representative decision making. They do, and it is called lobbying. Post's discussion of discursive democracy suggests that we should be giving greater attention to the ways in which corporate money undercuts postelection formation of public opinion and choice among policies. Here again, though, we have the problem that the communicative activity we would be regulating falls outside the "distinct managerial domain" of elections. The concept of electoral integrity does not give much of a handle on how to address corporate spending directed at changing public opinion on issues pending before governmental bodies or on lobbying activity. Indeed, the more robust the commitment to discursive democracy, the harder it may be to justify such regulation.

When we turn from the question whether political spending is the problem to whether regulations can improve electoral integrity, the evidence is similarly complicated. While somewhere between two-thirds and three-quarters of respondents in various polls support virtually any campaign finance reform proposal, roughly the same percentage respond in other polls that "no matter what new laws are passed, special interests will always find a way to maintain their power in Washington."[15] There is little "systematic evidence that directly supports or contradicts [the] claim" that campaign finance laws can "improve popular perceptions of the democratic process."[16] One recent study that compared citizens' responses to ANES questions about political efficacy across states with different campaign finance regimes concluded that while "[t]here may be some modest improvement in efficacy from disclosure laws, and perhaps even limits on contributions from organizations" such as corporations, "none of the campaign finance [restrictions] consistently has a statistically significant effect on every measure of political efficacy."[17] Even if campaign finance reforms in fact improve political efficacy or some other measure of democratic functioning, they will not increase electoral integrity unless the public perceives that improvement.

More fundamentally, our problems with political money may be a by-product, rather than the source, of the broken link between the public and its representatives. The week before Dean Post delivered his lectures, the Center for Voting and Democracy released the latest of its biennial *Monopoly Politics* reports projecting outcomes in 85 percent of the 435 U.S. House elections to be held in 2014.[18] Over the years, the Center has consistently predicted the results in these elections without feeling the need to know anything about the level of campaign spending, the economy, the district-specific issues, the identity of the challenger, or even the incumbent's performance in office. A few variables regarding the electoral performance of the district are enough. It is more accurate to say that every ten years, as part of the post-Census redistricting, legislators (and their political allies) go into a room to select their constituents than to pretend that every two years voters go into a booth to elect their representatives. Partisan gerrymandering and incumbent protection mean that even significant shifts in public opinion may sink beneath the waves without a trace.[19] As Dan Ortiz observed:

> A national swing of five percent in voter opinion—a sea change in most elections—will change very few seats in the current House of Representatives. Gerrymandering thus creates a kind of inertia that arrests the House's dynamic process. It makes it less certain that votes in the chamber will reflect shifts in popular opinion, and thus frustrates change and creates undemocratic slippage between the people and their government.[20]

Under these circumstances, tinkering with the regulation of spending in the electoral domain may do little to restore electoral integrity.

II.

Electoral integrity, Post tells us, "consists of public confidence that elected officials attend to public opinion." It is a fundamentally subjective quality that turns on what "people actually believe." But what happens when we unpack those beliefs, as surely courts must do if the principle is actually to be applied in a concrete case? If we ask *why* the public thinks a particular form of political money undermines electoral integrity, we are exceptionally likely to get an answer that sounds almost entirely in one of the three existing justifications for regulating political money—namely, that regulation vindicates principles of political equality, prevents existing inequalities in wealth from distorting the political process, or guards against corruption and the appearance of corruption. Nowhere in his lectures does Post identify some other reason why voters are likely to think that corporate political expenditures—or other forms of political spending—weaken the link between representatives and their constituents.

Public confidence in the electoral process is of course critical to its legitimacy. No one denies that. But let's assume that Post is right, for example, that the antidistortion principle "expresses a government interest that is incompatible with the structure of First Amendment rights" because in a discursive democratic world, "[t]here can be no 'baseline,' no Archimedean point, from which to normalize the content of public opinion." If he is, then it is not clear to me why taking the derivative of that argument—namely, saying that people lose confidence in representative government when they think the electoral process has been distorted by wealthy spenders—somehow gains traction as a constitutional argument. Skeptics of campaign finance reform, including the majority on the current Supreme Court, may well see arguments from electoral integrity not as a new "firm *common* ground" on which to reconstruct "the constitutional jurisprudence of campaign finance reform," but as a strategic attempt to rearticulate the old justifications they have already rejected using a more attractive vocabulary.

III.

Post's conception of democratic legitimacy accepts that "[i]f a government possesses the trust and confidence of its people, it will be democratically legitimate, even if the impartial verdict of reason declares that the people ought to withdraw allegiance from their government." This raises serious problems in a political system like ours, where constitutional precommitments should be understood to take certain confidence-inspiring measures off the table. Indeed, the very subjectivity of the concept of electoral integrity may threaten key characteristics of the representative process.

In the final section of the second lecture, Post sets out an argument that elections constitute a "distinct managerial domain," and therefore that "[l]ike every government institution, elections must manage speech as well as behavior" in order to accomplish their designated purposes. I confess that I was disconcerted to see that he relied on *Purcell v. Gonzalez*[21] to support his argument that "the state can and must" impose restrictions in the electoral domain "that would be unconstitutional if applied" elsewhere, and then used the example of the Australian ballot to illustrate justifiable restrictions in the service of electoral integrity.

To be fair, Post is relying on the canonical view of the secret ballot.[22] But there is a less rosy account. Morgan Kousser, for example, describes the connection between the adoption of secret ballots and the exclusion of illiterate and foreign-born immigrants in the North, and blacks in the South:

> The publicly printed ticket required the voter, sometimes without any aid from anyone, to scurry quickly through a maze of names of candidates running for everything from presidential elector to county court clerk, a list which was often arranged by office rather than party. He then had to mark an "X" by the names of the candidates for whom he wished to vote, or, in some states, mark through or erase those he opposed. Such a task demanded not merely literacy, but fluency in the English language. An ingenious lawmaker could make voting all but impossible. Florida totally abolished party designations on the ballot. A Populist or Republican who wished to vote for his presidential electors had to count down five, ten, or fifteen unfamiliar names before starting to mark. Voters in one Virginia congressional district in 1894 confronted a ballot printed in the German Fraktur script.[23]

In this contrary account, appeals to a form of electoral integrity are intimately bound up in exclusionary politics. The secret ballot was part and parcel of the change in American politics from what Michael Schudson calls a "democracy of partisanship" to a "democracy of information."[24] So, too, were other Progressive-era measures billed as attempts to restore electoral integrity, such as literacy tests and the move to at-large elections.[25] For those who believe that electoral integrity depends on citizens having the right to participate effectively in the electoral process, it should cause concern that the emergence of discursive democracy coincided with a sharp decline in actual political participation, particularly by poor and minority citizens.[26]

As for *Purcell,* where Post finds a contemporary invocation of electoral integrity, it is worth remembering the underlying statute being challenged. In 2004, Arizona adopted new and draconian voter identification requirements that required individuals both to present specified documentary proof of citizenship in order to register and to present certain forms of government-issued identification in order to cast a ballot on Election Day.[27] The Arizona initiative was an expression of a troubling anti-immigrant sentiment that has permeated politics in much of the country. In light of the potential impact of the new identification provisions on minority voters (not to mention on poor, elderly, and disabled citizens more generally), a number of individuals, civil rights organizations, and Indian tribes then brought suit, challenging the requirements on constitutional and statutory grounds.[28]

The Supreme Court permitted the identification requirements to be used in the 2006 election. In explaining its decision, the Court offered a highly contestable account of the interests at play. On the one hand, the plaintiffs had a "strong interest in exercising the 'fundamental political right' to vote."[29] The "possibility" that qualified voters might be precluded from voting by a lack of adequate identification should, the Court observed, "caution any . . . judge to give careful consideration to the plaintiffs' challenges."[30]

On the other side, the Court articulated the language Post cites: "A State indisputably has a compelling interest in preserving the integrity of its election process."[31] But the account the Court then gives of "integrity" places a huge thumb on the scale of denying the right to participate:

> Confidence in the integrity of our electoral processes is essential to the functioning of our participatory democracy. Voter fraud drives honest citizens out of the democratic process and breeds distrust of our government. Voters who fear their legitimate votes will be outweighed by fraudulent ones will feel disenfranchised.[32]

In a subsequent decision upholding Indiana's voter identification statute, *Crawford v. Marion County Election Board,*[33] six members of the

Court abandoned the idea that restrictions on the franchise should trigger strict scrutiny because, as Justice Stevens wrote in an opinion for himself, the Chief Justice, and Justice Kennedy, "'evenhanded restrictions that protect the integrity and reliability of the electoral process itself' are not invidious."[34] Strikingly, Justice Stevens acknowledged that the record contained no evidence of in-person voter impersonation "actually occurring in Indiana at any time in its history."[35] Nonetheless, relying on the language from *Purcell*, which tracks the subjectivity of Post's concept of integrity, Justice Stevens declared that "public confidence in the integrity of the electoral process has independent significance, because it encourages citizen participation in the democratic process."[36]

To me, it seems perverse that the remedy for some voters' skepticism about the legitimacy of the political process can be to deny other citizens the right to participate. But if arguments about electoral integrity rest on claims about "what people actually believe"—as opposed to what is, in fact, true—does it even matter that fears of voter fraud apparently "do not have any relationship to a [citizen's] likelihood of intending to vote or turning out to vote"?[37] Does the principle of electoral integrity offer any basis on which to choose between type I and type II errors—that is, between false positives (permitting ineligible individuals to vote) and false negatives (excluding eligible citizens from casting a vote)? Particularly in a polarized society, where one group thinks the greatest threat to electoral integrity is vote fraud and a competing group thinks the greatest threat lies in vote suppression, what is a court to do? There is an entire movement—ironically enough cloaking itself in the mantle of "voter integrity"—based on the wholly unproven premise that legions of aliens and disenfranchised offenders are infiltrating the election system.[38] "Electoral integrity" tethered only to popular belief, particularly in a world of wide-open, robust, unmediated discursive democracy of the kind we find on contemporary talk radio, may pose its own dangers to the principles of equality and access that lie at the heart of the logic of representation. The voter ID decisions, even more than the campaign finance cases, fit Post's charge that "[a] line of cases this misguided about matters of such fundamental importance to American politics is a frightful thing." In their wake, I worry that invocations of electoral integrity may undermine our democracy rather than strengthen it.

Post tries to reassure us by asserting that electoral integrity is "a unique kind of constitutional value, for it depends upon what people actually believe." By contrast, "[t]he 'equally effective voice' principle" embodied in cases like *Reynolds v. Sims*[39] "should be applied on the basis of the actual facts relevant to equality, rather than on the basis of subjective beliefs." But *Purcell* itself blurred that very distinction when it quoted *Reynolds* to support its assertion about the disenfranchising, integrity-undermining effect of citizen distrust: "'[T]he right of suffrage can be denied by a debasement or dilution of the weight of a citizen's vote just as effectively as by wholly prohibiting the free exercise of the franchise.' *Reynolds v. Sims*, 377 U.S. 533, 555 (1964)."[40] In the Court's view, if a voter's lack of confidence in the system drives him out of the process, then he *has* been denied his equally effective voice; the government can act to restore the confidence that produces participation.

To be sure, Post might respond that the Court must demand empirical proof that withdrawal will occur before it upholds an election law that restricts other citizens' rights. Or perhaps he would conclude that even the risk that some citizens will withdraw cannot justify impairing the participation rights of others. But note that these restrictions are less likely to take the form of outright repudiations of the principle of equally effective voice than they are to involve procedural provisions explicitly embedded in the heartland of the "managerial domain associated with elections." And that domain is precisely the one that Post himself identifies as an area where interests in electoral integrity have properly operated in the past.

Suggesting that courts should consider the underlying empirical basis for restrictions on speech, voting, or other rights associated with the political process is not the same thing as "repudiat[ing] the premise that democratic legitimacy depends upon actual beliefs about the responsiveness of elected officials to public opinion" or "prohibit[ing] courts from incorporating the premise into their reasoning." It is simply to recognize the continued constitutional vitality of the republican view that public sentiment regarding how the political process should operate must sometimes be "checked and channeled." Jimmy Carter once promised us a government as "good and honest and decent and truthful and competent and compassionate and as filled with love as are the American people."[41] But part of the Constitution's ambition is to give us a government that does better than that, or at least, in the words of Abraham Lincoln's First Inaugural Address, that reflects the better angels of our nature.

III

RESPONSE

7

REPRESENTATIVE DEMOCRACY

Robert C. Post

Among the great pleasures of the Tanner Lectures is the opportunity to respond to thoughtful and astute commentators. In this regard I have manifestly hit the jackpot. I am grateful indeed for their wise and helpful observations. I find I have very little to add to their remarks, and so this response shall be quite brief.

Larry Lessig's comment on the corruption of improper dependence is characteristically perceptive. I accept Lessig's claim that the Founders used the concept of corruption to refer to improper dependence. Because the Founders were devoted to the ideal of a representative republic, they could not have conceptualized a principle of electoral integrity that makes sense only in the context of *democratic* forms of self-government. I therefore also accept that the concept of dependence corruption has a greater claim to originalist authority than any I have advanced.

I confess that my inclination is to analyze constitutional issues in terms of our own contemporary constitutional convictions rather than in terms of those that are two centuries old. I believe that the chief attraction of modern originalism lies in its capacity to channel contemporary constitutional beliefs.[1] If the five majority members of the Court in *Citizens United* had prized the integrity of representative forms of self-government more than they valued democratic participation, as the Founders no doubt did, they would have decided the case differently. It is *because* the modern Court privileges freedom of speech over the workings of representative government that *Citizens United* came out the way it did.

The justices who joined the majority opinion in *Citizens United* did not seem aware that the constitutional value of electoral integrity is implicit in their own reliance on First Amendment rights. My hope in these Tanner Lectures is to build a bridge between the majority and the dissent by illuminating the entailments of our own contemporary commitment to First Amendment ideals. It may be that fidelity to originalist principles might effect a similar reconciliation, but I doubt it.[2]

Of course it is open to Lessig to observe that there might be little difference between his approach, which probes whether our election system produces officials who are improperly dependent upon the funders as distinct from the people, and the approach for which I advocate in these Tanner Lectures, which probes whether our election system produces officials who are improperly dependent upon the funders as distinct from public opinion. In the end, Lessig might argue, we are simply using different words to describe the identical phenomenon.

The phenomenon we seek to remedy depends upon the words we use to describe it. If the relevant phenomenon is described at a sufficient level of generality—if it is described, say, as money having too great an influence on politics—I quite agree that it is impossible to make important distinctions. But viewed with the particularity required by constitutional law, the phenomenon described by Lessig, and the phenomenon I identify, seem quite different.

A theory of electoral integrity postulates that elections must be structured to secure public confidence that elected officials are responsive to public opinion. There must be public confidence that elected officials are attentive to the meanings produced by the structure of communication policed by First Amendment rights. The connection between electoral integrity and First Amendment doctrine could not be tighter. Electoral integrity depends upon a concept of public opinion which is *defined* in terms of the processes established by First Amendment rights. Except in very unusual and strictly limited situations, First Amendment rights do not distinguish among speakers based upon their resources.

A theory of dependence corruption, by contrast, postulates that elections must be structured to secure public confidence that elected officials are responsive to the "People." But the theory has no intrinsic answer to the obvious question: Who are the People? If the People are defined by the public opinion they produce when communicating in the manner protected by First Amendment rights, there is indeed no difference between a theory of electoral integrity and a theory of dependence corruption. But there is strong reason to doubt that a theory of dependence corruption can define the People in this way. Lessig is quite clear that the People *excludes* "the funders," who "are less than .05 percent of America."

Why are the funders excluded from the People? Why don't the People *include* the funders? Suppose I were to claim that elected officials are responsive to "the writers"—those who participate in the public sphere by publishing in broadcast media, or on the Internet, or in books or magazines. And suppose I could demonstrate that the writers constitute less than .05 percent of the people. Would I establish that elected officials are corrupt if I can demonstrate that they are dependent upon the writers *instead of* the People?

You can see where I am going with this question. A theory of dependence corruption that purports to excise a class of persons from the body of the People, a class of persons whom the First Amendment would otherwise authorize to participate in the formation of public opinion, must offer a convincing account of how it defines the People.

The most sympathetic such account I can construct is that the People are defined by their collective will. Persons whose participation in public discourse distorts the expression of this will can be excluded from the People. This is accomplished by restricting their First Amendment rights. Obviously this account postulates that elected officials should be accountable to an entity quite different from, and antithetical to, the communicative structures defined and safeguarded by First Amendment rights.[3] It is an entity best captured by the antidistortion theory of campaign finance reform, which postulates that the will of the people can be known in some way other than their ongoing expression.

Nadia Urbinati's comment makes it quite clear that the United States cannot now be conceptualized either as a representative republic or as a pure democracy. It is instead a representative democracy. In a representative democracy, the people cannot be known solely by their will. Urbinati explains that in a representative democracy, the people must be known through a "diarchy of will and opinion (namely the process of authoritative decision making and the process of opinion formation)."

I entirely agree with Urbinati's analysis. In the United States today the value of self-government cannot lie solely in the province of freedom of expression or in that of representative integrity. We require both, and this means that we must join together two forms of self-government that abide by two very different logics. Diarchy is as accurate a way of describing this awkward joinder as any I can conceive.

In my second lecture, I attempted to derive the requirement of diarchy from the internal perspective of our First Amendment commitments. I argued that freedom of opinion requires electoral integrity if it is to serve the purpose of self-government. In my first lecture I attempted to show that the reverse is also true, that the need for diarchy derives from the internal perspective of representative integrity whenever historical conditions prevent representative government from serving the value of self-government without freedom of expression.

Urbinati short-circuits my long-winded appeals to constitutional law and history by deriving diarchy directly from a complex and fascinating political theory of representative institutions. She brings "theory" back, although not as "the application of an abstract blueprint" but instead as an immanent achievement of "the history of the American republic." It is a delight to learn from her in this regard. Her forthcoming book, *Democracy Disfigured: Opinion, Truth and the People,* the proofs of which I did not have the pleasure of reading until after the Tanner Lectures, offers a deep and satisfying discussion of this fundamental subject.

There is no doubt that Frank Michelman understands the fundamental tension at the heart of diarchy. He clearly perceives the necessity and difficulty of maintaining "the two integrities, of elections and of public discourse." But Michelman is concerned that judicial efforts to sustain this tension might be incompatible with the doctrine of strict scrutiny. Michelman sets out the black-letter elements of strict-scrutiny doctrine, and he asks how these elements could possibly be applied in the context of electoral integrity.

Michelman is right to see a tension between diarchy and strict scrutiny, but I am puzzled why he considers the doctrine of strict scrutiny to be constitutionally fundamental. Doctrine consists of rules or standards that courts use to guide them in their decision making. It both coordinates decision making among diverse courts and empowers higher courts to control the decision making of lower courts.[4] The ultimate point of doctrine, however, is not simple consistency, but the promotion of judicial decision making that correctly implements relevant legal values. If doctrine does not do this, it is subject to critique as mere formalism.

The modern doctrine of strict scrutiny first appeared in the 1940s when the Court expressed strong constitutional disapproval of state action inflicting racial stigmatization.[5] The doctrine assumed its modern form, explicated by Michelman, in the 1960s, when the Court concluded that racial classifications were a likely tool of racial stigmatization.[6] But as unanticipated uses of racial classifications developed, for example in the context of affirmative action, it became uncertain whether racial classifications in fact necessarily inflicted terrible racial stigmatization. In response to these concerns, the doctrine of strict scrutiny evolved into what Michelman calls "weak-form" strict scrutiny.[7] As Michelman correctly notes, last term the Court tacked to the right and seemed to move closer to a "strong-form" strict scrutiny in the context of affirmative action.[8]

What this history illustrates is that doctrine evolves as underlying constitutional values evolve. This is true of strict scrutiny, just as it is true of every doctrinal formulation. There is no ideal or canonical form of strict scrutiny. Strict scrutiny is merely an instrument to accurately express the constitutional values that should be brought to bear in a given case. Historians of constitutional law can easily demonstrate that the form and spirit of strict scrutiny have changed as these values have evolved.

Strict scrutiny was imported into First Amendment doctrine during the last third of the twentieth century in order to safeguard the "supremely precious"[9] resource of democratic legitimation. Strict scrutiny expresses the constitutional relationship between the value of democratic legitimation and whatever competing values may tempt government to regulate the content of public discourse. The thesis of these lectures is that electoral integrity is equally essential to democratic legitimation as the integrity of public discourse. If this thesis is correct, it would follow that courts cannot apply strict scrutiny to protect the integrity of public discourse *at the expense* of electoral integrity. Insofar as the function of First Amendment doctrine is to protect democratic legitimation, this would constitute an egregious doctrinal mistake.

It is an open question whether the weak form of strict scrutiny can accommodate both electoral integrity and the integrity of public discourse. It would depend largely upon the spirit with which courts apply the doctrine. But if weak-form strict scrutiny were to prove a successful avenue for protecting *both* electoral integrity *and* the integrity of public discourse, it is no objection at all to observe that in other contexts (like affirmative action) the Court has insisted on employing strong-form strict scrutiny.

If the Court is persuaded that weak-form strict scrutiny is necessary to reconcile electoral integrity with the integrity of public discourse, I am certain it will not be deterred from using weak-form strict scrutiny on the ground that strict scrutiny is a universal, invariant test that must always in all circumstances be applied in exactly the same manner. Constitutional significance attaches to constitutional values, not to doctrinal form.

Of course the Court might find that some other doctrinal test better serves to reconcile electoral integrity and the integrity of public discourse, and that would be fine with me. The form of doctrine is of less importance than a clear-headed understanding of what doctrine is designed to accomplish. Doctrinal form should follow doctrinal function.

I sense that Michelman's concern for the integrity of the strict-scrutiny test reflects a deeper worry that there is no doctrinal test at all that might be capable of expressing the constitutional value of electoral integrity. Because electoral integrity turns on public confidence that elections select officials who are attentive to public opinion, and because electoral integrity can be apprehended only through the exercise of political judgment, legislative efforts to preserve electoral integrity might prove to be a "political question" and thus resist all judicial supervision. In effect this would leave legislatures a free and unreviewable hand to shape the contents of public discourse. That would be a most undesirable outcome.

I accept with gratitude Michelman's fine and helpful reconstruction of how courts might conceptualize electoral integrity in a way that would avoid this result. As Michelman notes, electoral integrity must consist of what he aptly calls "a certain state of the public imagination." The law commonly aspires to protect subjective experience, like the experience of trust or confidence, by normalizing it,[10] which means linking it to what Michelman rightly terms the "intersubjective" dimension of social reality.[11] This is how the law conceives and protects the "relationships of trust and confidence"[12] that are known as fiduciary relationships. The law safeguards fiduciary relationships by using the concept of "reasonableness" to connect subjective individual experience with normalizing intersubjective expectations.

The point may be illustrated by the *Restatement of Trusts,* which obliges trustees to preserve the trust and confidence of beneficiaries by keeping them "reasonably informed"[13] and by exercising "reasonable care" to prevent breaches of trust and confidence.[14] Analogously, the tort of invasion of privacy, which is designed to protect persons from subjective experiences deemed violative of individual integrity, identifies these experiences by asking whether communications "would be highly offensive to a reasonable person."[15] In each case, the law grasps subjective experience through the medium of normalized intersubjective expectations. The upshot is that the law defines and safeguards "a certain state of the public imagination."

Despite the shift toward positivism that accompanied the triumph of the *Erie* doctrine in the 1930s,[16] it remains quite common for courts to construct constitutional law by appealing to intersubjective understandings of this kind.[17] This is what courts do whenever they determine the "reasonableness" of a search and seizure under the Fourth Amendment,[18] or interpret the meaning of "dignity" under the Fifth Amendment,[19] or of "cruel and unusual punishment" under the Eighth Amendment,[20] or of "undue burden" under the Fourteenth Amendment.[21]

Appeals to intersubjective experience cannot be made in a vacuum. They require an acute knowledge of relevant facts. My criticism of the Court's treatment of the Montana Corrupt Practices Act was its heedless conclusion that no facts in the world could justify the conclusion that independent corporate expenditures in Montana might compromise electoral integrity. The Court believed it unnecessary to consider the actual circumstances that had prompted the enactment of the Montana Corrupt Practices Act.

I did not mean to imply in my discussion of that case that electoral integrity was a matter of fact *rather than of law,* but rather that the law of electoral integrity cannot be applied without awareness of the material facts. One cannot interpret and apply relevant intersubjective understandings without knowledge of the material factual context. I am grateful to Michelman for the opportunity to clarify this issue.

In her knowing and careful comment, Pam Karlan makes three points. First, she observes that electoral integrity may be seriously endangered by structural features of our electoral system that do not involve issues of campaign finance reform. Second, she notes that the principle of electoral integrity "may ultimately collapse back into the existing, and largely unsuccessful, rationales" for campaign finance reform. Third, she fears that the subjective nature of electoral integrity may "in the hands of the current Supreme Court" be used to undermine democratic participation.

I have no quarrel with Karlan's first point. Other features of our electoral system may indeed be as destructive of electoral integrity as our system of campaign finance. I am not prepared to argue the question, one way or the other. It is enough for the purpose of the Tanner Lectures to affirm that aspects of our system of campaign finance are surely inimical to electoral integrity.[22] The lectures are an effort to uncover the forms of constitutional reasoning that ought to be applied to legislative attempts to protect electoral integrity; they do not attempt to recommend one policy option or another. My focus on *Citizens United* is in this regard exemplary, not exhaustive.

My hope is that if we can rightly understand the constitutional principles that should apply in a case like *Citizens United*, we can also apply these same principles in the many other contexts where electoral integrity may be threatened, including, most especially, in the context of partisan gerrymandering, which has received singularly obtuse constitutional treatment from the Court.[23] It is staggering to me that in the last general election only 47 percent of American voters cast their ballots for Republican representation in the House of Representatives, yet due in part to partisan gerrymandering the House ended up with a membership that was 54 percent Republican.[24] Given the polarization that has gripped Congress, this stunning disparity in the House portends serious repercussions for electoral integrity.

Karlan's second and third points seem to me in tension with each other. If electoral integrity is simply another name for what everyone already thinks, it cannot have the new and noxious effects she fears. But Karlan's second point is not quite right. Karlan observes: "If we ask *why* the public thinks a particular form of political money undermines electoral integrity, we are exceptionally likely to get an answer that sounds almost entirely in one of the three existing justifications for regulating political money—namely, that regulation vindicates principles of political equality, prevents existing inequalities in wealth from distorting the political process, or guards against corruption and the appearance of corruption."

I agree with Karlan that if we ask members of the public *why* they believe that their representative government is failing, they will give reasons that sound in the logic of representation. Equality, antidistortion, and anticorruption are all values that pertain to a well-functioning system of representation. It is because those advocating for campaign finance reform have adopted these values, and because the Court has in turn adopted them as the primary constitutional justifications for campaign finance reform, that the case for campaign finance reform has been set at such odds with First Amendment jurisprudence.

The Tanner Lectures seek to bypass this unproductive standoff by conceptualizing electoral integrity as a distinctly First Amendment value.

The constitutional argument for electoral integrity derives from the specific requirements of the First Amendment, not from those of representative integrity. This is because electoral integrity is a concept designed to evaluate First Amendment restrictions that judges have imposed on campaign finance legislation. Whether the public would identify electoral integrity as necessary for confidence in representative government is irrelevant to the question of whether judges should regard electoral integrity as necessary for the exercise of First Amendment rights. Judges have so far failed to appreciate the relevance of electoral integrity because they have instead focused on values associated with representative government, like equality, antidistortion, or anticorruption.

Karlan's third point is well taken. I agree with her hostility to *Purcell v. Gonzalez*[25] and *Crawford v. Marion Cnty. Election Bd.*[26] In both these decisions the Court applied the principle that "confidence in the integrity of our electoral processes is essential to the functioning of our participatory democracy"[27] in ways that were very disturbing. Both decisions have roots in Justice Souter's 2000 opinion in *Nixon v. Shrink Missouri Government PAC,*[28] which upheld state campaign contribution limitations, in part on the ground that "democracy works 'only if the people have faith in those who govern. . . .' "[29]

I should note at the outset that none of these cases precisely uses the term electoral integrity in the way I have sought to define it. All three of these cases refer to a general principle of trust in elections, rather than to the more specific issue of whether elected officials are responsive to public opinion. But of course these questions of confidence are interconnected, and I agree with Karlan that *Purcell* and *Crawford* illustrate how a perfectly sound principle of constitutional law can at times be abused.

It is significant that although Justice Souter dissented in *Crawford,* he did not repudiate the idea that confidence in the integrity of our electoral processes is a compelling government interest.[30] Instead he wrote:

> It should go without saying that none of this is to deny States' legitimate interest in safeguarding public confidence. The Court has, for example, recognized that fighting perceptions of political corruption stemming from large political contributions is a legitimate and substantial state interest, underlying not only campaign finance laws, but bribery and antigratuity statutes as well. See *Nixon v. Shrink Missouri Government PAC,* 528 U.S. 377, 390 (2000). But the force of the interest depends on the facts (or plausibility of the assumptions) said to justify invoking it. . . . While we found

in *Nixon* that "there is little reason to doubt that sometimes large contributions will work actual corruption of our political system, and no reason to question the existence of a corresponding suspicion among voters," there is plenty of reason to be doubtful here, both about the reality and the perception. It is simply not plausible to assume here, with no evidence of in-person voter impersonation fraud in a State, and very little of it nationwide, that a public perception of such fraud is nevertheless "inherent" in an election system providing severe criminal penalties for fraud and mandating signature checks at the polls. Cf. *id.*, at 390 ("[T]he perception of corruption [is] 'inherent in a regime of large individual financial contributions' to candidates for public office" (quoting *Buckley v. Valeo*, 424 U.S. 1, 27 (1976) *(per curiam)*).[31]

Souter seems to me exactly right. The problem with *Crawford* is not the validity of a government interest in confidence, but rather the absence of any factual demonstration that confidence was actually at risk despite severe and demonstrable curtailments of the right to vote.

To get a sense of how odd *Crawford* is, imagine that the Court were to acknowledge electoral integrity as a constitutionally compelling interest in the context of campaign finance reform. Imagine that in reliance on this interest a state were to enact strict limits on independent campaign expenditures. It is simply not conceivable that the Court would evaluate the constitutionality of these restrictions without somehow balancing the strength of the state's interest in maintaining electoral integrity against the impairment of First Amendment rights entailed by the restrictions. The Court would conduct this evaluation using whatever constitutional doctrine best suited its purpose—whether strong-form strict scrutiny, or weak-form strict scrutiny, or balancing,[32] or proportionality.[33]

The right criticism of *Crawford*, as Souter contends, is that the Court failed to perform any such balancing at all, in any form. The lesson to be learned from *Crawford* is that facile invocations of public confidence, unsupported by any record, and unqualified by any consideration of competing constitutional values, can be very dangerous indeed. *Crawford* utterly failed to balance the maintenance of confidence against the impairment of the right to exercise "equal influence" in an election.[34] This mistake has nothing to do with the "subjective" nature of the need for public confidence.[35]

At the conclusion of her commentary, Karlan invokes Lincoln's beautiful First Inaugural Address to gloss the "Constitution's ambition." Constitutional law, she writes, should reflect "the better angels of our nature." I could not agree more. Our constitutional ideals distill the hard-earned meanings of our national experience. Self-government is indisputably one such ideal. It is an ideal that can be realized only by those who believe themselves to be self-governing. It has been so since the days of the Revolution.

Surely, then, the ideal of self-government should count as one of the better angels of our nature. It deserves secure recognition in our constitutional doctrine.[36]

NOTES

1. First Lecture: A Short History of Representation and Discursive Democracy

1. 424 U.S. 1 (1976).

2. By 1994 *Buckley* could plausibly be characterized "as one of the most vilified Supreme Court decisions of the post–World War II era," a decision that in its structure and consequences is "the modern-day analogue of the infamous and discredited case of *Lochner v. New York.*" Cass R. Sunstein, *Political Equality and Unintended Consequences,* 94 COLUM. L. REV. 1390, 1394, 1397 (1994).

3. 558 U.S. 310 (2010). For a description of the circumstances of the opinion, see Jeffrey Toobin, *Annals of the Law: Money Unlimited: The Chief Justice and* Citizens United, NEW YORKER, May 21, 2012, at 36.

4. The Court did go out of its way to affirm the constitutionality of campaign finance disclosure requirements. 558 U.S. at 366–371.

5. *See* Dan Eggen, *Poll: Large Majority Opposes Supreme Court's Decision on Campaign Financing,* WASH. POST, Feb. 17, 2010, http://articles.washington post.com/2010-02-16/politics/36773318_1_corporations-unions-new-limits ("Americans of both parties overwhelmingly oppose a Supreme Court ruling that allows corporations and unions to spend as much as they want on political campaigns, and favor new limits on such spending, according to a new Washington Post–ABC News poll. Eight in 10 poll respondents say they oppose the high court's Jan. 21 decision to allow unfettered corporate political spending, with 65 percent 'strongly' opposed. . . . The polls reveal relatively little difference of opinion on the issue among Democrats (85 percent opposed to the ruling), Republicans (76 percent) and independents (81 percent)."). Public opinion polling ten months after the decision reflected continued hostility. According to a Constitutional Attitudes Survey conducted by Harvard and Columbia professors in October 2010, 58 percent of survey respondents disagreed that "Corporations ought to be able to spend their profits on TV advertisements urging

voters to vote for or against candidates," and 85 percent indicated that corporations should be required to get approval from shareholders for campaign-related expenditures. The results led one pollster to note that *Citizens United* is "very out of step with public opinion." Jon Hood, *Poll Finds Most Recent Supreme Court Decisions Popular: Corporate-Friendly* Citizens United *Ruling Highly Unpopular,* CONSUMER AFFAIRS (Oct. 18, 2010), http://www.consumeraffairs.com/news04/2010/10/poll-respondents-mostly-approve-of-recent-supreme-court-decisions.html. Reviewing the decision in the *New York Review of Books,* Ronald Dworkin observed that "No Supreme Court decision in decades has generated such open hostilities among the three branches of our government as has the Court's five-to-four decision in *Citizens United v. FEC* in January 2010." Ronald Dworkin, *The Decision That Threatens Democracy,* N.Y. REV. BOOKS, May 13, 2010); *see also* Richard H. Pildes, *Is the Supreme Court a "Majoritarian" Institution?,* 2010 SUP. CT. REV. 103, 126 ("[p]ublic support for campaign finance reform (other than public financing) has been extremely high for many years"); ibid., 157 ("*Citizens United* is the most countermajoritarian decision invalidating national legislation on an issue of high public salience in the last quarter century.").

6. 558 U.S. at 372.

7. Ibid., 382 (Stevens, J., dissenting).

8. *See* Lillian R. BeVier, *Full of Surprises—and More to Come:* Randall v. Sorrell, *The First Amendment, and Campaign Finance Regulation,* 2006 SUP. CT. REV. 173, 195 ("Debate on these issues has reached an impasse. . . . The chasm that separates the Justices from one another appears unbridgeable.").

9. I would exempt from this point some excellent scholarship that, in my view, points the way toward a constructive account of how campaign finance regulation may be reconciled with the First Amendment. This account, which I shall explore in these lectures, conceives elections as distinct managerial domains. To my knowledge, this account first appeared in C. Edwin Baker, *Campaign Expenditures and Free Speech,* 33 HARV. C.R.-C.L. REV. 1 (1998), and Burt Neuborne, *The Supreme Court and Free Speech: Love and a Question,* 42 ST. LOUIS U. L.J. 789 (1998). Their work was quickly followed by Richard Briffault, *Issue Advocacy: Redrawing the Elections/Politics Line,* 77 TEX. L. REV. 1751 (1999); and Frederick Schauer & Richard H. Pildes, *Electoral Exceptionalism and the First Amendment,* 77 TEX. L. REV. 1803 (1999). Recent excellent examples of this genre include Samuel Issacharoff, *The Constitutional Logic of Campaign Finance Regulation,* 36 PEPP. L. REV. 373 (2009); Dennis F. Thompson, *Election Time: Normative Implications of Temporal Properties of the Electoral Process in the United States,* 98 AM. POL. SCI. REV. 51 (2004); and Saul Zipkin, *The Election Period and Regulation of the Democratic Process,* 18 WM. & MARY. BILL OF RTS. J. 533 (2010). I myself was an early and tentative contributor to this line of thought. *See* Robert Post, *Regulating Election Speech Under the First Amendment,* 77 TEX. L. REV. 1837 (1999).

10. Austin v. Mich. Chamber of Commerce, 494 U.S. 652, 660–661 (1990), *overruled by Citizens United,* 558 U.S. 310.

11. *Buckley,* 424 U.S. at 48–49.

12. *See* Samuel Issacharoff & Pamela S. Karlan, *The Hydraulics of Campaign Finance Reform,* 77 Tex. L. Rev. 1705 (1999).

13. *See* Lawrence Lessig, Republic, Lost: How Money Corrupts Congress—and a Plan to Stop It (2011).

14. 558 U.S. at 339 (citation omitted).

15. Ibid., 340.

16. Ibid., 435 n.60 (Stevens, J., dissenting) (quoting Pipefitters v. United States, 407 U.S. 385, 450 (1972) (Powell, J., dissenting)).

17. Ibid., 446.

18. Ibid., 440 (some internal quotation marks omitted) (quoting McConnell v. FEC, 540 U.S. 93, 206–207 n.88 (2003)).

19. Daniel R. Ortiz, *The Engaged and the Inert: Theorizing Political Personality Under the First Amendment,* 81 Va. L. Rev. 1, 7–10 (1995).

20. Bruce Ackerman & James S. Fishkin, Deliberation Day 159–163 (2004).

21. Letter from Thomas Jefferson to Roger Weightman (June 24, 1826), *reprinted in* Thomas Jefferson: Writings 1517 (Merrill D. Peterson ed., 1984).

22. The Declaration of Independence, para. 2.

23. James Wilson, Considerations on the Nature and the Extent of the Legislative Authority of the British Parliament 3 (1774).

24. James Wilson, Commentaries on the Constitution of the United States of America 40 (1792).

25. 2 The Records of the Federal Convention of 1787, at 476 (Max Farrand ed., 1966) (quoting James Madison).

26. The Federalist No. 39, at 181–182 (James Madison) (Terence Ball ed., 2003).

27. The Federalist No. 10, note 26 above, at 43 (James Madison).

28. Thomas Paine, The Rights of Man 28 (1797).

29. John Adams, 3 Defence of the Constitutions of the Government of the United States 214 (1794).

30. The Federalist No. 63, note 26 above, at 308, 309 (James Madison). For a discussion of the shift from direct face-to-face democracy to representation, see James S. Fishkin, The Voice of the People: Public Opinion and Democracy 26–29 (1997). On the history of the idea of representation, see Edmund S. Morgan, Inventing the People: The Rise of Popular Sovereignty in England and America (1989); and J.R. Pole, Political Representation in England and the Origins of the American Republic (1966).

31. 2 The Records of the Federal Convention of 1787, note 25 above, at 9 (quoting James Madison).

32. 1 The Records of the Federal Convention of 1787, note 25 above, at 561 (quoting William Patterson).

33. Wilson, note 24 above, at 87–88.

34. Jean-Jacques Rousseau, An Inquiry into the Nature of the Social Contract; or Principles of Political Right 265–266 (London, G.G.J. & J. Robinson, 1791) (1762).

35. Ibid., 266.

36. Wilson, note 24 above, at 30–31.

37. Wilson, note 23 above, at 21; *see also* ibid. ("If a person is bound, only because he is represented, it must certainly follow that whenever he is *not* represented he is *not bound*.")

38. 1 The Writings of John Dickinson: Political Writings 1764–1774, at 357 (Paul Leicester Ford ed., 1895).

39. The Controversy Between Great Britain and Her Colonies Reviewed 67 (1769).

40. Thomas Whately, The Regulations Lately Made Concerning the Colonies and the Taxes Imposed upon Them Considered 108 (3d ed. 1775) (1765); *see* Ian R. Christie, *A Vision of Empire: Thomas Whately and the Regulations Lately Made Concerning the Colonies,* 113 Eng. Hist. Rev. 300 (1998).

41. Whately, note 40 above, at 109.

42. Ibid. Whately believed that the rights and interests of British commons ought to be the sole consideration of each member of Parliament:

> [H]owever his own Borough may be affected by general Dispositions, . . . to sacrifice these to a partial Advantage in favour of the Place where he was chosen, would be a Departure from his Duty; if it were otherwise, *Old Sarum* would enjoy Privileges essential to Liberty, which are denied to *Birmingham* and to *Manchester;* but as it is, they and the Colonies, and all *British* Subjects whatever, have an equal Share in the general Representation of the Commons of *Great Britain,* and are bound by the Consent of the Majority of that House, whether their own particular Representatives consented to or opposed the Measures there taken, or whether they had, or had not particular Representatives there.

Ibid. Writing on the subject of Irish Catholics in 1792, Edmund Burke would later develop a theoretical framework for the concept of "virtual" representation invoked by Whately:

> Virtual representation is that in which there is a communion of interests and a sympathy in feelings and desires between those who act in the name of any description of people and the people in whose name they act, though the trustees are not actually chosen by them. This is virtual representation. Such a representation I think to be in many cases even better than the actual. It possesses most of its advantages, and is free from many of its inconveniences; it corrects the irregularities in the literal

representation, when the shifting current of human affairs or the acting of public interests in different ways carry it obliquely from its first line of direction. . . . But this sort of virtual representation cannot have a long or sure existence, if it has not a substratum in the actual.

Edmund Burke, *Letter to Sir Hercules Langrishe, in* 4 THE WRITINGS AND SPEECHES OF THE RIGHT HONOURABLE EDMUND BURKE 293 (Beaconsfield ed., 1901).

43. Because the colonists had no intention of themselves establishing universal manhood suffrage, much less of allowing women to vote, they could not completely reject the concept of virtual representation, which they cashed out much in the manner of Burke (as discussed in note 42 above):

> The Security of the Non-Electors against Oppression, is, that their Oppression will fall also upon the Electors and the Representatives. The one can't be injured, and the other indemnified. . . .
>
> The Electors, who are inseparably connected in their Interests with the Non-Electors, may be justly deemed to be the representatives of the Non-Electors, at the same Time they exercise their personal Privilege in their Right of Election, and the Members chosen, therefore, the Representatives of both. This is the only rational Explanation of the Expression, *virtual Representation.*

DANIEL DULANY, CONSIDERATIONS ON THE PROPRIETY OF IMPOSING TAXES IN THE BRITISH COLONIES FOR THE PURPOSE OF RAISING A REVENUE BY ACT OF PARLIAMENT (1765), *reprinted in* PROLOGUE TO REVOLUTION: SOURCES AND DOCUMENTS ON THE STAMP ACT CRISIS, 1764–1766, at 8 (Edmund S. Morgan ed., 1973).

44. THE DECLARATIONS OF THE STAMP ACT CONGRESS (1765), *reprinted in* PROLOGUE TO REVOLUTION, note 43 above, at 63.

45. Hence the subsequent rejection of the concept of representation by lot, which might be thought the most accurate form of selection if, as the colonists sometimes said, "the representative assembly should be an exact portrait, in miniature, of the people at large." 6 THE WORKS OF JOHN ADAMS 205 (1851) (1776). Representation by lot continues in institutions like juries, but for two centuries it has had no place in the selection of governmental representatives. The story of how the principle of consent altered the nature of representation is told in BERNARD MANIN, THE PRINCIPLES OF REPRESENTATIVE GOVERNMENT (1997).

46. THE DECLARATIONS OF THE STAMP ACT CONGRESS (1765), *reprinted in* PROLOGUE TO REVOLUTION, note 43 above, at 63.

47. A LETTER FROM A PLAIN YEOMAN (1765), *reprinted in* PROLOGUE TO REVOLUTION, note 43 above, at 75–76.

48. 1 JOURNALS OF THE CONTINENTAL CONGRESS 1774–1789 at 68 (Oct. 14, 1774) (1904).

49. 2 THE RECORDS OF THE FEDERAL CONVENTION OF 1787, note 25 above, at 135 (quoting James Madison).

50. DULANY, note 43 above, at 82. The principle of commonality of interests underlay the colonists' own invocation of virtual representation in the context of women and disenfranchised white males. *See* ibid. There are obvious tensions between the principle of consent and the principle of commonality of interests, tensions that over the past centuries have been resolved by a secular trend toward universal suffrage. For a discussion of these two principles in the intellectual universe of the founding generation, see Richard Buel, Jr., *Democracy and the American Revolution: A Frame of Reference,* in THE REINTERPRETATION OF THE AMERICAN REVOLUTION 1763–1789 (Jack P. Greene ed., 1968).

51. 2 THE RECORDS OF THE FEDERAL CONVENTION OF 1787, note 25 above, at 321 (quoting James Madison).

52. 2 ibid., 50 (quoting James Madison).

53. *See, e.g.,* AKHIL REED AMAR, AMERICA'S CONSTITUTION: A BIOGRAPHY 64–84 (2005); JACK N. RAKOVE, ORIGINAL MEANINGS: POLITICS AND IDEAS IN THE MAKING OF THE CONSTITUTION 203–243 (1996).

54. 4 THE DEBATES IN THE SEVERAL STATE CONVENTIONS ON THE ADOPTION OF THE FEDERAL CONSTITUTION 288 (Jonathan Elliot ed., 1836) (quoting Rawlins Lowndes of South Carolina). In Virginia, Patrick Henry thundered:

> The honorable gentleman was pleased to say that the representation of the people was the vital principle of this government. I will readily agree that it ought to be so. But I contend that this principle is only nominally, and not substantially, to be found there. We contended with the British about representation. They offered us such representation as Congress now does. They called it a virtual representation. . . . Is there but a virtual representation in the upper house? The states are represented, *as states,* by two senators each. This is virtual, not actual. They encounter you with Rhode Island and Delaware. This is not an actual representation. What does the term *representation* signify? It means that a certain district—a certain association of men—should be represented in the government, for certain ends. . . . Here, sir, this populous state has not an adequate share of legislative influence. The two petty states of Rhode Island and Delaware, which, together, are infinitely inferior to this state in extent and population, have double her weight, and can counteract her interest. I say that the representation in the Senate, as applicable to states, is not actual. Representation is not, therefore, the vital principle of this government.

3 THE DEBATES IN THE SEVERAL STATE CONVENTIONS ON THE ADOPTION OF THE FEDERAL CONSTITUTION, above, at 324.

55. 2 THE RECORDS OF THE FEDERAL CONVENTION OF 1787, note 25 above, at 48 (quoting George Mason).

56. 2 ibid., 49–50 (quoting James Madison).

57. 2 ibid., 58 (quoting Edmund Randolph); *see* ibid., 517 (quoting Gouverneur Morris) (discussing "the turbulency of democracy").

58. 2 ibid., 289 (quoting Alexander Hamilton).

59. 2 ibid., 430 (quoting James Madison).

60. 2 ibid., 432 (quoting Alexander Hamilton); *see also* Lycurgus, *Observations on the Present Situation and the Future Prospects of This and the United States*, NEW HAVEN GAZETTE & CONN. MAG., Mar. 23, 1786, at 1 ("In a democracy the power remains in the people, and every subject enjoys his full share of liberty and legislation. But there is a great difference between an absolute democracy and a form of government either wholly or partly democratical; for an absolute democracy, in which all power should remain in the hands of the people, undelegated to any magistrate or representative, is a perfect anarchy, and deserves not the name of a government: but in a democratical government, all power is entrusted in the hands of the magistrates, judges, representatives, and other officers, eligible only by the people, chosen for stated periods, and accountable for their conduct in office to proper judicatures. Between an absolute democracy and a democratical government, there is a certain mode of political existence, in which all forms of government are preserved, magistrates, judges and other officers duly elected, nominal authority amply bestowed, but no real power given out of the hands of the people. This mode is the most favourable to the liberties of the subject, and I congratulate my country that it is completely adopted in the general constitution of our empire. . . .").

61. JOHN MARSHALL, THE LIFE OF GEORGE WASHINGTON 467 (2000).

62. THE FEDERALIST NO. 63, note 26 above, at 309 (James Madison); *see also* 1 ZEPHANIAH SWIFT, A SYSTEM OF THE LAWS OF THE STATE OF CONNECTICUT 21 (1795) ("Nothing can be more erroneous than the opinion that the government of the United States is a democracy. It has not a single feature of that form of government. The people have no power but that of electing the representatives, which they have not in a democracy; they can not do a single act in framing the laws or administering the government, any more than they can in the most despotic government on the globe. Some have called it a representative democracy; but this is a contradiction in terms.")

63. THE FEDERALIST NO. 10, note 26 above, at 43–44 (James Madison).

64. Ibid., 44.

65. Ibid.

66. Ibid., 45.

67. Ibid. An extended sphere of governance also meant that the state could encompass a "greater variety of parties and interests," so that it would be "less probable that a majority of the whole will have a common motive to invade the rights of other citizens; or if such a common motive exists, it will be more difficult for all who feel it to discover their own strength, and to act in unison with each other." Ibid.

68. ROBERT H. WIEBE, SELF-RULE: A CULTURAL HISTORY OF AMERICAN DEMOCRACY 18 (1995); *see also* ibid., 17 ("[H]ierarchies . . . had organized

18th century life everywhere in the Western world, including America. In economic opportunities and political prerogatives, in dress and language, in the control of information and the right to speak, in all aspects of public life, obvious and subtle, hierarchy's privileges came graded along a social scale, and society's function depended upon a general acceptance of those differences.").

69. *See* THOMAS BENTON, 1 ABRIDGEMENT OF THE DEBATES OF CONGRESS 1789–96, at 138 (1857) (Aug. 15, 1789).

70. *See* MASS. CONST. art. XIX (1780); N.C. CONST., Declaration of Rights XVIII (1776); N.H. CONST., Bill of Rights XXXII (1784); PA. CONST., Declaration of Rights XVII (1776); VT. CONST. ch. 1, XXII (1786).

71. BENTON, note 69 above, at 143 (remarks of Rep. John Page of Virginia).

72. Ibid., 139 (remarks of Rep. John Page of Virginia). Page continued: "Under a democracy, whose great end is to form a code of laws congenial with the public sentiment, the popular opinion ought to be collected and attended to." Elberidge Gerry of Massachusetts hammered home this point:

> The friends and patrons of this constitution have always declared that the sovereignty resides in the people, and that they do not part with it on any occasion; to say the sovereignty vests in the people, and that they have not a right to instruct and control their representatives, is absurd to the last degree.

Ibid., 140.

73. Ibid., 138 (remarks of Rep. Thomas Hartley of Pennsylvania). Hartley continued:

> It appears to my mind, that the principle of representation is distinct from an agency, which may require written instructions. The great end of meeting is to consult for the common good; but can the common good be discerned without the object is reflected and shown in every light. A local or partial view does not necessarily enable any man to comprehend it clearly; this can only result from an inspection into the aggregate. Instructions viewed in this light will be found to embarrass the best and wisest men.

Ibid., 138–139.

74. Ibid., 139 (remarks of Rep. George Clymer of Pennsylvania).

75. Ibid., 139; *see also* SWIFT, note 62 above, at 35 ("A government by representation, implies the idea that the representatives stand in the place of the people, and are vested with all their power, within the constitution. In the legislature, therefore, consisting of the representatives, is concentered the majesty of the people, and the supremacy of the government. They are neither bound to obey the instruction, nor to consult the will of the people—but being in their place, and vested with all their power, they have a right to adopt and pursue such measures as in their judgment, are best calculated to promote the happiness and welfare of the community, in the same manner as the people them-

selves would act, if it were possible for them to assemble and deliberate on their common concerns. The reason why the instructions of the people are not to be regarded is, because it is impossible that the general sense should be collected: and even if that could be done, they have not those means of information which are necessary to qualify them to deliberate and decide. As to the instructions from any particular district, to the representative by them elected, they ought to have no influence, because when elected, a person becomes the representative of the community at large; he cannot therefore regard the instructions of his immediate constituents, but must consult the general good of the community and not the particular advantage of a district.").

76. The right of instruction was nevertheless frequently claimed in later years on behalf of state legislatures seeking to control their senators. *See* Clement Eaton, *Southern Senators and the Right of Instruction, 1789–1860,* 18 J.S. HIST. 303 (1952); William S. Hoffmann, *Willie P. Mangum and the Whig Revival of the Doctrine of Instructions,* 22 J.S. HIST. 338 (1956).

77. *See, e.g.,* David Rabban, *The Ahistorical Historian: Leonard Levy on Freedom of Expression in Early American History,* 37 STAN. L. REV. 795 (1985).

78. BENTON, note 69 above, at 141. For a discussion, see MANIN, note 45 above, at 170–173. To Madison's list should be added the revolutionary implications of requiring Congress to keep a public journal. U.S. CONST. art. I, § 5. On the implications of opening up legislative debates, see J.R. POLE, THE GIFT OF GOVERNMENT 117–140 (2008). Pole observes:

> Neither political representation nor popular government was a new idea at the time of the American Revolution. What was new in the politics of the time was the use of representation as a clearly defined institutional bridge between people and government. The two-way traffic over this bridge was a traffic in knowledge.

Ibid., 140.

79. 2 THE RECORDS OF THE FEDERAL CONVENTION OF 1787, note 25 above, at 50 (quoting James Madison).

80. JAMES MADISON, THE REPORT OF 1800 (1800), *reprinted in* 17 THE PAPERS OF JAMES MADISON 344 (David B. Matern et al. eds., 1991).

81. 2 THE RECORDS OF THE FEDERAL CONVENTION OF 1787, note 25 above, at 381 (quoting Nathaniel Gorham).

82. 2 ibid., 423 (quoting Roger Sherman).

83. THE FEDERALIST NO. 57, note 26 above, at 277 (James Madison).

84. THE FEDERALIST NO. 52, note 26 above, at 256–257 (James Madison).

85. Ibid., 258.

86. THE FEDERALIST NO. 57, note 26 above, at 277 (James Madison).

87. THE FEDERALIST NO. 53, note 26 above, at 264 (James Madison) (concluding that "biennial elections will be as useful to the affairs of the public, as we have seen that they will be safe to the liberty of the people").

88. The Federalist No. 52, note 26 above, at 255 (James Madison) ("The definition of the right of suffrage is very justly regarded as a fundamental article of republican government.").

89. The Federalist No. 56, note 26 above, at 274 (James Madison) (stating that the representative assembly should be large enough to fulfill the "sound and important principle that the representative ought to be acquainted with the interests and circumstances of his constituents").

90. *Essays of Brutus*, N.Y. J., Oct. 18, 1787, *in* The Anti-Federalist: Writings by the Opponents of the Constitution 114 (Herbert J. Storing & Murray Dry eds., 1985); *see also* ibid. ("In a free republic, although all laws are derived from the consent of the people, yet the people do not declare their consent by themselves in person, but by representatives, chosen by them, who are supposed to know the minds of their constituents, and to be possessed of integrity to declare this mind.")

91. Ibid., 125.

92. Ibid., 129.

93. Ibid., 129–130.

94. Ibid., 130–131.

95. The Federalist No. 57, note 26 above, at 277 (James Madison).

96. Ibid., 279.

97. Ibid.

98. The Federalist No. 57, note 26 above, at 279 (James Madison) ("Such will be the relations between the House of Representatives and their constituents. Duty, gratitude, interest, ambition itself, are the chords by which they will be bound to fidelity and sympathy with the great mass of the people.").

99. *Essays of Brutus,* note 90 above, at 124–125. The legislative body "ought to be so constituted, that a person, who is a stranger to the country, might be able to form a just idea of their character, by knowing that of their representatives. They are the sign—the people are the things signified." Ibid., 124.

100. Ibid., 129. Brutus articulated what scholars would now call a theory of "descriptive representation." *See* Hanna Fenichel Pitkin, The Concept of Representation 60–91 (1967); Jane Mansbridge, *Should Blacks Represent Blacks and Women Represent Women? A Contingent "Yes,"* 61 J. Pol. 628 (1999).

101. The point was not controversial in the founding period. *See, e.g.,* 1 The Records of the Federal Convention of 1787, note 25 above, at 49 (quoting James Wilson) ("No government could long subsist without the confidence of the people. In a republican Government this confidence was peculiarly essential."); 2 The Records of the Federal Convention of 1787, note 25 above, at 451 (quoting George Mason) ("If Govt is to be lasting, it must be founded in the confidence & affections of the people, and must be so constructed as to obtain these.").

102. The story is well told in WIEBE, note 68 above. *See generally* SEAN WI-
LENTZ, THE RISE OF AMERICAN DEMOCRACY: JEFFERSON TO LINCOLN (2005).

103. WIEBE, note 68 above, at 38–39.

104. James Madison, *Public Opinion,* NAT'L GAZETTE, Dec. 19, 1791, *reprinted in* 14 THE PAPERS OF JAMES MADISON, note 80 above, at 170. A month
later Madison repeated the thought: "All power has been traced up to opinion.
The stability of all governments and security of all rights may be traced to the
same source. The most arbitrary government is controlled where the public
opinion is fixed. . . . How devoutly is it to be wished, then, that the public opinion of the United States should be enlightened, that it should attach itself to
their governments as delineated in the *great charters,* derived . . . from the legitimate authority of the people." *Charters,* NAT'L GAZETTE, Jan. 18, 1792, *reprinted
in* 14 THE PAPERS OF JAMES MADISON, note 80 above, at 468. Madison's conception of public opinion seems to be deeply indebted to David Hume: "As FORCE is
always on the side of the governed, the governors have nothing to support them
but opinion. It is, therefore, on opinion only that government is founded; and
this maxim extends to the most despotic and most military governments, as well
as to the most free and most popular." DAVID HUME, OF THE FIRST PRINCIPLES
OF GOVERNMENT (1777), *in* 1 ESSAYS: MORAL, POLITICAL AND LITERARY 110
(T.H. Green & T.H. Grose eds., 1889).

105. *Public Opinion,* note 104 above. With startling profundity, and antici-
pating the insights a generation later of Tocqueville, Madison went on to
observe:

> The larger a country, the less easy for its real opinion to be ascertained, and the
> less difficult to be counterfeited; when ascertained or presumed, the more respectable
> it is in the eyes of individuals. This is favorable to the authority of government. For
> the same reason, the more extensive a country, the more insignificant is each indi-
> vidual in his own eyes. This may be unfavorable to liberty.
>
> Whatever facilitates a general intercourse of sentiments, as good roads, domestic
> commerce, a free press, and particularly a circulation of newspapers through the
> entire body of the people, and representatives going from and returning among every
> part of them, is equivalent to a contraction of territorial limits, and is favorable to
> liberty, where these may be too extensive.

106. JAMES MADISON, NOTES FOR THE *NATIONAL GAZETTE* ESSAYS (circa
1791–1793), *reprinted in* 4 THE PAPERS OF JAMES MADISON, note 80 above, at
168.

107. COLLEEN A. SHEEHAN, JAMES MADISON AND THE SPIRIT OF REPUBLI-
CAN SELF-GOVERNMENT 105 (2009).

108. William Leggett, *Direct Taxation,* EVENING POST, Apr. 22, 1834, *reprinted in* 1 A COLLECTION OF THE POLITICAL WRITINGS OF WILLIAM LEGGETT
262 (Theodore Sedgwick, Jr., ed., 1840).

109. Ibid.

110. 1 Alexis De Tocqueville, Democracy in America 33 (Henry Reeve trans., D. Appleton & Co. 1899).

111. *See* Alexander Keyssar, The Right to Vote: The Contested History of Democracy in the United States (2000).

112. 1 De Tocqueville, note 110 above, at 210–211; *see* John Stuart Mill, Considerations on Representative Government 160 (1875) ("It is an admitted fact that in the American democracy . . . the highly-cultivated members of the community, except such of them as are willing to sacrifice their own opinions and modes of judgment, and become the servile mouthpieces of their inferiors in knowledge, do not even offer themselves for Congress or the State Legislatures, so certain is it that they would have no chance of being returned.").

113. 1 De Tocqueville, note 110 above, at 272.

114. 1 ibid., 175.

115. George Bancroft, Oration Delivered on the Fourth of July 1826 at Northampton, Mass. 20 (1826).

116. 2 De Tocqueville, note 110 above, at 493.

117. *The Democratic Principle—The Importance of Its Assertion, and Application to Our Political System and Literature,* 1 U.S. Mag. & Democratic Rev. 1, 4–5 (1837).

118. 2 Reg. Deb. 1729–1730 (March 22, 1826) (statement of Rep. Thomas R. Mitchell).

119. Benjamin Franklin Butler, Representative Democracy in the United States: An Address Delivered Before the Senate of Union College 20 (C. Van Benthuysen ed., 1841).

120. James Madison, *Government of the United States,* Nat'l Gazette (Feb. 4, 1792).

121. President Andrew Jackson, State of the Union Address (Dec. 8, 1829), *reprinted in* Cong. Globe, 21st Cong., 1st Sess. 3, 7 (1829).

122. Woodrow Wilson, Division and Reunion 1829–1898, at 12 (1895). Compare Bancroft in 1826: "With the people the power resides, both theoretically and practically. The government is a democracy, a determined, uncompromising democracy; administered immediately by the people, or by the people's responsible agents." Bancroft, note 115 above, at 19.

123. George Bancroft, *Eulogy on the Life and Character of General Jackson* (June 27, 1845), *in* Life and Public Services of Gen. Andrew Jackson, Seventh President of the United States, Including the Most Important of His State Papers 209 (John S. Jenkins ed., 1852).

124. *The Democratic Principle,* note 117 above, at 3.

125. The depth of this transformation is difficult to appreciate. As late as 1821 Alexander Hill Everett could write that "where the representative principle is introduced, the form in which the elections are made is altogether indifferent. The result will be the same, whether they are made by a small or a large

proportion of the citizens, by the rich or the poor, on the same or on various principles, at one degree, at two, or at three. The same individuals will in fact be designated by all these different methods. The number of persons to whom the confidence of the public attaches itself is not very great: and every form of election that can be indicated is only another mode of proclaiming them." Alexander Hill Everett, *Dialogue on the Principles of Representative Government, Between the President de Montesquieu and Dr. Franklin,* 12 N. AM. REV. 346, 360 (Apr. 1821). On the complexities of the transition from a deference society, see Ronald P. Formisano, *Deferential-Participant Politics: The Early Republic's Political Culture, 1789–1840,* 68 AM. POL. SCI. REV. 473 (1974).

126. In 1828, Andrew Jackson had campaigned as "the People's Candidate" and the "Farmer of Tennessee." PAUL F. BOLLER JR., PRESIDENTIAL CAMPAIGNS: FROM GEORGE WASHINGTON TO GEORGE W. BUSH 44 (2004). By the 1840 campaign, Whig candidate William Henry Harrison had raised the stakes by proclaiming his affinity for the "hard cider," "log cabins," and "homely fare" of the common man. Whigs cast incumbent Martin Van Buren as an out-of-touch elitist, sipping from "a china cup" and eating with "a golden spoon." CHARLES OGLE, SPEECH OF MR. OGLE, OF PENNSYLVANIA, ON THE REGAL SPLENDOR OF THE PRESIDENT'S PALACE: DELIVERED IN THE HOUSE OF REPRESENTATIVES, APRIL 14, 1840 (1840); A. B. NORTON, THE GREAT REVOLUTION OF 1840: REMINISCENCES OF THE LOG CABIN AND HARD CIDER CAMPAIGN (1888); Wilcomb E. Washburn, *The Great Autumnal Madness: Political Symbolism in Mid-Nineteenth-Century America,* 49 Q. J. OF SPEECH 417, 419 (1963); Robert G. Gunderson, *Log-Cabin Canvass, Hoosier Style,* 53 IND. MAG. OF HIST. 245, 250 (1957). This rhetoric represents a triumph of the kind of descriptive representation imagined by Brutus. *See* note 100 above.

127. For a general historical and theoretical discussion of the etiology of political parties, see JOHN H. ALDRICH, WHY PARTIES? THE ORIGIN AND TRANSFORMATION OF POLITICAL PARTIES IN AMERICA (1995). On the emergence of party politics during the Jacksonian era, see GERALD LEONARD, THE INVENTION OF PARTY POLITICS: FEDERALISM, POPULAR SOVEREIGNTY, AND CONSTITUTIONAL DEVELOPMENT IN JACKSONIAN ILLINOIS (2002).

128. *The Democratic Principle,* note 117 above, at 1.

129. WILENTZ, note 102 above, at 516.

130. Ibid.

131. David J. Russo, *The Major Political Issues of the Jacksonian Period and the Development of Party Loyalty in Congress, 1830–1840,* 62 TRANSACTIONS AM. PHIL. SOC'Y 3, 48 (1972).

132. For contemporary work theorizing how parties can continue to serve this function, see, for example, Christopher S. Elmendorf & David Schleicher, Essay, *Districting for a Low Information Electorate,* 121 YALE L.J. 1846 (2012); and David Schleicher, *What If Europe Held an Election and No One Cared?,* 52

Harv. Int'l L.J. 110 (2011). Elmendorf and Schleicher build on the foundational work of Morris Fiorina in Morris P. Fiorina, Retrospective Voting in American National Elections (1981).

133. William Leggett, *Small Note Circulation,* Evening Post, Aug. 6, 1834, *reprinted in* 1 A Collection of the Political Writings of William Leggett, note 108 above, at 41.

134. William Leggett, *Rich and Poor,* Evening Post, Dec. 6, 1834, *reprinted in* 1 A Collection of the Political Writings of William Leggett, note 108 above, at 109; *see also* Leggett, *Monopolies,* Evening Post, Nov. 1834, *reprinted in* 1 A Collection of the Political Writings of William Leggett, note 108 above, at 91 ("What have the People, the Democracy, been struggling for in the last election? Was it merely to satisfy a personal predilection in favour of a few leaders, and to gratify a personal dislike to a few others; or was it for certain great principles, combined in the one great general term of equal rights?").

135. William Leggett, *Prefatory Remarks,* The Plaindealer, Dec. 3, 1836, *reprinted in* 2 A Collection of the Political Writings of William Leggett, note 108 above, at 110. Leggett explicitly invokes Edmund Burke, Thoughts on the Present Cause of the Present Discontents 110 (1770), in which Burke writes that "[p]arty is a body of men united for promoting by their joint endeavours the national interest, upon some particular principle in which they are all agreed." Burke reasons:

> For my part, I find it impossible to conceive that any one believes in his own politics, or thinks them to be of any weight, who refuses to adopt the means of having them reduced into practice. It is the business of the speculative philosopher to mark the proper ends of Government. It is the business of the politician, who is the philosopher in action, to find out proper means towards those ends, and to employ them with effect. Therefore, every honourable connection will avow it as their first purpose to pursue every just method to put the men who hold their opinions into such a condition as may enable them to carry their common plans into execution, with all the power and authority of the State. . . . Without a proscription of others, they are bound to give to their own party the preference in all things, and by no means, for private considerations, to accept any offers of power in which the whole body is not included, nor to suffer themselves to be led, or to be controlled, or to be overbalanced, in office or in council, by those who contradict, the very fundamental principles on which their party is formed, and even those upon which every fair connection must stand. Such a generous contention for power, on such manly and honourable maxims, will easily be distinguished from the mean and interested struggle for place and emolument.

Ibid., 110–112.

136. Woodrow Wilson, Constitutional Government in the United States 203 (1908).

137. Ibid., 205.

138. Ibid., 206; *see* Formisano, note 125 above, at 475 ("Indeed, the party's inherent ambition to unify various levels of government violated the Whig heritage of the Revolution and some of the most sacred values of eighteenth-century political culture.").

139. WILSON, note 136 above, at 217.

140. Ibid., 207.

141. 1 DE TOCQUEVILLE, note 110 above, at 271; *see* E.E. SCHATTSCHNEIDER, PARTY GOVERNMENT 208 (1942) ("Party government is good democratic doctrine because the parties are the special form of political organization adapted to the mobilization of majorities. How else can the majority get organized? If democracy means anything at all it means that the majority has the right to organize for the purpose of taking over the government. Party government is strong because it has behind it the great moral authority of the majority and the force of a strong traditional belief in majority rule.").

142. Daryl J. Levinson & Richard H. Pildes, *Separation of Parties, Not Powers,* 119 HARV. L. REV. 2311, 2322–2323 (2006).

143. THE POLITICAL PHILOSOPHY OF ROBERT M. LA FOLLETTE AS REVEALED IN HIS SPEECHES AND WRITINGS 14 (Ellen Torelle ed., 1920) (1903); *see* ibid., 21–25.

144. For contemporary statements of this position, see *FEC v. Colo. Republican Fed. Campaign Comm.,* 518 U.S. 604, 615–616 (1996) (plurality opinion of Breyer, J.) ("A political party's independent expression not only reflects its members' views about the philosophical and governmental matters that bind them together, it also seeks to convince others to join those members in a practical democratic task, the task of creating a government that voters can instruct and hold responsible for subsequent success or failure."); ibid., 646 (Thomas, J., concurring in part and dissenting in part) ("What could it mean for a party to 'corrupt' its candidate or to exercise 'coercive' influence over him? The very aim of a political party is to influence its candidate's stance on issues and, if the candidate takes office or is reelected, his votes. When political parties achieve that aim, that achievement does not, in my view, constitute 'a subversion of the political process.' For instance, if the Democratic Party spends large sums of money in support of a candidate who wins, takes office, and then implements the Party's platform, that is not corruption; that is successful advocacy of ideas in the political marketplace and representative government in a party system.").

145. *See, e.g., Our Electoral Machinery,* 117 N. AM. REV. 383, 394 (1873).

146. For a thorough overview of the development of new electoral practices and structures during the Reconstruction era, see RICHARD FRANKLIN BENSEL, THE AMERICAN BALLOT BOX IN THE MID-NINETEENTH CENTURY (2004). *See also* Scott C. James, *Patronage Regimes and American Party Development from 'The Age of Jackson' to the Progressive Era,* 36 BRIT. J. POL. SCI. 39, 41 (2006).

After the Civil War, augmented government spending increased the potential benefits of controlling government expenditures. *See* ELISABETH S. CLEMENS, THE PEOPLE'S LOBBY: ORGANIZATION INNOVATION AND THE RISE OF INTEREST GROUP POLITICS IN THE UNITED STATES, 1890–1925, at 219–220 (1997) (citing FRANCES CAHN & VALESKA BARY, WELFARE ACTIVITIES OF FEDERAL, STATE, AND LOCAL GOVERNMENTS IN CALIFORNIA, 1850–1934, at 175 (1936)).

147. BENSEL, note 146 above, at 16–17.

148. W.R. Ware, *The Machinery of Politics and Proportional Representation,* in BRISTOL SELECTED PAMPHLETS 6 (1872).

149. JAMES BRYCE, 2 THE AMERICAN COMMONWEALTH 344–345 (1888); *see, e.g.,* RICHARD HOFSTADTER, THE AMERICAN POLITICAL TRADITION AND THE MEN WHO MADE IT 164–179 (1954) (describing Republicans and Democrats as "divided over spoils, not issues"). For a different view, see Charles W. Calhoun, *Major Party Conflict in the Gilded Age: A Hundred Years of Interpretation,* OAH MAG. HIST., Summer 1999, at 5; and Charles W. Calhoun, *Political Economy in the Gilded Age: The Republican Party's Industrial Policy,* 8 J. POL. HIST. 291 (1996).

150. Worth Robert Miller, *The Lost World of Gilded Age Politics,* 1 J. GILDED AGE & PROGRESSIVE ERA 49 (2002).

151. Ronald P. Formisano, *The "Party Period" Revisited,* 86 J. AM. HIST. 93, 94 (1999).

152. Richard McCormick, *The Party Period and Public Policy: An Exploratory Hypothesis,* 66 J. AM. HIST. 279, 282 (1979).

153. Ibid., 282, 283.

154. WILLIAM L. RIORDON, PLUNKITT OF TAMMANY HALL: A SERIES OF VERY PLAIN TALKS ON VERY PRACTICAL POLITICS 47 (1905) (ch. 23).

155. The Tammany district leader "seeks direct contact with the people, does them good turns when he can, and relies on their not forgetting him on election day." Ibid.

156. Mark Voss-Hubbard, *The "Third Party Tradition" Reconsidered: Third Parties and American Public Life, 1830–1900,* 86 J. AM. HIST. 121, 123 (1999).

157. Ibid., 130 (quoting Jay Burroughs, leader of the Nebraska Farmer's Alliance). The platform of the Prohibition Party proclaimed in 1869 that "[a] lamentable evil is the education of the people into the belief that a permanent political party is a great good." Ibid., 123.

158. Ibid., 134.

159. Peter H. Argersinger, *No Rights on This Floor: Third Parties and the Institutionalization of Congress,* 22 J. INTERDISC. HIST. 655, 687 (1992).

160. THE FARMERS TRIBUNE, May 12, 1897, at 3 (quoting the *Des Moines News*).

161. Myra Peppers, *Representative Government,* THE FARMERS TRIBUNE, May 12, 1897, at 2.

162. Voss-Hubbard, note 156 above, at 131.

163. WIEBE, note 68 above, at 134.

164. *See* Walter Dean Burnham, *The Changing Shape of the American Political Universe,* 59 AM. POL. SCI. REV. 7, 22–23 (1965). The old political order "eroded away very rapidly after 1900." Ibid., 23.

165. McCormick, note 152 above, at 295.

166. WIEBE, note 68 above, at 135–136.

167. In promoting causes like the professional civil service and the Australian ballot, Mugwumps, who were typically disaffected northeastern intellectuals, condemned political parties as (in the words of former Columbia president F.A.P. Barnard) run by "professional or 'machine'" politicians, "a pernicious class of men who devote themselves to the control of elections as a business, and make a systematic study and practice of the arts by which the will of the people may be suppressed, or its expression falsified." F.A.P. Barnard, *Republican Government Under the American Constitution,* 8 CHAUTAUQUAN 11, Oct. 1887, at 11, 13. "The consequence is that government in the United States, whether national, state or municipal . . . has long since ceased to be representative of the popular sovereignty; but has passed into the hands of a comparatively small number of unscrupulous men, who employ it for the advancement of their own personal interests, and direct their efforts both in legislation and in administration, not for the promotion of the public welfare, but for the maintenance of themselves in power." Ibid.

168. F.N. Judson, *The Future of Representative Government,* 2 AM. POL. SCI. REV. 185, 185 (1908).

169. A. LAWRENCE LOWELL, PUBLIC OPINION AND POPULAR GOVERNMENT 131 (1914).

170. THE POLITICAL PHILOSOPHY OF ROBERT M. LA FOLLETTE AS REVEALED IN HIS SPEECHES AND WRITINGS, note 143 above, at 55.

171. Ibid.

172. J. ALLEN SMITH, THE SPIRIT OF AMERICAN GOVERNMENT: A STUDY OF THE CONSTITUTION: ITS ORIGIN, INFLUENCE AND RELATION TO DEMOCRACY 208 (1907).

173. Ibid., 211.

174. Ibid., 209.

175. Ibid., 210.

176. Ibid., 211.

177. Ibid., 211.

178. Ibid., 216. *"Political corruption, then, is a force by which a representative democracy is transformed into an oligarchy, representative of special interests, and the medium of the revolution is the party."* Lincoln Steffens, *Enemies of the Republic,* 23 McCLURE'S MAG. 395, 396 (1904).

179. SMITH, note 172 above, at 372.

180. Ibid., 216.

181. Ibid., 371.

182. Richard L. McCormick, *The Discovery That Business Corrupts Politics: A Reappraisal of the Origins of Progressivism*, 86 AM. HIST. REV. 247, 252, 270 (1981).

183. Ibid., 265.

184. ALBERT SHAW, POLITICAL PROBLEMS OF AMERICAN DEVELOPMENT 149 (1907).

185. Edward A. Ross, *Political Decay—An Interpretation*, 61 INDEPENDENT 123, 124 (1906).

186. Ibid., 123.

187. Ibid., 124–125.

188. As Ross tells the story:

> The transformation of popular government into government by special interests presents four stages: First, ordinary "political" legislators or officials are influenced or bought for specific purposes. This is the era of lobby and bribe. Second, scenting "easy money" vultures . . . sell legislation for what they can get. This is the age of boodle. Third, financed by the Interests the party machines send up "safe" men who will vote as they are told on bills affecting corporations. . . . This is the epoch of blackmail and petty graft. Fourth, the Interests, falling gradually into a system cease to be customers of the bosses. They own them and are able to grow their own legislators. This brings into politics a more respectable type that scorns miscellaneous graft and takes his reward in business favors or professional connections. . . . This decent conduct of public affairs, free from the odium of grafting and blackmail, is known as "good government," and is the fine flower of perfected commercial oligarchy.

Ibid., 125.

189. *See* HERBERT CROLY, PROGRESSIVE DEMOCRACY 10 (1914) ("As soon as public opinion began to realize that business exploitation had been allied with political corruption, and that reformers were confronted, not by disconnected abuses, but by a perverted system, the inevitable and salutary inference began to be drawn. Just as business exploitation was allied with political corruption, so business reorganization must be allied with political reorganization.").

190. McCormick, note 182 above, at 252, 268. McCormick writes:

> From 1905 to 1907 alone, fifteen new state railroad commissions were established, and at least as many existing boards were strengthened. Most of the commissions were "strong" ones, having rate-setting powers and a wide range of administrative authority to supervise service, safety, and finance. In the years to come, many of them extended their jurisdiction to other public utilities, including gas, electricity, telephones, and telegraphs. . . .
>
> The adoption of these measures marked the moment of transition from a structure of economic policy based largely on the allocation of resources and benefits to one in which regulation and administration played permanent and significant roles.

Ibid., 268.

191. Woodrow Wilson, *The Study of Administration,* 2 Pol. Sci. Q. 197 (1887).

192. Ibid., 210. "Self-government," Wilson wrote, "does not consist in having a hand in everything, any more than housekeeping consists necessarily in cooking dinner with one's own hands. The cook must be trusted with a large discretion as to the management of the fires and the ovens." Ibid., 214.

193. The story of the federal statute, 34 Stat. 864, is told in *United States v. International Union United Automobile, Aircraft and Agricultural Implement Workers of America,* 352 U.S. 567, 570–576 (1957). More generally, "[m]any states passed laws explicitly designed to curtail illicit business influence in politics. These included measures regulating legislative lobbying, prohibiting corporate campaign contributions, and outlawing the acceptance of free transportation passes by public officials." McCormick, note 182 above, at 266.

194. Charles Zeublin, Democracy and the Overman 182 (1910).

195. Elihu Root, Addresses on Government and Citizenship 144 (Robert Bacon & James Brown Scott eds., 1916).

196. Ibid., 141.

197. Theodore Roosevelt, The New Nationalism 13–14, 29–30 (1910).

198. *See* Ross, note 185 above, at 125 ("[T]he special interests must, of course, guard their means of control, and hence they are adamant against the merit system, direct primary, referendum, ballot reform, anti-pass regulation, corrupt practices act and the like 'fads' tending to strengthen the people."). The progressive era was well known for developing "regular means . . . for newer interest groups to participate in government," McCormick, note 182 above, at 258, thus bypassing party government.

199. George H. Haynes, The Election of Senators 166–167 (1906) ("Democracy is certainly an illusion unless it works out for itself a government which is, in some genuine fashion, responsible to the people. [But a Senator elected by a state legislature] almost inevitably . . . renounces any attempt to keep in sensitive touch with the people. It is not to them that he standeth or falleth. He feels that he must put his political faith in some power that abides; and hence he turns to the 'organization' and relies upon that to secure for him his reëlection as the reward for his subservience.").

200. McCormick, note 182 above, at 266–267.

201. The Political Philosophy of Robert M. La Follette as Revealed in His Speeches and Writings, note 143 above, at 28.

202. Ibid., 30, 33, 40. "Great corporations, such as the railways, would not then be able to rule, as they do now, by controlling the springs and sources of power—the primary party meeting and the party convention." Nathan Cree, Direct Legislation by the People 140 (1892).

203. Walter E. Weyl, The New Democracy 300 (1912).

204. ELLIS PAXSON OBERHOLTZER, THE REFERENDUM IN AMERICA 392–396 (1900).

205. ROOT, note 195 above, at 269.

206. Ibid.

207. "Under party government all representation is party representation, and its constitution rests with those who control those first or primary meetings of the parties which are the real springs and sources of power." CREE, note 202 above, at 71; *see* Judson, note 168 above, at 195–197. For a superb discussion of the progressive anti-partyism and its various institutional manifestations, see NANCY L. ROSENBLUM, ON THE SIDE OF THE ANGELS: AN APPRECIATION OF PARTIES AND PARTISANSHIP 165–209 (2008).

208. CREE, note 202 above, at 16.

209. As the University of Chicago sociologist Charles Zeublin remarked with some pride, "[N]ot only has there been a greater volume of progressive and aggressive legislation than in several previous decades, but it has been accomplished by appeals to public opinion, frequently in disregard of party." ZEUBLIN, note 194 above, at 176. Zeublin indignantly observed of the 1908 presidential election that "one might expect a universal protest against Mr. Taft's sublime presumption when he says: 'If ever a *party* earned the verdict of well done by the record of the last seven years, and the reward of a renewed mandate of power, it is the Republican party under Theodore Roosevelt.'" Ibid., 177–178.

210. WEYL, note 203 above, at 298–310.

211. RICHARD HOFSTADTER, THE AGE OF REFORM 18 (1955).

212. Judson, note 168 above, at 194.

213. 2 DE TOCQUEVILLE, note 110 above, at 752. Tocqueville also saw that "[w]hen the right of every citizen to co-operate in the government of society is acknowledged, every citizen must be presumed to possess the power of discriminating between the different opinions of his contemporaries, and of appreciating the different facts from which inferences may be drawn. The sovereignty of the people and the liberty of the press may therefore be looked upon as correlative institutions; just as the censorship of the press and universal suffrage are two things which are irreconcilably opposed, and which can not long be retained among the institutions of the same people." 1 ibid., 187.

214. 3 JAMES BRYCE, THE AMERICAN COMMONWEALTH 3 (1888). "We talk of public opinion as a new force in the world," Bryce writes, "conspicuous only since governments began to be popular. Statesmen, even in the last generation, looked on it with some distrust or dislike. Sir Robert Peel, for instance, in a letter written in 1820, speaks with the air of a discoverer, of 'that great compound of folly, weakness, prejudice, wrong feeling, right feeling, obstinacy, and newspaper paragraphs, which is called public opinion.'" Ibid., 14.

215. Ibid., 24.

216. Ibid., 27.

217. "The obvious weakness of government by opinion is the difficulty of ascertaining it." Ibid., 144.

218. Ibid., 47; *see* V.O. KEY, JR., PUBLIC OPINION AND AMERICAN DEMOCRACY 17 (1961).

219. 3 BRYCE, note 214 above, at 159. With remarkable foresight, Bryce seems to have anticipated the advent of modern polling, speculating about what would happen "if the will of the majority of the citizens were to become ascertainable at all times, and without the need of its passing through a body of representatives, possibly even without the need of voting machinery at all. In such a state of things the sway of public opinion would have become more complete. . . . Popular government would have been pushed so far as almost to dispense with, or at any rate to anticipate, the legal modes in which the majority speaks its will at the polling booths; and this informal but direct control of the multitude would dwarf, if it did not supersede, the importance of those formal but occasional deliverances made at the elections of representatives." 3 BRYCE, note 214 above, at 19. For an explanation of how polling began in the 1940s to shape public discourse and the concept of the American "public," see SARAH IGO, THE AVERAGED AMERICAN: SURVEYS, CITIZENS, AND THE MAKING OF THE MASS PUBLIC 168–180, 282 (2008). For an exploration of the constitutional consequences of modern public opinion polling, see Or Bassok, *The Two Countermajoritarian Difficulties,* 31 ST. L. U. PUB. L. REV. 333 (2012).

220. 3 BRYCE, note 214 above, at 159. In Great Britain, Goldwin Smith was simultaneously making an analogous observation:

> Parliaments are losing much of their importance, because the real deliberation is being transferred from them to the press and the general organs of discussion by which the great questions are virtually decided, parliamentary speeches being little more than reproductions of arguments already used outside the House, and parliamentary divisions little more than registrations of public opinion. It is not easy to say how far, with the spread of public education, this process may go, or what value the parliamentary debate and division list will in the end retain.

Goldwin Smith, *The Machinery of Elective Government,* 20 POPULAR SCI. MONTHLY 628, 629–630 (1882).

221. 3 BRYCE, note 214 above, at 160.

222. Ibid., 161.

223. Hence Charles Horton Cooley could define democracy as "the organized sway of public opinion." CHARLES HORTON COOLEY, SOCIAL ORGANIZATION 118 (1910). He observed that "our government, under the Constitution, was not originally a democracy, and was not intended to be so by the men that framed it. It was expected to be a representative republic, the people choosing men of character and wisdom, who would proceed to the capital, inform themselves there upon current questions, and deliberate and decide regarding them."

Ibid., 86. In Cooley's view, America evolved into a democracy as public opinion expanded based "upon the telegraph, the newspaper and the fast mail." Ibid.

224. JOHN DEWEY, THE PUBLIC AND ITS PROBLEMS (1927); *see* JOHN DEWEY, ORGANIZATION IN AMERICAN EDUCATION (1916), *in* 10 THE COLLECTED WORKS OF JOHN DEWEY 397, 404 (Jo Ann Boydston ed., 1989) ("If, then, we have a state, if we have a real social organization and unity, it is in virtue of the existence and the influence of that impalpable thing called public opinion: the common mind, the common intention, resulting from free exchange and communication of ideas, from teaching and from being taught.").

225. M.P. FOLLETT, THE NEW STATE: GROUP ORGANIZATION THE SOLUTION OF POPULAR GOVERNMENT (1926).

226. Follett stressed that "the vote in itself does not give us democracy." Ibid., 179. "The ballot-box ... *creates nothing*—it merely registers what is already created. ... The essence of democracy is an educated and responsible citizenship evolving common ideas and *willing* its own social life." Ibid., 180.

227. CROLY, note 189 above, at 228.

228. Ibid., 228–229.

229. Ibid., 229. "It would be absurd to attach the prerogatives of sovereignty to the electorate, although the absurdity of so doing does not prevent many progressives from doing it." Ibid., 227; *see, e.g.,* ROBERT H. FULLER, GOVERNMENT BY THE PEOPLE 1 (1908) ("In the government of the United States sovereignty is divided equally among the qualified voters and it is exercised by a plurality of those who vote.").

230. CROLY, note 189 above, at 263.

231. ROOT, note 195 above, at 39.

232. CROLY, note 189 above, at 308.

233. Ibid., 265.

234. Ibid., 267.

235. Ibid., 283.

236. Ibid., 281.

237. Ibid., 283.

238. Ibid., 272. Croly forcefully opposed those who sought "to hinder the unrestrained movement of the popular will ... by praise of the virtues of representative government." Herbert Croly, *State Political Reorganization,* 6 AM. POL. SCI. REV. 122, 126 (Supp. Feb. 1912).

239. CROLY, note 189 above, at 284.

240. Ibid.

241. Croly, note 238 above, at 131. Croly spoke of the executive's "inevitable responsibilities to public opinion." Ibid., 132. He also believed that "The value of executive leadership consists in its peculiar serviceability not merely as the agent of prevailing public opinion, but also as the invigorator and concentrator of such opinion." CROLY, note 189 above, at 304.

242. Croly, note 238 above, at 132. On the radical increase in executive power contemplated by Croly, *see* CROLY, note 189 above, at 303.

243. The progressive solution to the problem of representative integrity might be thought to depend upon the weakness of parties as a medium for political identification. The appeal to public opinion as a solution to representative integrity is thus connected to the phenomenon of independent voters, with its attendant "elevation of the individual, educated, rational voter as the model citizen." Michael Schudson, *Politics as Cultural Practice*, 18 POL. COMM. 421, 427 (2001). Schudson writes that "the model of the informed citizen" separates us

> dramatically from the politics of most other democratic systems in the world where an anti-party reformation did not take place. . . . As the Progressives abandoned politics for science, party for city manager, parades for pamphlets, streets for parlors . . . so we have accepted an ideal of citizenship at once privatized, effortful, cerebral, not much fun. Citizenship became spinach, if you will, distasteful but good for you.

Ibid., 429; *see* MICHAEL SCHUDSON, THE GOOD CITIZEN: A HISTORY OF AMERICAN CIVIC LIFE (1998).

The rise of independent voters has been a long-term secular trend. *See* THOMAS R. PEGRAM, PARTISANS AND PROGRESSIVES: PRIVATE INTEREST AND PUBLIC POLICY IN ILLINOIS, 1870–1922, at 155–158 (1992) (noting that during the Progressive era candidates began designing campaigns to appeal to uncommitted voters); Larry M. Bartels, *Electoral Continuity and Change, 1868–1996*, 17 ELECTORAL STUD. 301, 307 (1998) (conducting an empirical study and concluding that "the persistence of partisan loyalties appears to have declined throughout the first half of the 20th century from the very high level of the Gilded Age"). This trend continues through the present day. By 1952, roughly a quarter of the population identified as independent. *See* RUSSELL J. DALTON, THE APARTISAN AMERICAN: DEALIGNMENT AND CHANGING ELECTORAL POLITICS 17–21 (2013) (noting that reliable data about partisan affiliation became available only in the middle of the twentieth century, when Gallup and the American National Election Survey (ANES) began asking voters about their partisan affiliations). This percentage held steady or increased throughout the second half of the twentieth century (ibid., 17–21), reaching a high of 40 percent in 2011 and 2012. Jeffrey M. Jones, *In U.S., Democrats Re-Establish Lead in Party Identification*, GALLUP, Jan. 9, 2013 (visited Mar. 12, 2013), *available at* http://www .gallup.com/poll/159740/democrats-establish-lead-party-affiliation.aspx (noting that Gallup asks: "In politics today, do you consider yourself a Republican, a Democrat, or an independent?"); *see also* DALTON, above, at 181 (noting that as of 2008 roughly 40 percent of Americans lacked a partisan identification). The percentage of the population identifying as independent was 40 percent or greater in 32 of 65 Gallup polls conducted between January 2010 and March

2013, and never fell below 33 percent during that period. *Party Affiliation*, GAL-LUP, Mar. 11, 2013, *available at* http://www.gallup.com/poll/15370/party-affili ation.aspx (last visited Mar. 12, 2013).

While some political scientists argue that independents are really partisans in disguise and that the "decline of parties" hypothesis is overstated, *see, e.g.*, Larry M. Bartels, *Partisanship and Voting Behavior, 1952–1996,* 44 AM. J. POL. SCI. 35, 44 (2000), independents may vote for candidates of a particular party without feeling any strong allegiance to that party. Studies suggest that independents who report a lean toward one party or another are significantly more likely than self-described "weak" partisans to switch their partisan preference or to begin affiliating as pure independents. DALTON, above, at 22–23. Empirical studies suggest that the major parties have become more polarized over the past thirty years at the elite level (particularly in government). *See* Marc J. Hetherington, *Putting Polarization in Perspective,* 39 BRIT. J. POL. SCI. 413, 415–419 (2009) (surveying empirical studies of elite polarization and concluding that "little doubt remains that elites are polarized today"). But empirical studies have failed to find similar polarization in the general populace. *See* Morris P. Fiorina & Samuel J. Abrams, *Political Polarization in the American Public,* 11 ANN. REV. POL. SCI. 563, 584 (2008) (surveying empirical studies of mass polarization and concluding that "the American public as a whole is no more polarized today than it was a generation ago"); Hetherington, above, at 431–436. It is possible that moderate and independent voters may increasingly view the party they favor as the lesser of two evils, especially if parties serve elite interests rather than the interests of the general population. *See* Kathleen Bawn et al., *A Theory of Political Parties: Groups, Policy Demands and Nominations in American Politics,* 10 PERSP. ON POL. 571, 571 (2012). Partisan identification may well serve for some people as a component of individual identity. *See, e.g.,* DONALD GREEN ET AL., PARTISAN HEARTS AND MINDS: POLITICAL PARTIES AND THE SOCIAL IDENTITIES OF VOTERS 78 (2002). If so, independent voters may be those who resist the socializing pull of partisan identity.

244. Consider:

> Analysts report that for the electorate as a whole, parties are less objects of dissatisfaction than insignificant. "The parties are currently perceived with almost complete indifference by a large proportion of the population." . . . Voters see parties as irrelevant for solving problems and inconsequential for government outcomes. Roughly one-third of voters prefer that "candidates run as individuals without party labels." . . . In surveys, fewer than 10 percent of respondents disagree with the statement "The best rule in voting is to pick the best candidate, regardless of party label."

ROSENBLUM, note 207 above, at 326–328; *see also* ibid., 524 n.16 ("Polling in the United States indicates that only a bare majority of respondents, 53%, feels well represented by the two major parties.").

245. *See, e.g.,* Frederic C. Howe, *The Constitution and Public Opinion,* 5 Proc. Acad. Pol. Sci. in N.Y.C. 7, 18 (1914) ("Adequate responsiveness to public opinion involves provision for direct legislative action by the people themselves, through the initiative and referendum. . . . The initiative is the final step in democracy; it involves a government which mirrors public opinion.").

246. Judson, note 168 above, at 194–195 ("The sober advocate of the referendum no longer claims that it will be a substitute for representative government, but that it will furnish an additional and needed restraint upon our legislative bodies. . . . In a great political crisis it may represent the sovereign will of the people, but its warmest friends must admit that it is not and cannot be a means of working out the necessary details of legislation.").

247. 3 Bryce, note 214 above, at 30; *see* Adrian Vermeule, *"Government by Public Opinion": Bryce's Theory of the Constitution* (Harvard Pub. Law Working Paper No. 11–13, 2011), *available at* http://papers.ssrn.com/sol3/papers.cfm ?abstract_id=1809794.

248. *See* text accompanying notes 217–218 above.

249. For a discussion of democratic legitimation, see Robert Post, Democracy, Expertise, Academic Freedom: A First Amendment Jurisprudence for the Modern State (2012).

250. *See* Shaun Bowler & Todd Donovan, Opinion, Voting, and Direct Democracy 4–5 (2000).

251. Weyl, note 203 above, at 310.

252. Thus Weyl could write that "although men are crying that representative government is dead and that the occupation of the legislator is gone, the fundamental issue in America is in reality not between representative and direct government (both of which systems have merits, inconveniences, and perils), but between a *misrepresentative,* plutocratic government and a democratic government, whether representative, direct, or mixed." Ibid., 308.

253. *See* text accompanying note 228 above.

254. Key, note 218 above, at 538–539 ("If an elite is not to monopolize power and thereby to bring an end to democratic practices, its rules of the game must include restraints in the exploitation of public opinion. . . . A body of customs that amounts to a policy of 'live and let live' must prevail. In constitutional democracies some of these rules are crystalized into fundamental law in guarantees such as those of freedom of speech, freedom of press, and the right to appeal to the electorate for power.").

255. Bernard Manin, Elly Stein & Jane Mansbridge, *On Legitimacy and Political Deliberation,* 15 Pol. Theory 338, 352 (1987).

256. The story is well told in David M. Rabban, *Free Speech in Progressive Social Thought,* 74 Tex. L. Rev. 951 (1996). An exception might be made for Theodore Schroeder and the Free Speech League. *See* Theodore Schroeder, Freedom of the Press and "Obscene" Literature: Three Essays (1906),

except that Schroeder tended to support communicative rights because of their importance to individual liberty rather than discursive democracy. On the hostility of Progressives to constitutional rights, see KEY, note 218 above, at 4–5:

> Democratic hopes and expectations reached a great peak in the United States in the years before World War I, when the doughty Progressives fought their battles against privilege and preached the righteousness of the popular will. To see that the popular will prevailed, they contrived no end of means to involve the people in the process of government. . . . The courts, regarded as the sturdiest bastion of the special interest, were to be subjected to the humiliation of a popular review of their constitutional decisions.

257. *See* CHRISTOPHER CAPOZZOLA, UNCLE SAM WANTS YOU: WORLD WAR I AND THE MAKING OF THE MODERN AMERICAN CITIZEN 144–173 (2008); DAVID M. KENNEDY, OVER HERE: THE FIRST WORLD WAR AND AMERICAN SOCIETY 75–92 (1980). The 1918 amendments to the Espionage Act of 1917, which were known informally as the Sedition Act, made it a crime to "utter, print, write or publish any disloyal, profane, scurrilous, or abusive language about the form of government of the United States, or the Constitution of the United States, or the military or naval forces of the United States, or the flag . . . or the uniform of the Army or Navy of the United States, or any language intended to bring the form of government . . . or the Constitution . . . or the military or naval forces . . . or the flag . . . of the United States into contempt, scorn, contumely, or disrepute." Sedition Act of 1918, 40 Stat. 553; *see also* Espionage Act of 1917, 40 Stat. 217 (proscribing "mak[ing] or convey[ing] false reports or false statements" with intent to undermine the ability of the United States military to prevail in war); Geoffrey R. Stone, *Judge Learned Hand and the Espionage Act of 1917: A Mystery Unraveled*, 70 U. CHI. L. REV. 335, 356 n.95 (2003) ("The purpose of the 1918 Act was quite clearly to broaden and strengthen the prohibitions of the Espionage Act. A year of war, with all of its casualties, had significantly changed the mood of the country and the Congress. Whatever tolerance may have existed for dissent in 1917 was largely dissipated after a year of brutal conflict and unrelenting government-sponsored anti-German propaganda.").

The first great scholarly treatment of freedom of speech was ZECHARIAH CHAFEE, FREEDOM OF SPEECH (1920), which on its first page makes clear the motivation for its publication:

> Never in the history of our country, since the Alien and Sedition Laws of 1798, has the meaning of free speech been the subject of such sharp controversy as to-day. Over nineteen hundred prosecutions and other judicial proceedings during the war, involving speeches, newspaper articles, pamphlets, and books, have been followed since the armistice by a widespread legislative consideration of bills punishing the advocacy of extreme radicalism. It is becoming increasingly important to determine the true limits of freedom of expression, so that speakers and writers may know how

much they can properly say, and governments may be sure how much they can lawfully and wisely suppress.

Ibid., 1.

258. In the words of the editor of the *New York World,* Frank I. Cobb:

> For five years there has been no free play of public opinion in the world.
>
> Confronted by the inexorable necessities of war, Governments conscripted public opinion as they conscripted men and money and materials.
>
> Having conscripted it, they dealt with it as they dealt with other raw recruits. They mobilized it. They put it in charge of drill sergeants. They goose-stepped it. They taught it to stand at attention and salute.
>
> This governmental control over public opinion was exerted through two different channels—one the censorship and the other propaganda. . . . As the war progressed the censorship became less and less a factor, and propaganda increased in importance. . . . Governments relied on propaganda to equip and sustain their armies, to raise money, to furnish food and munitions, and to perform all those services without which armies would be vain and helpless. The organized manipulation of public opinion was as inevitable a development of modern warfare as airplanes, tanks, and barbed-wire entanglements.

Frank I. Cobb, *Public Opinion,* S. Doc. No. 175, at 3–4 (1920). Cobb's perspective should be contrasted to that of Edward Bernays, who in his 1928 book *Propaganda* recognized and celebrated the power of government to manipulate public opinion:

> [The politician] sends up his trial balloon. He may send out an anonymous interview through the press. He then waits for reverberations to come from the public—a public which represents itself in mass meetings, or resolutions, or telegrams, or even such obvious manifestations as editorials in the partisan or nonpartisan press. On the basis of these repercussions he then publicly adopts his originally tentative policy, or rejects it, or modifies it to conform to the sum of public opinion which has reached him. . . .
>
> [This] is a method which has little justification. If a politician is a real leader, he will be able, by the skillful use of propaganda, to lead the people, instead of following the people by means of the clumsy instrument of trial and error.
>
> The propagandist's approach is the exact opposite of that of the politician just described. The whole basis of propaganda is to have an objective and then to endeavor to arrive at it through an exact knowledge of the public and modifying circumstances to manipulate and sway that public.

Edward Bernays, Propaganda 125–126 (1928). The era of the First World War was also when mass consumer *private* advertising began to expand, spearheaded by none other than Edward Bernays.

259. Cobb, note 258 above, at 6.

260. Ibid., 6–8. On the linkage of First Amendment rights to self-government, Cobb writes:

> Either the people are fit to govern or they are not. If they are fit to govern it is no function of government to protect them from any kind of propaganda. They will protect themselves. That capacity for self-protection is the very essence of self-government. Without it popular institutions are inconceivable, and the moment that a republican form of government sets itself up as the nursemaid of the people to train their immature minds to suit its own purposes and to guard them from all influences that it considers contaminating, we already have a revolution and a revolution backward, a revolution by usurpation.

Ibid. As early as October 1917, Herbert Croly had written to President Wilson to protest "the censorship over public opinion" in which the administration was engaged. Letter from Herbert Croly to Woodrow Wilson (Oct. 19, 1917), *in* 44 THE PAPERS OF WOODROW WILSON 408 (Arthur S. Link ed., 1983). After the war, Croly explicitly recognized the necessity of communicative rights to protect the processes that form public opinion. In 1919 he wrote an article in the *New Republic* praising Holmes's dissent in *Abrams v. United States,* 250 U.S. 616, 624 (1919), which had specifically and for the first time acknowledged that First Amendment rights should be used to invalidate government action. Croly wrote:

> Democracy is capable of curing the ills it generates by means of peaceful discussion and unhesitating acquiescence in the verdict of honestly conducted elections but its self-curative properties are not unconditional. They are the creation of a body of public opinion which has access to the facts, which can estimate their credibility and significance and which is in effective measure open to conviction. The most articulate public opinion in America is temporarily indifferent to the facts and impervious to conviction. . . . American educators and lawyers no longer act as if the government and Constitution of the United States is, as Justice Holmes says, an experiment which needs for its own safety an agency of self-adjustment and which seeks it in the utmost possible freedom of opinion. They act as good Catholics formerly acted in relation to the government and the creed of the Catholic Church—as if the government and Constitution were the embodiment of ultimate political and social truth, which is to be perpetuated by persecuting and exterminating its enemies rather than by vindicating its own qualifications to carry on under new conditions the difficult job of supplying political salvation to mankind. If they begin by sacrificing freedom of speech to what is supposed to be the safety of constitutional government they will end by sacrificing constitutional government to the dictatorship of one class.

The Call to Toleration, NEW REPUBLIC, Nov. 26, 1919, at 360, 362. On Croly's authorship, see Rabban, note 256 above, at 1014–1015. Croly had written Holmes directly on November 13 to praise Holmes's *Abrams* dissent. *See* THOMAS HEALY, THE GREAT DISSENT: HOW OLIVER WENDELL HOLMES CHANGED HIS MIND—AND CHANGED THE HISTORY OF FREE SPEECH IN AMERICA 220 (2013).

261. JOHN DEWEY & JAMES H. TUFTS, ETHICS 398 (rev. ed. 1936). Dewey and Tufts explained that freedom of speech "is central because the essence of the

democratic principle is appeal to voluntary disposition instead of to force, to persuasion instead of coercion. Ultimate authority is to reside in the needs and aims of individuals as these are enlightened by a circulation of knowledge, which in turn is to be achieved by free communication, conference, discussion. . . . The idea [of freedom of speech] is implicit in our Constitution because whatever interferes with the free circulation of knowledge and opinions is adverse to the efficient working of democratic institutions." Ibid., 398–399. On the shift in Dewey's position in the years after World War I, see Rabban, note 256 above, at 1021–1026. For a good statement of Dewey's postwar position, see JOHN DEWEY, CONTRIBUTION TO *DEMOCRACY IN A WORLD OF TENSIONS* (1951), *in* 16 THE COLLECTED WORKS OF JOHN DEWEY, note 224 above, at 399, 402 ("Yet the place occupied in the organic law of the United States by guaranty of Civil Rights: rights of free speech, free press, free assembly, and freedom of belief and worship in religious matters, is fundamental and central. Taken collectively they constitute nothing less than an express recognition in the fundamental law of the land of the indispensable place held in a democracy by freedom of discussion and publicity. Philosophers had previously written about the importance of leaving mind free; but in the absence of explicit legal recognition of the right to free public communication, freedom "of mind" hardly amounted to more than a pious wish—of concern doubtless to writers on political philosophy and jurisprudence, but of slight importance in the actual conduct of organized social life."); ibid., 403–404 ("Given the present state of affairs both at home and in connection with other states, the way and degree in which we use or fail to use freedom of inquiry and public communication may well be the criterion by which in the end the genuineness of our democracy will be decided in all issues.").

For a discussion of the shift of another key progressive, John Lord O'Brien, see PAUL L. MURPHY, THE MEANING OF FREEDOM OF SPEECH: FIRST AMENDMENT FREEDOMS FROM WILSON TO FDR 97–98 (1972), which notes that O'Brien was one of many progressives who, during and after World War I, "realized that the state could be an instrument for evil as well as good" and as a result "suddenly entered the fray in defense of free expression. . . ."

262. For the story, see DAVID M. RABBAN, FREE SPEECH IN ITS FORGOTTEN YEARS (1997).

263. *See, e.g.,* MICHAEL CURTIS, FREE SPEECH: THE PEOPLE'S DARLING PRIVILEGE: STRUGGLES FOR FREEDOM OF EXPRESSION IN AMERICAN HISTORY (2000); Charles Beard, *The Great American Tradition: A Challenge for the Fourth of July,* NATION, July 7, 1926, at 7.

264. David Rabban, *The First Amendment in Its Forgotten Years,* 90 YALE L.J. 514, 523 (1981). I should note that in the prewar years at least two state supreme courts used state freedom of speech guarantees to invalidate progressive campaign regulations. *See* Nebraska ex rel. Ragan v. Junkin, 85 Neb. 1 (1909)

(striking down a direct primary); Wisconsin v. Pierce, 163 Wisc. 615 (1916) (striking down Wisconsin restrictions on third-party campaign expenditures).

265. Patterson v. Colorado, 205 U.S. 454, 462 (1907) (Holmes, J.); *see* TIMOTHY WALKER, INTRODUCTION TO AMERICAN LAW 188–189 (1837) ("The doctrine then is, that the liberty of speech and of the press consists in freedom from previous censorship or restraint, and not in exemption from subsequent liability for the injury which may thereby be done."); 3 JOSEPH STORY, COMMENTARIES ON THE CONSTITUTION OF THE UNITED STATES 731–746 (1833); THEOPHILUS PARSONS, THE PERSONAL AND PROPERTY RIGHTS OF A CITIZEN OF THE UNITED STATES 185–186 (1877); CHRISTOPHER G. TIEDEMAN, A TREATISE ON THE LIMITATIONS OF POLICE POWER IN THE UNITED STATES 189–193 (1886). A notable dissenter from this consensus was THOMAS M. COOLEY, A TREATISE ON THE CONSTITUTIONAL LIMITATIONS 420–421 (3d ed. 1874). Zachariah Chafee would subsequently emphasize Cooley's views in order to reconstruct a history of First Amendment "rights" in the United States. *See* CHAFEE, note 257 above. For an illuminating discussion of Cooley and the largely lost tradition of conservative libertarianism, see MARK A. GRABER, TRANSFORMING FREE SPEECH: THE AMBIGUOUS LEGACY OF CIVIL LIBERTARIANISM (1991).

266. SAMUEL FREEMAN MILLER, LECTURES ON THE CONSTITUTION OF THE UNITED STATES 645 (1893).

267. Abrams v. United States, 250 U.S. 616, 624 (1919). For a discussion of the constitutional innovations of *Abrams,* see Robert Post, *Reconciling Theory and Doctrine in First Amendment Jurisprudence,* 88 CALIF. L. REV. 2353 (2000).

268. *Abrams,* 250 U.S. at 630 (Holmes, J., dissenting).

269. *See* Vince Blasi, *Propter Honores Respectum: Reading Holmes Through the Lens of Schauer: The Abrams Dissent,* 72 NOTRE DAME L. REV. 1343, 1349, 1351 (1997). We know that Holmes's epistemological perspective was associated with that of Charles Peirce, who was quite explicit that a free market in ideas was no way to determine scientific truth:

> Some persons fancy that bias and counter-bias are favorable to the extraction of truth—that hot and partisan debate is the way to investigate. This is the theory of our atrocious legal procedure. But Logic puts its heel upon this suggestion. It irrefragably demonstrates that knowledge can only be furthered by the real desire for it, and that the methods of obstinacy, of authority, and every mode of trying to reach a foregone conclusion, are absolutely of no value. These things are proved. The reader is at liberty to think so or not as long as the proof is not set forth, or as long as he refrains from examining it. Just so, he can preserve, if he likes, his freedom of opinion in regard to the propositions of geometry; only, in that case, if he takes a fancy to read Euclid, he will do well to skip whatever he finds with A, B, C, etc., for, if he reads attentively that disagreeable matter, the freedom of his opinion about geometry may unhappily be lost forever.

CHARLES SANDERS PEIRCE, 2 COLLECTED PAPERS 635 (Charles Hartshorne, Paul Weiss & Arthur Burks eds., 1932). On the connection between Holmes and Peirce, see Note, *Holmes, Peirce and Legal Pragmatism*, 84 YALE L.J. 1123 (1975).

270. Gilbert v. Minnesota, 254 U.S. 325, 337–338 (1920) (Brandeis, J., dissenting). Before Brandeis, of course, there was the great opinion of Learned Hand in Masses Publishing Co. v. Patten, 244 F. 535 (S.D.N.Y.), *rev'd,* 246 F. 24 (2d Cir. 1917), which verged on explaining judicially enforceable First Amendment rights as necessary to protect the formation "of that public opinion which is the final source of government in a democratic state." *See* James Weinstein, *The Story of* Masses Publishing Co. v. Patten: *Judge Learned Hand, First Amendment Prophet, in* R. GARNETT & A. KOPPELMAN, FIRST AMENDMENT STORIES (2011). By 1920 Hand was willing to be more explicit, writing in a letter to Zechariah Chafee:

> I prefer a test based upon the nature of the utterance itself. If, taken in its setting, the effect upon the hearers is only to counsel them to violate the law, it is unconditionally illegal. . . .
>
> As to other utterances, it appears to me that regardless of their tendency they should be permitted. The reason is that any State which professes to be controlled by public opinion, cannot take sides against any opinion except that which must express itself in the violation of law. On the contrary, it must regard all other expression of opinion as tolerable, if not good. . . .
>
> Nothing short of counsel to violate law should be itself illegal. . . .
>
> Therefore, to be a real protection to the expression of egregious opinion in times of excitement, I own I cannot see any escape from construing the privilege as absolute, so long as the utterance, objectively regarded, can by any fair construction be held to fall short of counselling violence.

Letter from Learned Hand to Zechariah Chafee, Jr., Jan. 8, 1920 (on file in the Chafee Papers, Box 4, Folder 20, Harvard Law Library, Treasure Room), *as reprinted in* Gerald Gunther, *Learned Hand and the Origins of Modern First Amendment Doctrine: Some Fragments of History,* 27 STAN. L. REV. 719, 764–766 (1975).

271. Whitney v. California, 274 U.S. 357, 377 (1927) (Brandeis, J., concurring).

272. Ibid., 375. Compare Edward Everett Hale in 1889:

> In truth . . . the business of voting is only a small part of the duty of a good citizen in a Republic. . . . The people we choose at elections are the people's servants in a very pathetic sense. This is no statement of a demagogue; it is the simple statement of the truth that public opinion governs the country. . . .
>
> The business of the citizen, then, consists very largely in what he can do in the right moulding of public opinion. This he does all the time; in the street-cars he may do it; he may do it in waltzing in the german; he may do it in his pew at church; he

may do it as he talks with the foreman in the mill. The public opinion of the country is improved in proportion as he does it, and the country is the better governed. And the really valuable magistrates and officers in this Republic are, invariably, men who are in close connection with all sorts of people, who have that delicate touch by which they find out what the people means to have done, and then, with promptness and willingness, do it.

Edward Everett Hale, *The Tree of Political Knowledge,* 148 N. Am. Rev. 564, 566–567 (1889).

273. 283 U.S. 359, 369 (1931).

274. Garrison v. Louisiana, 379 U.S. 64, 74–75 (1964). "Political speech is the primary object of First Amendment protection." Nixon v. Shrink Missouri Government, 528 U.S. 377, 410 (2000) (Thomas, J., dissenting).

275. New York Times Co. v. Sullivan, 376 U.S. 254, 270 (1964).

276. Connick v. Myers, 461 U.S. 138, 145 (1983) (quoting NAACP v. Claiborne Hardware Co., 458 U.S. 886, 913 (1982)).

277. *Buckley,* 424 U.S. at 14.

278. Globe Newspaper Co. v. Superior Court, 457 U.S. 596, 604 (1982).

279. Post, note 249 above.

280. Knox v. Serv. Emps. Int'l Union, Local 1000, 132 S. Ct. 2277, 2288 (2012).

281. Brown v. Hartlage, 456 U.S. 45, 60 (1982).

282. Jürgen Habermas, Between Facts and Norms: Contributions to a Discourse Theory of Law and Democracy 486 (William Rehg trans., MIT Press 1996).

283. Michael Walzer, Spheres of Justice: A Defense of Pluralism and Equality 310 (1983).

284. Clemens, note 146 above.

285. Schattschneider, note 141 above, at 107–109 ("American politics is remarkable for the exaggerated role played by pressure groups. . . . The executive agencies cannot resist pressures if Congress will not support them. Congress in its turn is prodigal in its concessions to organized minorities because the parties are too decentralized to impose an effective discipline on their congressional representation."). For reasons analogous to those of J. Allen Smith, Schattschneider concluded that the American Constitution has "made impossible the rise of responsible cabinet government and all that a responsible cabinet system might mean in terms of party government." Ibid., 126. "If the tendency of the system of separation of powers to frustrate central party control were not sufficient to disorganize the parties, the federal system would complete the task." Ibid., 128.

286. Arthur F. Bentley, The Process of Government: A Study of Social Pressures 210 (1908).

287. CLEMENS, note 146 above, at 320–321.

288. *See, e.g.,* Issacharoff, note 9 above, at 383–388. On the weakness of American political parties, see Paul S. Edwards, *Madisonian Democracy and Issue Advocacy: An Argument for Deregulating,* 50 CATH. UNIV. L. REV. 49, 61 (2000) ("Despite the emerging consensus that healthy, competitive parties are an essential, intermediating institution in modern democracies, American political parties are relatively weak. . . ."); Paul L. McKaskle, *Of Wasted Votes and No Influence: An Essay on Voting Systems in the United States,* 35 HOUS. L. REV. 1119, 1131–1132 (1998) ("Party organizations can be divided into two types. The first type, such as exists in the United States, . . . are very weak . . . in that their leadership has little formal control over the party's membership or candidates. . . . Moreover, there is no formal ability to discipline those elected under the party banner for voting contrary to the wishes of the party."); Terri Peretti, *The Virtues of "Value Clarity" in Constitutional Decisionmaking,* 55 OHIO ST. L.J. 1079, 1090–1091 (1994) ("United States political institutions are not well-designed or structured so as to ascertain and respond to majority desires effectively. Political parties in the United States, for example, have traditionally been weak and highly decentralized organizations . . . [and thus] have only a limited capacity for organizing that morass of preferences into coherent and comprehensive policy packages and for enforcing adherence to that platform by all of the party's candidates."). For one explanation of this fact, see Jeff Bowen & Susan Rose-Ackerman, *Partisan Politics and Executive Accountability: Argentina in Comparative Perspective,* 10 SUP. CT. ECON. REV. 157, 195 (2003) ("[P]olitical parties are likely to be relatively weak in presidential systems because they are not required to form the government. For example, in a weak party system, such as the United States, legislative majorities are frequently cobbled together across party lines.").

2. Second Lecture: Campaign Finance Reform and the First Amendment

1. 558 U.S. 310 (2010).

2. Ibid., 339 (citation omitted).

3. Ibid. (some internal quotation marks omitted) (quoting Eu v. S.F. Cnty. Democratic Cent. Comm., 489 U.S. 214, 223 (1989)).

4. MICHEL DE MONTAIGNE, ON LIARS (1574), *reprinted in* ESSAYS 28, 31 (J.M. Cohen trans., 1958).

5. United States v. Windsor, 133 S. Ct. 2675, 2698 (2013) (Scalia, J., dissenting).

6. Buckley v. Valeo, 424 U.S. 1, 14 (1976).

7. Nixon v. Shrink Mo. Gov't PAC, 528 U.S. 397, 398–399 (2000) (Stevens, J. dissenting).

8. Ibid; *see* Jim Leach, Citizens United: *Robbing America of Its Democratic Idealism*, DAEDALUS, Spring 2013, at 95, 96–97; J. Skelly Wright, *Politics and the Constitution: Is Money Speech?*, 85 YALE L.J. 1001 (1976).

9. The argument is elaborated in Robert Post, *Recuperating First Amendment Doctrine*, 47 STAN. L. REV. 1249 (1995).

10. Elena Kagan, *Private Speech, Public Purpose: The Role of Governmental Motive in First Amendment Doctrine*, 63 U. CHI. L. REV. 413 (1996); Jed Rubenfeld, *The First Amendment's Purpose*, 53 STAN. L. REV. 767 (2001).

11. Sorrell v. IMS Health, Inc., 131 S. Ct. 2653, 2667 (2011).

12. *See, e.g.,* Simon & Schuster, Inc. v. Members of N.Y. State Crime Victims Bd., 502 U.S. 105 (1991), in which the Court invoked the First Amendment to strike down the New York "Son of Sam" law, which required that the income received by authors accused or convicted of a crime be put into an escrow account for the benefit of the victims of the crime, whenever such authors described the reenactment of their crime by way of a movie, book, magazine article, tape recording, phonograph record, radio or television presentation, or live entertainment of any kind, or whenever they expressed their thoughts, feelings, opinions, or emotions regarding their crime. *See also* United States v. Nat'l Treasury Emps. Union, 513 U.S. 454 (1995) (striking down a ban on receipt of honoraria by federal employees).

Those defending the position that First Amendment scrutiny should not apply to campaign finance regulation sometimes assert the distinction between the regulation of "pure speech" and the regulation of "a form of conduct related to speech—something roughly equivalent to the physical act of picketing." Wright, note 8 above, at 1006. I think the distinction is indefensible. There is no such thing as "pure speech." All communication requires a physical substrate, whether it is the sound vibrations of oral speech or the paper required by old-fashioned books or leaflets. The regulation of the substrate is not separable from the regulation of the speech.

13. *See* Watchtower Bible & Tract Soc'y v. Vill. of Stratton, 536 U.S. 150, 163 (2002); Ladue v. Gilleo, 512 U.S. 43 (1994).

14. The Court has in at least one instance struck down state campaign finance regulation on this basis. Randall v. Sorrell, 548 U.S. 230 (2006).

15. *Citizens United,* 558 U.S. at 319.

16. Ibid., 340 (quoting FEC v. Wisc. Right to Life, Inc., 551 U.S. 449, 464 (2007)).

17. Reynolds v. Sims, 377 U.S. 533, 565 (1964). In actuality, the story may be a bit more complicated. Every court to consider the issue has held that jurisdictions may, consistent with the "one person, one vote" principle of *Reynolds*, design districts with equal total populations, rather than equal numbers of eligible voters. *See* Chen v. City of Houston, 206 F.3d 502, 528 (5th Cir. 2000); Garza v. Cnty. of L.A., 918 F.2d 763, 775 (9th Cir. 1990); Calderon v. City of L.A., 481

P.2d 489, 494 (Cal. 1971). Judge Kozinski has referred to this as a choice between "electoral equality" and "equality of representation." Under "electoral equality," each eligible voter must have an equally weighted vote; under "equality of representation," each resident must have an equal ability to petition for constituent services. *Garza*, 918 F.2d at 781 (Kozinski, J., dissenting).

18. *See* Edward B. Foley, *Equal-Dollars-Per-Voters: A Constitutional Principle of Campaign Finance*, 94 COLUM. L. REV. 1204 (1994); Frank Pasquale, *Reclaiming Egalitarianism in the Political Theory of Campaign Finance Reform*, 2008 U. ILL. L. REV. 599 (2008); David A. Strauss, *Corruption, Equality, and Campaign Finance Reform*, 94 COLUM. L. REV. 1369 (1994).

19. Harper v. Canada, 2004 SCCC 33, at ¶ 62.

20. Ibid. The Canadian Supreme Court conceives the problem of campaign finance regulation as exemplifying a fundamental tension between what it calls "the democratic values of freedom of expression," Libman v. Quebec, [1997] 3 S.C.R. 569, at ¶ 61, and what it calls "the right to 'effective representation,'" *Harper*, 2004 S.C.J. at ¶ 68. The egalitarian model adopted by *Harper* privileges the latter right.

21. 424 U.S. at 48.

22. Ibid., 48–49.

23. Ibid., 49 n.55.

24. Thus *Reynolds v. Sims* turns explicitly on the idea that representative government is a form of self-government that requires decision making through elections:

> But representative government is in essence self-government through the medium of elected representatives of the people, and each and every citizen has an inalienable right to full and effective participation in the political processes of his State's legislative bodies. Most citizens can achieve this participation only as qualified voters through the election of legislators to represent them.

377 U.S. 533, 565 (1964).

25. In the United States this rule is violated by the election of the president by the Electoral College.

26. *See, e.g.,* Synder v. Phelps, 131 S. Ct. 1207, 1220 (2011); Rosenberger v. Univ. of Va., 515 U.S. 819, 831 (1995); Hustler Magazine v. Falwell, 485 U.S. 46, 55 (1988).

27. This is a difficult concept to articulate within the context of representation. As David Runciman observes, "When a government is voted out of office following . . . elections, many individuals will have voted for the defeated party, yet we do not say that these individuals altogether cease to be represented by the new government that replaces their preferred choice. This is because we do not believe that governments simply represent individuals and their choices; they also represent the people as a whole. . . ." David Runciman, *The Paradox of*

Political Representation, 15 J. POL. PHIL. 93, 102 (2007). But how can it be that governments "represent" those who did not vote for them? Runciman concludes that we must draw a distinction "between the public on whose behalf political representatives act, and the public whose opinions of the actions of those representatives determine whether or not they can plausibly claim to be representing the people as a whole." Ibid., 106. The views of the latter public, however, cannot by definition be captured by any election, since every election will have winners and losers. It is more accurate to say, therefore, that the views of the latter public concern the general and diffuse question of democratic legitimacy, which is not a matter of representation but rather of the legitimacy of the government qua government. This suggests that democratic legitimacy makes possible the legitimacy of any given election.

28. First Amendment rights are a necessary but not sufficient condition for the creation of democratic legitimacy.

29. Of course, the usual qualifications apply. The First Amendment rights of one individual must be consistent with the First Amendment rights of other individuals. Ordinary "rules of the road," typically formulated as content-neutral "time, place, and manner" regulations, may also be applicable.

30. For a more developed discussion, see Robert Post, *Democracy and Equality,* 1 LAW, CULTURE & HUMAN. 142 (2005); and Robert Post, *Equality and Autonomy in First Amendment Jurisprudence,* 95 MICH. L. REV. 1517 (1997).

31. Cohen v. California, 403 U.S. 15 (1971).

32. Ariz. Free Enter. Club's Freedom Club PAC v. Bennett, 131 S. Ct. 2806, 2825–2826 (2011) ("We have repeatedly rejected the argument that the government has a compelling state interest in 'leveling the playing field' that can justify undue burdens on political speech. . . . 'Leveling the playing field' can sound like a good thing. But in a democracy, campaigning for office is not a game. It is a critically important form of speech. The First Amendment embodies our choice as a Nation that, when it comes to such speech, the guiding principle is freedom . . . not whatever the State may view as fair."). William Douglas, dissenting in the *Automobile Workers* decision about twenty years before *Buckley,* expressed the thought this way: "Undue influence . . . cannot constitutionally form the basis for making it unlawful for any segment of our society to express its views on the issues of a political campaign." 353 U.S. at 598 n.2.

33. *Citizens United,* 558 U.S. at 348.

34. 494 U.S. 654 (1990), *overruled by Citizens United,* 558 U.S. 310.

35. 494 U.S. at 660.

36. Ibid.; *see also* ibid., 684–685 (Scalia, J., dissenting); ibid., 705–706 (Kennedy, J., dissenting); Elizabeth Garrett, *New Voices in Politics: Justice Marshall's Jurisprudence on Law and Politics,* 52 HOWARD L.J. 655 (2009).

37. 494 U.S. at 660.

38. Ibid.

39. George F. Edmunds, *Corrupt Political Methods,* 7 FORUM 349, 350 (1889).

40. 494 U.S. at 659 (quoting FEC v. Mass. Citizens for Life, Inc., 479 U.S. 238, 258 (1986)). In dissent Justice Scalia critiqued this reasoning, arguing that it was "entirely irrational. Why is it perfectly all right if advocacy by an individual billionaire is out of proportion with 'actual public support' for his positions?" 494 U.S. at 685 (Scalia, J., dissenting). Scalia does have a point. As Judge Calabresi has observed in a deep and excellent opinion, "money does not measure intensity of desire equally for rich and poor. . . . [A] large contribution by a person of great means may influence an election enormously, and yet may represent a far lesser intensity of desire than a pittance given by a poor person. . . . [I]ntensity of desire is not well-measured by money in a society where money is not equally distributed." Landell v. Sorrell, 406 F.3d 159, 161–162 (2d Cir. 2005) (en banc).

In favor of the Michigan statute, however, it might be said that individual expenditures are registers of individual beliefs, and that elections are supposed to reflect individual beliefs. Corporate expenditures, by contrast, do not express personal beliefs, but rather corporate decision making, which elections are not supposed to reflect. Scalia may be correct that in a perfect world all campaign expenditures would be regulated so as to ensure, in Judge Calabresi's words, that "one's intensity of desire, as expressed in monetary terms, be measured equally." Ibid., 162. Compared with such regulation, the Michigan statute may be underinclusive. But that does not render it "entirely irrational." It merely makes it practical.

41. LAWRENCE LESSIG, REPUBLIC, LOST: HOW MONEY CORRUPTS CONGRESS—AND A PLAN TO STOP IT 128 (2011).

42. Ibid., 95.

43. *See* ibid. at 127.

44. Ibid., 128.

45. Ibid.

46. Ibid., 151.

47. Ibid., 232.

48. Ibid., 232–233.

49. There is of course the distinct question of who should constitutionally be recognized as appropriate participants in public discourse. I address this question in the text accompanying notes 112–147. Ordinary commercial corporations should not be constitutionally regarded as participants in public discourse.

50. Insofar as direct democracy aspires to a popular authority that is imagined as a genuine manifestation of popular sentiment, it has strong theoretical affinities with populism, see Nadia Urbinati, *Democracy and Populism,* 5 CONSTELLATIONS 110 (1998), or, more darkly, with the full-throated acclamation of "a present, genuinely assembled people" theorized in the scholarship of Carl Schmitt. *See* CARL SCHMITT, CONSTITUTIONAL THEORY 272 (Jeffrey Seitzer trans., 2008); Duncan Kelly, *Carl Schmitt's Political Theory of Representation,* 65 J. HIST. IDEAS 113 (2004).

51. Jürgen Habermas, Between Facts and Norms: Contributions to a Discourse Theory of Law and Democracy 486 (William Rehg trans., MIT Press 1996).

52. Claude Lefort, Democracy and Political Theory 17 (David Macey trans., 1988) ("DPT"). See Claude Lefort, The Political Forms of Modern Society: Bureaucracy, Democracy, Totalitarianism 279 (John B. Thompson ed., 1986). For Lefort this is most true at the moment of an election. "Nothing . . . makes the paradox of democracy more palpable than the institution of universal suffrage. It is at the very moment when popular sovereignty is assumed to manifest itself, when the people is assumed to actualize itself by expressing its will, that social interdependence breaks down and that the citizen is abstracted from all the networks in which his social life develops and becomes a mere statistic. Number replaces substance." Lefort, DPT, above, at 18–19. Like Habermas, Lefort identifies the emptiness of democracy with the "public space," which is "negative" in that it cannot be identified with any "group, not even the majority." Lefort, DPT, above, at 41. The public space is "so constituted that everyone is encouraged to speak and to listen without being subject to the authority of another. . . . This space, which is always indeterminate, has the virtue of belonging to no one, of being large enough to accommodate only those who recognize one another within it." Ibid. As such, a "democratic society is instituted as a society without a body, as a society which undermines the representation of an organic totality. . . . [N]either the state, the people nor the nation represent substantial entities. Here representation is itself, in its dependence upon political discourse and upon a sociological and historical elaboration, always bound up with ideological debate." Ibid., 18.

53. Sofia Näsström, *Representative Democracy as Tautology: Ankersmit and Lefort on Representation,* 5 Eur. J. Pol. Theory 321, 332 (2006); see Nadia Urbinati, Representative Democracy: Principles and Genealogy 33 (2006) (rejecting the idea of "a single or collective sovereign that seeks pictorial representation through election"); Lisa Disch, *Toward a Mobilization Conception of Democratic Representation,* 105 Am. Pol. Sci. Rev. 100, 104 (2011) (repudiating a "metaphysics of presence" that assumes "the fantasy of a reality that is self-evident, unmediated by social processes, and sovereign so that it can be imagined to provide an origin and point of reference for assessing the accuracy and faithfulness of any attempt to represent it"). Bryan Garsten seeks to arrive at this same conclusion through the logic of representation. He writes that "[b]y locating the source of sovereignty in an abstract entity, 'the people,' whose voice can be heard only through the various interpretations of its many spokespeople, representative government instigates constant debate about what the popular will actually is. . . . Representation properly understood requires a distinction between representatives and the people. This is the distinction that demagogues aim to obscure whenever they claim to fully represent the people;

it is the distinction that representative government, with its indirectness, aims to preserve." Bryan Garsten, *Representative Government and Popular Sovereignty, in* POLITICAL REPRESENTATION 105 (Ian Shapiro et al. eds., 2009); *see also* ibid., 91 ("representative government aims . . . to provoke debate about precisely what the popular will is and thereby to prevent any one interpretation of the popular will from claiming final authority"). This view is precisely the opposite of Schmitt's, who writes that "[b]y its *presence,* specifically, the people initiate the public. Only the present, truly assembled people are the people and produce the public." SCHMITT, note 50 above, at 272. *"Public opinion,"* Schmitt writes, *"is the modern type of acclamation."* Ibid., 275.

54. *See* URBINATI, note 53 above, at 228 ("Politics keeps the sovereign in perpetual motion, so to speak, while transforming its presence into an exquisite and complex manifestation of political influence.").

55. MICHAEL WALZER, SPHERES OF JUSTICE: A DEFENSE OF PLURALISM AND EQUALITY 309–310 (1983).

56. *Buckley,* 424 U.S. at 25.

57. FEC v. Nat'l Conservative PAC ("NCPAC"), 470 U.S. 448, 496–497 (1985); *see* Davis v. FEC, 554 U.S. 724, 741–742 (2008).

58. There is a massive and illuminating literature on this topic. I have found especially helpful Lillian R. BeVier, *Money and Politics: A Perspective on the First Amendment and Campaign Finance Reform,* 73 CALIF. L. REV. 1045 (1985); Thomas F. Burke, *The Concept of Corruption in Campaign Finance Law,* 14 CONST. COMMENT. 127 (1997); Bruce M. Cain, *Moralism and Realism in Campaign Finance Reform,* 1995 U. CHI. LEGAL F. 111 (1995); Samuel Issacharoff, *On Political Corruption,* 124 HARV. L. REV. 118 (2010); Daniel Hays Lowenstein, *Campaign Contributions and Corruption: Comments on Strauss and Cain,* 1995 U. CHI. LEGAL F. 163 (1995); Strauss, note 18 above; David A. Strauss, *What Is the Goal of Campaign Finance Reform?,* 1995 U. CHI. LEGAL F. 141 (1995); Zephyr Teachout, *The Anti-Corruption Principle,* 94 CORNELL L. REV. 341 (2009); and Dennis F. Thompson, *Two Concepts of Corruption: Making Campaigns Safe for Democracy,* 73 GEO. WASH. L. REV. 1036 (2005).

59. *Citizens United,* 558 U.S. at 447 (Stevens, J., dissenting). Indeed, the Court originally introduced the antidistortion principle as a variant of the corruption rationale. *See Austin,* 494 U.S. at 659–660 ("Michigan's regulation aims at a different type of corruption in the political arena. . . .").

60. "[I]n the context of the real world only a single definition of corruption has been found to identify political corruption successfully and to distinguish good political responsiveness from bad—that is *quid pro quo.* Favoritism and influence are not, as the Government's theory suggests, avoidable in representative politics. . . . Democracy is premised on responsiveness. *Quid pro quo* corruption has been, until now, the only agreed upon conduct that represents the bad form of responsiveness and presents a justiciable standard with a relatively

clear limiting principle: Bad responsiveness may be demonstrated by pointing to a relationship between an official and a *quid*." McConnell v. FEC, 540 U.S. 93, 297 (2003) (Kennedy, J., concurring in part and dissenting in part), *overruled in part on other grounds by Citizens United*, 558 U.S. 310.

61. Although the Court has occasionally employed language suggesting that the appearance of corruption is of concern because it itself erodes public trust in government (as in *McConnell*, 540 U.S. at 136–138; *Nixon*, 528 U.S. at 390; and *Buckley*, 424 U.S. at 27), the Court seems to have accepted the "appearance of corruption" rationale primarily because an appearance of corruption suggests a high likelihood of actual corruption. *See* Nathaniel Persily & Kelli Lammie, *Perceptions of Corruption and Campaign Finance: When Public Opinion Determines Constitutional Law*, 153 U. Pa. L. Rev. 119, 135 (2004) ("[T]he unique position of 'appearance of corruption' in the campaign finance jurisprudence has more to do with the difficulties of proving actual corruption . . . than the importance of the state interest in combating such negative perceptions."). On this account, the constitutional force of the "appearance of corruption" rationale depends upon the constitutional force of the actual corruption rationale.

Several scholars have suggested that an "appearance of corruption" can produce harms regardless of the presence of actual corruption. *See* Dennis F. Thompson, Ethics in Congress: From Individual to Institutional Corruption 125–126 (1995) (arguing that prohibiting the appearance of corruption not only serves as a proxy for preventing corruption but also promotes public trust in government and, "because appearances are usually the only window that citizens have on official conduct," facilitates "democratic accountability"); Deborah Hellman, *Judging by Appearances: Professional Ethics, Expressive Government, and the Moral Significance of How Things Seem*, 60 Md. L. Rev 653, 668 (2001) (arguing that as long as the relationship between a representative and her constituents is conceptualized as a "joint enterprise," "the representative [must] avoid, where possible, providing her constituents with a reason to doubt her. The fact that citizens are often justified in drawing conclusions on the basis of appearances provides a reason for legislators to avoid appearing corrupt."); Mark E. Warren, *Democracy and Deceit: Regulating Appearances of Corruption*, 50 Am. J. Pol. Sci. 160, 172 (2006) ("Democratic systems of representation depend upon the integrity of appearances, not simply because they are an indication of whether officials are upholding their public trust, but because they provide the means through which citizens can judge whether, in any particular instance, their trust in public officials is warranted. . . . Likewise, institutions that fail to support citizens' confidence in appearances produce political exclusions and generate a form of disempowerment. Together these failures amount to a corruption of democratic processes.").

62. *Buckley*, 424 U.S. at 26–27.

63. *NCPAC*, 470 U.S. at 497.

64. *NCPAC*, 470 U.S. at 497–498. Consider as well *McCormick v. United States:*

> Serving constituents and supporting legislation that will benefit the district and individuals and groups therein is the everyday business of a legislator. It is also true that campaigns must be run and financed. Money is constantly being solicited on behalf of candidates, who run on platforms and who claim support on the basis of their views and what they intend to do or have done. Whatever ethical considerations and appearances may indicate, to hold that legislators commit the federal crime of extortion when they act for the benefit of constituents or support legislation furthering the interests of some of their constituents, shortly before or after campaign contributions are solicited and received from those beneficiaries, is an unrealistic assessment of what Congress could have meant by making it a crime to obtain property from another, with his consent, "under color of official right." To hold otherwise would open to prosecution not only conduct that has long been thought to be well within the law but also conduct that in a very real sense is unavoidable so long as election campaigns are financed by private contributions or expenditures, as they have been from the beginning of the Nation. . . .
>
> This is not to say that it is impossible for an elected official to commit extortion in the course of financing an election campaign. Political contributions are of course vulnerable if induced by the use of force, violence, or fear. The receipt of such contributions is also vulnerable under the Act as having been taken under color of official right, but only if the payments are made in return for an explicit promise or undertaking by the official to perform or not to perform an official act. In such situations the official asserts that his official conduct will be controlled by the terms of the promise or undertaking. This is the receipt of money by an elected official under color of official right within the meaning of the Hobbs Act.
>
> This formulation defines the forbidden zone of conduct with sufficient clarity. As the Court of Appeals for the Fifth Circuit observed in *United States v. Dozier,* 672 F.2d 531, 537 (1982):
>
> > "A moment's reflection should enable one to distinguish, at least in the abstract, a legitimate solicitation from the exaction of a fee for a benefit conferred or an injury withheld. Whether described familiarly as a payoff or with the Latinate precision of *quid pro quo,* the prohibited exchange is the same: a public official may not demand payment as inducement for the promise to perform (or not to perform) an official act."

500 U.S. 257, 272–273 (1991); *see also* Evans v. United States, 504 U.S. 255 (1992).

65. Burke, note 58 above, at 128.

66. In *Caperton v. A.T. Massey Coal Co.,* 556 U.S. 868 (2009), the Court, per Justice Kennedy, held that large independent expenditures on behalf of a candidate for judicial office could so undermine public confidence in the fairness of the candidate's subsequent judgment as to violate the Due Process Clause. What is particularly striking about the case is that there were no allegations of

contributions to the judge's campaign. Instead the allegation was that someone who was a party to a case that would subsequently be heard by the judge had made *independent expenditures* on behalf of the judge's election. The distinction between contributions and independent expenditures was so immaterial to the potential loss of public confidence in the disinterest of the judge that Justice Kennedy conflated the two terms throughout his opinion. *See* Pamela S. Karlan, *Electing Judges, Judging Elections, and the Lessons of* Caperton, 123 HARV. L. REV. 80, 91 (2009).

67. *See, e.g.,* Citizens Against Rent Control/Coalition for Fair Housing v. Berkeley, 454 U.S. 290, 294–299 (1981) ("Contributions by individuals to support concerted action by a committee advocating a position on a ballot measure is beyond question a very significant form of political expression.").

68. *See, e.g.,* JOHN SAMPLES, THE FALLACY OF CAMPAIGN FINANCE REFORM (2006).

69. McCormick v. United States, 500 U.S. 257, 272–273 (1991).

70. *Citizens United,* 558 U.S. at 359; *see also McConnell,* 540 U.S. at 153 ("[M]ere political favoritism or opportunity for influence alone is insufficient to justify regulation."); Colo. Republican Fed. Campaign Comm. v. FEC, 518 U.S. 604, 646 (1996) (Thomas, J., concurring in part and dissenting in part); *NCPAC,* 470 U.S. at 498 ("The fact that candidates and elected officials may alter or reaffirm their own positions on issues in response to political messages paid for by the PACs can hardly be called corruption, for one of the essential features of democracy is the presentation to the electorate of varying points of view."); Kathleen Sullivan, Comment, *Political Money and Freedom of Speech,* 30 U.C. DAVIS L. REV. 663, 680 (1997) ("Legislators respond disproportionately to the interests of some constituents all the time, depending, for example, on the degree of their organization, the intensity of their interest in particular issues, and their ability to mobilize voters to punish the legislator who does not act in their interest. On one view of democratic representation, therefore, there is nothing wrong with private interest groups seeking to advance their own ends through electoral mobilization and lobbying, and for representatives to respond to these targeted efforts to win election and reelection. It is at least open to question why attempts to achieve the same ends through amassing campaign money are more suspect, at least in the absence of personal inurement.").

71. David Strauss, for example, has famously argued that quid pro quo contributions, as distinct from outright bribes, are not improper at all, since they amount to nothing more than "delivering a certain number of votes." Strauss, note 18 above, at 1373. Our opposition to quid pro quo contributions, Strauss contends, reflects either our deeper opposition to the inequality that quid pro quo contributions facilitate, or our worry that candidates may commit themselves to constituent interest groups and so fail to engage in the "duty" of "deliberation" that should attach to the role of a representative.

72. Perhaps, for example, quid pro quo contributions are improper because they require representatives to make binding promises, and such promises are inconsistent with the duty of a representative fully to participate in the deliberations required by a legislative assembly. *See* Chapter 1, notes 69–76. But this interpretation would rule out all campaign promises and pledges, and it therefore does not seem a plausible account of representation. *See* Brown v. Hartlage, 456 U.S. 45, 55–56 (1982).

Perhaps quid pro quo contributions are corrupt because it is improper for representatives to undertake official action in return for gifts of value. The federal antibribery statute, 18 U.S.C. § 201, prohibits offering or promising "anything of value" to any public official "with intent to influence any official act." This view of corruption would have far-reaching consequences. Money is one form of value, but there are many others. Offers of money do not seem any more intrinsically "coercive" than other forms of valuable support. *See, e.g.,* FEC v. Democratic Senatorial Campaign Comm., 454 U.S. 27, 41 (1981); Richard L. Hasen, *Campaign Finance Laws and the Rupert Murdoch Problem,* 77 TEX. L. REV. 1627, 1665 n.80 (1999); Ofer Raban, *Constitutionalizing Corruption:* Citizens United, *Its Conceptions of Political Corruption and the Implications for Judicial Election Campaigns,* 46 U.S.F. L. REV. 359 (2011); United States v. Girard, 601 F.2d 69, 71 (2d Cir. 1979). Does it follow that a candidate who promises to vote for legislation in return for valuable contributions like volunteer labor or a newspaper endorsement should be condemned for "improper commitments"? Does it follow that a candidate who pledges to support his party's platform in return for his party's active support is guilty of corruption? On the whole, this is not the way that quid pro quo corruption has been conceptualized or policed. Daniel Hays Lowenstein, *Political Bribery and the Intermediate Theory of Politics,* 32 UCLA L. REV. 784 (1985).

Perhaps quid pro quo contributions are corrupt only because they promise official action in return for support that is not otherwise constitutionally valuable. It may be valuable to our constitutional system for persons to write editorials and to canvass for voters, or for parties actively to participate in campaigns, so that official promises to act in return for these forms of support serve democratic ends and should not be condemned as corrupt. But why would we regard giving financial support to candidates as an activity that we wish to discourage or that is not otherwise valuable? We regard charitable contributions as quite valuable. Why are political contributions not analogous?

It may be that a candidate's promise to take official action in return for valuable support is corrupt because it commits the candidate to act on behalf of only some constituents, rather than on behalf of all constituents. *See, e.g.,* Ariz. Free Enter. Club's Freedom Club PAC v. Bennett, 131 S. Ct. 2806, 2830 (2011) (Kagan, J., dissenting). The Court has sometimes spoken of the obligation of elected officials to represent "their constituency as a whole." In the context of reapportionment plans, for example, the Court has struck down districts that appear to be drawn to provide representation of a particular racial group: "When a district obviously is created solely to effectuate the perceived common interests of one racial group, elected officials are more likely to believe that their primary obligation is to represent only the members of that group, rather than their constituency as a whole. This is altogether antithetical to our system of representative democracy." Shaw v. Reno, 509 U.S. 630, 648 (1993).

Yet American candidates routinely pledge to act at the behest of some of their constituents rather than all their constituents. Constituencies are commonly divided. If a candidate runs on a controversial platform to battle public employee unions, for example, it is not inconsistent with the role of an elected representative to speak for those constituents who oppose public employee unions, rather than for the "constituency as a whole." Candidates frequently pledge to act in support of those constituents who offer them valuable support, as for example members of their own party.

Quid pro quo contributions might be improper because they require a candidate to pledge to act in response to the wishes of a smaller number of constituents than would be required to win an election. There is no opprobrium attached to a candidate who pledges to act in a certain way, and who on the basis of that pledge attracts enough votes to gain election. Does it follow that there would be no objection to a candidate who receives quid pro quo contributions from an organization that represents 51 percent of her constituents? Does it equally follow that a representative who stubbornly pledges to act on behalf of the views of a minority of her constituents is guilty of improper behavior?

These potentially distinct interpretations are illuminated by the actual practices of justification in modern American political life. Consider how a candidate would be judged if he were to make the following statements in the press (these examples are inspired by the work of Daniel Lowenstein, see Lowenstein, note 58 above):

1. "I am voting for Statute X because if I do, I shall receive a large campaign donation."
2. "I am voting for Statute X because if I do, labor unions shall donate labor to my reelection campaign."
3. "I am voting for Statute X because if I do, the *New York Times* will endorse my candidacy."
4. "I am voting for Statute X because if I do, I shall be reelected."
5. "I am voting for Statute X because if I do, a majority of my constituents shall donate substantial campaign contributions."
6. "I am voting for Statute X because it is in the public good."
7. "I am voting for Statute X because my constituents want it."
8. "I am voting for Statute X because my party supports it."

My intuition is that it would be acceptable for a candidate to affirm propositions 6 through 8, but that a candidate who openly avows propositions 1 through 5 would suffer severe public opprobrium. This may be because statements 1 through 5 have in common the idea that a candidate will take official action merely because of a personal desire to obtain (or retain) official power. By contrast, a candidate may take official action because it is in the public good (statement 6), or because it is desired by her constituents (statement 7), or because those with whom he is politically affiliated believe that it serves the public good (statement 8).

One can perhaps generalize from these intuitions that although political representatives in the United States can choose to be delegates, trustees, or even party flunkies, they cannot choose to undertake official action *for the mere purpose of retaining or obtaining political power.* Such a purpose corrupts fundamental republican principles. *See* Jack M. Balkin, Living Originalism 244–245 (2011); Teachout, note 58 above, at 374 ("The Framers believed that an individual is corrupt if he uses his public office primarily to serve his own ends. . . . If corruption—writ large—is the rotting of positive ideals of civic virtue and public integrity, political corruption is a particular kind of conscious or reckless abuse of the position of trust. While political virtue is pursuing the public good in public life, political corruption is using public life for private gain. . . . A corrupt public actor will not only consider the good in public life for himself, he will make it is his goal and daily habit to pursue it. The public good does not motivate him.").

Perhaps Americans agree that quid pro quo contributions are corrupt because such contributions so manifestly evidence the improper purpose of seeking to obtain or retain power. If so, the subjectively unethical motivations of representatives would provide a slippery foundation on which to institutionalize any general account of corruption.

73. *See* Thompson, note 58 above, at 1040–1046.

74. *McConnell v. FEC,* 540 U.S. 93, 153 (2003), *overruled in part on other grounds by Citizens United,* 558 U.S. 310; *see* FEC v. Beaumont, 539 U.S. 146, 155–156 (2003); Heather Gerken, *Lobbying as the New Campaign Finance,* 27 Ga. St. U. L. Rev. 1155, 1158 (2011).

75. *McConnell,* 540 U.S. at 154.

76. *See* note 64 above.

77. I agree, however, that it is improper for a representative to accept contributions merely for the purpose of obtaining or retaining power. *See* note 72 above.

78. Empirical studies purport to find that campaign donations are unlikely to influence policy outcomes. *See* Steven Ansolabehere, John M. de Figueiredo & James M. Snyder, Jr., *Why Is There So Little Money in U.S. Politics?,* J. Econ. Persp., Winter 2003, 105, 110–117. Yet they also conclude that such donations

can have "under the radar screen" effects. *See* John M. de Figueiredo & Elizabeth Gilbert, *Paying for Politics*, 78 S. CAL. L. REV. 591 (2005) ("What does money buy? It likely buys access, small favors, energy in casework, intercession with regulators, and a place on the legislative agenda.").

79. *See, e.g.*, Martin Gilens, *Under the Influence*, BOS. REV., July 1, 2012, http://bostonreview.net/forum/lead-essay-under-influence-martin-gilens.

80. *Citizens United*, 558 U.S. at 359; *see also* McConnell v. FEC, 540 U.S. 93, 297 (2003) (Kennedy, J., concurring in part and dissenting in part). This same disagreement is also visible in the context of controversies about the "appearance of corruption." *Compare McConnell*, 540 U.S. at 297–298 (Kennedy, J., concurring in part and dissenting in part), *with* ibid., 153–154 (majority opinion of Stevens & O'Connor, JJ.).

81. *Citizens United*, 558 U.S. at 356–361.

82. 2 THE RECORDS OF THE FEDERAL CONVENTION OF 1787, at 381 (Max Farrand ed., 1966) (quoting Nathaniel Gorham).

83. HABERMAS, note 51 above, at 299. Among political theorists there has recently been a renewed appreciation of this fusion between the republican and democratic traditions. *See, e.g.*, URBINATI, note 53; Disch, note 53; Garsten, note 53; Bernard Manin, Elly Stein & Jane Mansbridge, *On Legitimacy and Political Deliberation*, 15 POL. THEORY 338, 352 (1987); David Plotke, *Representation Is Democracy*, 4 CONSTELLATIONS 19 (1997); Nadia Urbinati, *Continuity and Rupture: The Power of Judgment in Democratic Representation*, 12 CONSTELLATIONS 194 (2005); Nadia Urbinati & Mark E. Warren, *The Concept of Representation in Contemporary Democratic Theory*, 11 ANN. REV. POL. SCI. 387 (2008). In essence, this work affirms that representative government generates democratic legitimacy by provoking an endless public conversation about who truly represents the people. So, far from settling political controversies, elections keep "the political contestation going." Näsström, note 53 above, at 334. Of course any such account of representation would be incomplete without a specification of the communicative rights that define legitimate "political contestation."

84. *See* note 53 above. Nadia Urbinati argues that representation is structurally important precisely *because* it keeps the identity of the people occluded, so that there can be no unilateral Schmittian acclamation. "A political representative is unique *not* because he substitutes for the sovereign in passing laws, but precisely because he *is not* a substitute for an absent sovereign (the part replacing the whole) since he needs to be constantly recreated and dynamically linked to society in order to pass laws." URBINATI, note 53 above, at 20. On this account, representation merges with discursive democracy insofar as it must focus attention on the communicative structures necessary to maintain representation, and insofar as it must rule out the possibility of a fully present people overriding the communicative framework that facilitates the legitimate formation of public opinion.

85. *See* HANNA FENICHEL PITKIN, THE CONCEPT OF REPRESENTATION 224, 234 (1967) ("The representative system must look after the public interest and be responsive to public opinion, except insofar as non-responsiveness can be justified in terms of the public interest. . . . Our concern with elections and electoral machinery, and particularly with whether elections are free and genuine, results from our conviction that such machinery is necessary to ensure systematic responsiveness. . . . We require functioning institutions that are designed to, and really do, secure a government responsive to public interest and opinion.").

86. For an analogous idea, formulated in terms of the "self-government rationale," see Richard H. Pildes, *Foreword: The Constitutionalization of Democratic Politics,* 118 HARV. L. REV. 29, 149–150 (2004). *See also* Samuel Issacharoff, *On Political Corruption,* 124 HARV. L. REV. 118, 127–129 (2010) (emphasizing the dangers of "clientelism").

87. In his academic writing, Justice Breyer has advanced a closely analogous idea:

> The [First] Amendment in context also forms a necessary part of a constitutional system designed to sustain that democratic self-government. The Amendment helps to sustain the democratic process both by encouraging the exchange of ideas needed to make sound electoral decisions and by encouraging an exchange of views among ordinary citizens necessary to their informed participation in the electoral process. It thereby helps to maintain a form of government open to participation (in Constant's words, by "all the citizens, without exception"). The relevance of this conceptual view lies in the fact that the campaign finance laws also seek to further the latter objective. They hope to democratize the influence that money can bring to bear upon the electoral process, thereby building public confidence in that process, broadening the base of a candidate's meaningful financial support, and encouraging greater public participation. They consequently seek to maintain the integrity of the political process—a process that itself translates political speech into governmental action. Seen in this way, campaign finance laws, despite the limits they impose, help to further the kind of open public political discussion that the First Amendment also seeks to encourage, not simply as an end, but also as a means to achieve a workable democracy.

Stephen Breyer, *Our Democratic Constitution,* 77 N.Y.U. L. REV. 245, 252–253 (2002).

88. Jack Dennis & Diana Owen, *Popular Satisfaction with the Party System and Representative Democracy in the United States,* 22 INT'L POL. SCI. REV. 399, 401 (2001) ("In a fully operative democracy, people are likely to have developed the firm expectation that they have the right to be heard, and that officials should be responsible to their needs and take action. If people have come to feel that their own needs, wants, interests, concerns, values, or demands are not being effectively represented in the policy process, then no matter how felicitous

the nature of system outputs is perceived to be, popular resentment likely will result.").

89. *Brown*, 456 U.S. at 52; *see* Knox v. Serv. Emps. Int'l Union, Local 1000, 132 S. Ct. 2277, 2288 (2012); Nev. Comm'n on Ethics v. Carrigan, 131 S. Ct. 2343, 2353 (2011) (Kennedy, J., concurring); Cal. Democratic Party v. Jones, 530 U.S. 567, 574 (2000); *Buckley*, 424 U.S. at 26–27. Although Zelphaniah Swift had in 1795 excoriated the term "representative democracy" as a "contradiction in terms," 1 Zephaniah Swift, A System of the Laws of the State of Connecticut 21 (1795), the term has been used since the founding of the Republic. *See, e.g.,* Joel Barlow, Letters from Paris, to the Citizens of the United States 51–52 (1800); St. George Tucker, 1 Blackstone's Commentaries 297 (1803); James Fenimore Cooper, The American Democrat: Hints on the Social and Civic Relations of the United States of America 104–105 (1838); Benjamin Franklin Butler, Representative Democracy in the United States: An Address Delivered Before the Senate of Union College (C. Van Benthuysen ed., 1841). The United States Supreme Court did not begin to use the term until the First Amendment era, and then typically to emphasize the important relationship between elected representatives and public opinion. *See, e.g.,* E.R.R. Presidents Conference v. Noerr Motor Freight, Inc., 365 U.S. 127, 137 (1961); Thomas v. Collins, 323 U.S. 516, 546 (1945) (Jackson, J., concurring).

90. Pitkin, note 85 above, at 221.

91. Ibid.

92. *Buckley,* 424 U.S. at 27.

93. Ibid.

94. *See, e.g.,* 147 Cong. Rec. 13,083 (July 12, 2001) (statement of Rep. Rosa DeLauro) ("Mr. Speaker, the time has come to pass meaningful campaign finance reform. . . . [T]he bipartisan Shays-Meehan Campaign Reform Act will . . . help us to restore the integrity to our political system. It will help us today to restore the confidence that the American public needs to have in people who serve in public life, restore their confidence in our government that, in fact, we can act on behalf of the interests of the people that we represent and not the interests of the moneyed interests in this country."); *Campaign Finance Reform: Hearing Before the H. Comm. on H. Admin.,* 107 Cong. 3 (2002) (statement of Rep. Steny Hoyer) ("Last November's election revealed a sharp and disturbing rise in the unregulated issue adds by third-party groups which most of us would agree are essentially campaign adds; a doubling of soft money contributions to political parties compared to the 1996 elections; and one of the lowest voter turnouts in a Presidential election in more than 50 years, due in large part perhaps to the public's growing cynicism about the influence of money in our political system.").

95. A. Lawrence Lowell, Public Opinion and Popular Government 138 (1914).

96. 148 Cong. Rec. 1709 (2002) (statement of Rep. Rodney Freylinghuysen) ("This issue is not about winning elections, it can't be. It is about restoring the public's faith and confidence in what we do. . . . It is about cleaning up a flawed system, where whether true or not, the perception is we are all bought and sold."). The argument was effectively made to the Court in *McConnell v. FEC*, 540 U.S. 93 (2003), *overruled in part on other grounds by Citizens United,* 558 U.S. 310, although it was couched in the misleading language of corruption. *See, e.g.,* Brief for Intervenor-Defendants Senator John McCain et al. at 11, *McConnell,* 540 U.S. 93 (No. 02–1674), 2003 WL 21999280, at *11 ("Since the Tillman Act of 1907, which prohibited corporate campaign contributions, Congress has endeavored to prevent the corruption and appearance of corruption of federal elected officials by reducing their dependence on large campaign contributions. Congress's concerns, as relevant now as they were in the time of Theodore Roosevelt, are that public officials will be particularly attentive to the interests of those who make large contributions to candidates and their political parties, and that citizens will perceive such official responsiveness to large donors as characteristic of a degraded system that does not deserve public confidence.").

97. 528 U.S. 377, 390 (2000); *see* Richard L. Hasen, *Buckley Is Dead, Long Live Buckley: The New Campaign Finance Incoherence of* McConnell v. Federal Election Commission, 153 U. Pa. L. Rev. 31, 42–47 (2004). Justice Souter has been alert to the issue of electoral integrity, although frequently he blends it with concerns about corruption and distortion. In his dissent in *FEC v. Wisconsin Right to Life, Inc.,* for example, he writes:

> Campaign finance reform has been a series of reactions to documented threats to electoral integrity obvious to any voter, posed by large sums of money from corporate or union treasuries, with no redolence of "grassroots" about them. Neither Congress's decisions nor our own have understood the corrupting influence of money in politics as being limited to outright bribery or discrete *quid pro quo;* campaign finance reform has instead consistently focused on the more pervasive distortion of electoral institutions by concentrated wealth, on the special access and guaranteed favor that sap the representative integrity of American government and defy public confidence in its institutions. From early in the 20th century through the decision in *McConnell,* we have acknowledged that the value of democratic integrity justifies a realistic response when corporations and labor organizations commit the concentrated moneys in their treasuries to electioneering.

551 U.S. at 522 (Souter, J., dissenting); *see also Buckley v. Valeo,* 424 U.S. 1, 265 (1976) (White, J., concurring in part and dissenting in part).

98. *Citizens United,* 558 U.S. at 360 (citation omitted) (some internal quotation marks omitted) (quoting *McConnell,* 540 U.S. at 144).

99. *See* Speechnow.org v. FEC, 599 F.3d 686, 694 (D.C. Cir. 2010) (interpreting *Citizens United* as holding "as a matter of law that independent expenditures do not corrupt or create the appearance of *quid pro quo* corruption," so that "contributions to groups that make only independent expenditures also cannot corrupt or create the appearance of corruption"), *cert. denied sub nom.* Keating v. FEC, 131 S. Ct. 553 (2010) (mem.).

100. W. Tradition P'ship v. Att'y Gen., 363 Mont. 220, 236 (2011).

101. Jeff Wiltse, *The Origins of Montana's Corrupt Practices Act: A More Complete History,* 73 Mont. L. Rev. 299, 318–319 (2012).

102. Am. Tradition P'ship, Inc., v. Bullock, 132 S. Ct. 2490 (2012).

103. A 2010 ANES study revealed a 21-percentage-point increase in the number of citizens who said that the government is "pretty much run by a few big interests" (from 48 percent in 2002 to 69 percent in 2008). *Is Government Run for the Benefit of All 1964–2008,* Am. Nat'l Elections Stud. (Aug. 5, 2010), http://www.electionstudies.org/nesguide/toptable/tab5a_2.htm. The poll showed a similar 21-percentage-point rise in the number of people who felt that "quite a few" of the people running the government are "crooked" (from 30 percent in 2002 to 51 percent in 2008). *Are Government Officials Crooked 1958–2008,* Am. Nat'l Elections Stud. (Aug. 5, 2010), *available at* http://www.electionstudies.org/nesguide/toptable/tab5a_4.htm. Gallup polls indicate that dissatisfaction with Congress reached a record high in 2011, with 69 percent of respondents indicating that they had "not very much" or no "trust and confidence" in Congress and almost two-thirds of people indicating that a majority of Congress did not deserve to be reelected. *Trust in Government,* Gallup (last visited Feb. 3, 2013), *available at* http://www.gallup.com/poll/5392/trust-government.aspx. A majority of respondents (53 percent) had "not very much" or no "trust and confidence" in the men and women "who either hold or are running for elective office." Ibid.

104. William P. Marshall, *The Constitutionality of Campaign Finance Regulation: Should Differences in a State's Political History and Culture Matter?,* 74 Mont. L. Rev. 79 (2013).

105. *See* Jeffrey Toobin, *Annals of the Law: Money Unlimited: The Chief Justice and* Citizens United, New Yorker, May 21, 2012, at 40.

106. Ibid., 40–41. On reargument of the case, then solicitor general Elena Kagan sought to contain the damage by avowing that Congress could not in fact prohibit a corporation from using funds to publish a book of express advocacy. Ibid., 44. Although firm in this conclusion, General Kagan was less clear about why Congress might be prohibited from banning books, and indeed in her argument she may have conceded that Congress could prohibit corporations from publishing pamphlets:

> *JUSTICE GINSBURG:* May I ask you one question that was highlighted in the prior argument, and that was if Congress could say no TV and radio ads, could it also

say no newspaper ads, no campaign biographies? Last time the answer was, yes, Congress could, but it didn't. Is that—is that still the government's answer?

GENERAL KAGAN: The government's answer has changed, Justice Ginsburg.

(Laughter.)

GENERAL KAGAN: It is still true that BCRA 203, which is the only statute involved in this case, does not apply to books or anything other than broadcast; 441b does, on its face, apply to other media. And we took what the Court—what the Court's—the Court's own reaction to some of those other hypotheticals very seriously. We went back, we considered the matter carefully, and the government's view is that although 441b does cover full-length books, that there would be quite good as-applied challenge to any attempt to apply 441b in that context.

And I should say that the FEC has never applied 441b in that context. So for 60 years a book has never been at issue. . . .

CHIEF JUSTICE ROBERTS: But we don't put our—we don't put our First Amendment rights in the hands of FEC bureaucrats; and if you say that you are not going to apply it to a book, what about a pamphlet?

GENERAL KAGAN: I think a—a pamphlet would be different. A pamphlet is pretty classic electioneering, so there is no attempt to say that 441b only applies to video and not to print. It does—

JUSTICE ALITO: Well, what if the particular—what if the particular movie involved here had not been distributed by Video on Demand? Suppose that people could view it for free on Netflix over the internet? Suppose that free DVDs were passed out. Suppose people could attend the movie for free in a movie theater; suppose the exact text of this was distributed in a printed form. In light of your retraction, I have no idea where the government would draw the line with respect to the medium that could be prohibited.

GENERAL KAGAN: Well, none of those things, again, are covered.

JUSTICE ALITO: No, but could they? Which of them could and which could not? I understand you to say books could not.

GENERAL KAGAN: Yes, I think what you—what we're saying is that there has never been an enforcement action for books. Nobody has ever suggested—nobody in Congress, nobody in the administrative apparatus has ever suggested that books pose any kind of corruption problem, so I think that there would be a good as-applied challenge with respect to that.

JUSTICE SCALIA: So you're—you are a lawyer advising somebody who is about to come out with a book and you say don't worry, the FEC has never tried to send somebody to prison for this. This statute covers it, but don't worry, the FEC has never done it. Is that going to comfort your client? I don't think so. . . .

Transcript of Oral Argument at 64–67 (reargued Sept. 9, 2009), *Citizens United*, 558 U.S. 310 (2009) (No. 08-205), *available at* http://www.supremecourt.gov/oral_arguments/argument_transcripts/08-205[Reargued].pdf.

107. *See Citizens United*, 558 U.S. at 349.

108. *See* note 72 above.

109. *See* note 106 above.

110. *Citizens United,* 558 U.S. at 340–341 (citations omitted).

111. *See* Robert Post, *Informed Consent to Abortion: A First Amendment Analysis of Compelled Physician Speech,* 2007 U. ILL. L. REV. 939.

112. *See* ROBERT POST, DEMOCRACY, EXPERTISE, ACADEMIC FREEDOM: A FIRST AMENDMENT JURISPRUDENCE FOR THE MODERN STATE (2012).

113. *Citizens United,* 558 U.S. at 340–341.

114. Viewpoint discrimination is in fact quite routine outside of public discourse. *See* Robert Post, *Between Governance and Management: The History and Theory of the Public Forum,* 34 UCLA L. REV. 1713, 1824–1829 (1987); Robert Post, *Viewpoint Discrimination and Commercial Speech,* 41 LOY. L.A. L. REV. 169 (2007).

115. *See* Martin Redish & Peter B. Siegal, *Constitutional Adjudication, Free Expression, and the Fashionable Art of Corporation Bashing,* 91 TEX. L. REV. 1447 (2013).

116. Rumsfeld v. Forum for Academic & Institutional Rights, Inc., 547 U.S. 47, 68 (2006) (citations omitted).

117. N.Y. State Club Ass'n, Inc. v. City of N.Y., 487 U.S. 1, 13 (1988).

118. Bd. of Dirs. of Rotary Int'l v. Rotary Club of Duarte, 481 U.S. 537, 544 (1987). First Amendment rights of freedom of association are thus distinct from due process rights of association. The latter protect "choices to enter into and maintain certain intimate human relationships . . . against undue intrusion by the State because of the role of such relationships in safeguarding the individual freedom that is central to our constitutional scheme." Roberts v. U.S. Jaycees, 468 U.S. 609, 617–618 (1984). These forms of intimate association receive "protection as a fundamental element of personal liberty." Ibid., 618.

119. NAACP v. Alabama ex rel. Patterson, 357 U.S. 449, 458–460 (1958).

120. Boy Scouts of Am. v. Dale, 530 U.S. 640, 647–648 (2000); *N.Y. State Club Ass'n,* 487 U.S. at 13.

121. 479 U.S. 238 (1986).

122. Wash. State Grange v. Wash. State Republican Party, 552 U.S. 442, 467 (2008) (Scalia, J., dissenting); *see* FCC v. Beaumont, 539 U.S. 146, 162 (2003).

123. *See also Boy Scouts,* 530 U.S. 640.

124. 435 U.S. 765 (1978).

125. Ibid., 775–776.

126. Ibid., 775. Alexander Meiklejohn famously viewed democracy as a process of "the voting of wise decisions." ALEXANDER MEIKLEJOHN, POLITICAL FREEDOM: THE CONSTITUTIONAL POWERS OF THE PEOPLE 26 (1965).

127. *Bellotti,* 435 U.S. at 777.

128. On the distinction between original and derivative rights, see MEIR DAN-COHEN, RIGHTS, PERSONS, AND ORGANIZATIONS: A LEGAL THEORY FOR BUREAUCRATIC SOCIETY (1986). The Court in *Citizens United* is quite blurry about the nature of the First Amendment rights possessed by commercial corpora-

tions. Like *Bellotti,* however, the Court in *Citizens United* states that "it is inherent in the nature of the political process that voters must be free to obtain information from diverse sources in order to determine how to cast their votes." 558 U.S. at 341. For a thoughtful analysis of institutional speech rights, see Randall P. Bezanson, *Institutional Speech,* 80 IOWA L. REV. 735 (1995).

129. *See, e.g.,* Riley v. Nat'l Fed'n of the Blind of N.C., Inc., 487 U.S. 781, 796–797 (1988).

130. Wooley v. Maynard, 430 U.S. 705, 714 (1977).

131. To compel a person to speak in public discourse is to alter that person's subjective experience of public discourse in a manner that may render participation in public discourse less meaningful.

132. *Citizens United,* 558 U.S. at 343.

133. NAACP v. Button, 371 U.S. 415, 433 (1963).

134. Whitney v. California, 274 U.S. 357, 375 (1927) (Brandeis, J., concurring).

135. *Citizens United,* 558 U.S. at 340–341.

136. Gilbert v. Minnesota, 254 U.S. 325, 338 (1920) (Brandeis, J., dissenting).

137. *See, e.g.,* Tom Bennigson, Nike *Revisited: Can Commercial Corporations Engage in Non-Commercial Speech?,* 39 CONN. L. REV. 379, 413 (2006); Thomas W. Joo, *Corporate Governance and the Constitutionality of Campaign Finance Reform,* 1 ELECTION L.J. 361, 370–371 (2002).

138. *See* Cent. Hudson Gas & Elec. Corp. v. Pub. Serv. Comm'n, 447 U.S. 557 (1980). For a discussion, see Robert Post, *The Constitutional Status of Commercial Speech,* 48 UCLA L. REV. 1 (2000).

139. United States v. Alvarez, 132 S. Ct. 2537 (2012).

140. *See* Edenfield v. Fane, 507 U.S. 761, 768 (1993) (quoting *Va. State Bd. of Pharmacy,* 425 U.S. at 771–772); Post, note 138 above.

141. David Shelledy, *Autonomy, Debate, and Corporate Speech,* 18 HASTINGS CONST. L.Q. 541, 576 (1991).

142. The acronym stands for Political Action Committees. To speak more precisely, the statute permits corporations to make independent expenditures for express advocacy or electioneering communications from separate segregated funds (SSFs), which are especially created for this purpose by corporations and which are supported by donations from stockholders and employees of the corporation. SSFs are a distinct kind of PAC.

143. *Citizens United,* 558 U.S. at 337, 339 (citation omitted).

144. Ibid., 329, 333–334, 357.

145. 1 BRUCE ACKERMAN, WE THE PEOPLE: FOUNDATIONS 230–265 (1991).

146. *See* Va. Pharmacy Bd. v. Va. Consumer Council, 425 U.S. 748, 772 n.24 (1976); Post, note 138 above. *Compare* In re Primus, 436 U.S. 412 (1978), *with* Ohralik v. Ohio State Bar Ass'n., 436 U.S. 447 (1978); *see also* Bates v. State Bar of Ariz., 433 U.S. 350, 380 (1977).

147. By allowing PACs, BCRA essentially empowers persons connected to the corporation to use the organizational structure of the corporation to create their own expressive association. Because nothing would prohibit such persons from creating their own expressive association outside the context of the corporation, BCRA is actually speech promoting from the perspective of persons connected to the corporation.

148. MEIKLEJOHN, note 126 above, at 6.

149. Ibid.

150. Ibid., 24.

151. Ibid., 26.

152. Ibid.; *see* Owen Fiss, *Money and Politics,* 97 COLUM. L. REV. 2470 (1997).

153. 395 U.S. 367 (1969).

154. Ibid., 388–389.

155. Ibid., 390.

156. Ibid., 389. As the broadcasting industry matured, and as scarcity diminished, the Court came gradually to regard broadcasters more as speakers in their own right than as fiduciaries for the general public. The constitutional law of broadcasting evolved accordingly. *See* Robert Post, *Subsidized Speech,* 106 YALE L.J. 151, 158–161 (1996).

157. *Red Lion,* 395 U.S. at 390.

158. Ibid.

159. Ibid., 392.

160. WALTER LIPPMANN, PUBLIC OPINION 44–46, 244 (1922).

161. He came close to this position three years later in WALTER LIPPMANN, THE PHANTOM PUBLIC (1925), which expressed a strong inclination to entrust government to qualified experts. *See* EDWARD A. PURCELL, JR., THE CRISIS OF DEMOCRATIC THEORY: SCIENTIFIC NATURALISM AND THE PROBLEM OF VALUE 105–107 (1973).

162. LIPPMANN note 160 above, at 402.

163. Ibid. For a modern version of this solution, see BRUCE ACKERMAN & JAMES S. FISHKIN, DELIBERATION DAY (2004).

164. Harper v. Canada, 2004 SCCC 33, § 72. The British House of Lords has come to a very similar conclusion:

> The fundamental rationale of the democratic process is that if competing views, opinions and policies are publicly debated and exposed to public scrutiny the good will over time drive out the bad and the true prevail over the false. It must be assumed that, given time, the public will make a sound choice when, in the course of the democratic process, it has the right to choose. But it is highly desirable that the playing field of debate should be so far as practicable level. This is achieved where, in public discussion, differing views are expressed, contradicted, answered and debated.

It is the duty of broadcasters to achieve this object in an impartial way by presenting balanced programmes in which all lawful views may be ventilated. It is not achieved if political parties can, in proportion to their resources, buy unlimited opportunities to advertise in the most effective media, so that elections become little more than an auction. Nor is it achieved if well-endowed interests which are not political parties are able to use the power of the purse to give enhanced prominence to views which may be true or false, attractive to progressive minds or unattractive, beneficial or injurious. The risk is that objects which are essentially political may come to be accepted by the public not because they are shown in public debate to be right but because, by dint of constant repetition, the public has been conditioned to accept them.

On the Application of Animal Defenders International v. Secretary of State for Culture, Media and Sport, [2008] H.R.L.R. 25 (Mar. 12, 2008), at ¶ 28 (Opinion of Lord Bingham of Cornhill).

165. For a discussion of the difference between Meiklejohnian principles and public discourse, see Robert Post, *Meiklejohn's Mistake: Individual Autonomy and the Reform of Public Discourse,* 64 U. Colo. L. Rev. 1109 (1993); and Robert Post, *Reconciling Theory and Doctrine in First Amendment Jurisprudence,* 88 Calif. L. Rev. 2353, 2369–2374 (2000).

166. *Citizens United,* 558 U.S. at 341.

167. The theory of speech rights within government organizations is discussed in Robert Post, *Between Governance and Management: The History and Theory of the Public Forum,* 34 UCLA L. Rev. 1713 (1987).

168. *Shrink,* 528 U.S. at 401 (Breyer, J., concurring).

169. *See* Louis Massicotte, André Blais & Anotine Yoshinaka, Establishing the Rules of the Game: Election Laws in Democracies (2004); Pildes, note 86 above, at 50–52.

170. Pildes, note 86 above, at 51–52.

171. Burdick v. Takushi, 504 U.S. 428, 433 (1992); Buckley v. Am. Constitutional Law Found., 525 U.S. 182, 191 (1999) ("States allowing ballot initiatives have considerable leeway to protect the integrity and reliability of the initiative process, as they have with respect to the election process generally."); Anderson v. Celebrezze, 460 U.S. 780, 787 n.9 (1982) ("We have upheld generally-applicable and evenhanded restrictions that protect the integrity and reliability of the electoral process itself.").

172. Purcell v. Gonzalez, 549 U.S. 1, 4 (2006) (quoting Eu v. S.F. Cnty. Democratic Cent. Comm., 489 U.S. 214, 231 (1989)).

173. Clingman v. Beaver, 544 U.S. 581, 593 (2005).

174. Burson v. Freeman, 504 U.S. 191, 200–205 (1992). As Elihu Root recalled in 1916:

I have seen a file of men marched out of a tramp lodging house with their ballots held aloft in one hand continuously in plain sight until they had deposited them in the ballot box, in order to give the necessary evidence that they were voting according to the contract under which they were immediately thereafter to be paid. Now . . . [t]he ballot is furnished by the state; the method of voting upon the Australian ballot in all its forms, by marking it in secret, makes bribery uncertain and unprofitable, because it is impossible to tell how any one votes, and the man who would take money for his vote cannot be depended upon to vote as he has agreed. . . . The change from dishonest and unfair elections to honest and fair elections is fundamental to the successful working of popular government. . . .

Elihu Root, Addresses on Government and Citizenship 69 (Robert Bacon & James Brown Scott eds., 1916).

175. F.N. Judson, *The Future of Representative Government,* 2 Am. Pol. Sci. Rev. 185, 197 (1908).

176. *Compare* Grovey v. Townsend, 295 U.S. 45 (1935), *with* Smith v. Allwright, 321 U.S. 649 (1944) *and* Terry v. Adams, 345 U.S. 461 (1953). The story is told in Michael J. Klarman, *The White Primary Rulings: A Case Study in the Consequences of Supreme Court Decisionmaking,* 29 Fla. St. U. L. Rev. 55 (2001).

177. Timmons v. Twin City Area New Party, 520 U.S. 351, 369 (1997).

178. *See, e.g.,* Robert Brett Dunham, *Defoliating the Grassroots: Election Day Restrictions on Political Speech,* 77 Geo. L. J. 2138 (1989).

179. W.R. Scott, Organizations: Rational, Natural, and Open Systems 180 (1981); *see* John Freeman, *The Unit of Analysis in Organizational Research, in* Environments and Organizations 336–338 (Marshall W. Meyer et al. eds., 1978).

180. Fremont E. Kast & James E. Rosenzweig, *General Systems Theory: Applications for Organization and Management,* 15 Acad. Mgmt. J. 447, 450 (1972).

181. Jeffrey Pfeffer & Gerald R. Salancik, The External Control of Organizations: A Resource Dependence Perspective 113 (1978); *see* James D. Thompson, Organizations in Action: Social Science Bases of Administrative Theory 39–44 (1967); *see also* Oliver E. Williamson, Markets and Hierarchies: Analysis and Antitrust Implications (1975).

182. San Diego v. Roe, 543 U.S. 77, 84 (2004).

183. U.S. Postal Serv. v. Council of Greenburgh Civic Ass'ns, 453 U.S. 114, 128–129 (1981).

184. Ibid., 126.

185. Ibid., 133.

186. Doninger v. Niehoff, 527 F.3d 41 (2d Cir. 2008); *see* Kowalski v. Berkeley Cnty. Sch., 652 F.3d 565 (4th Cir. 2011). Courts have even expanded the managerial domain of schools to include the parents of students. *See* Blasi v. Pen Argyl Area Sch. Dist., No. 11–3982, 512 Fed. Appx. 173 (Table), 2013 WL 343175 (3d Cir. Jan. 30, 2013).

187. For a discussion of this distinction, as well as of how the Court sets the boundaries of government institutions, see Post, note 167.

188. Allen Thorndike Rice, *Recent Reforms in Balloting,* 143 N. Am. Rev. 628, 631 (1886).

189. *See* Peter H. Argersinger, Structure, Process, and Party: Essays in American Political History 59 (1992) ("The adoption of the Australian ballot necessarily transformed state and local parties from private organizations into public agencies, and a corollary of its official recognition of parties on the ballot was state involvement in their nomination process.").

190. Bluman v. FEC, 800 F. Supp. 2d 281 (D.D.C. 2011), *aff'd mem.,* 132 S. Ct. 1087 (2012). The statute at issue in *Bluman* did not prohibit foreign nationals from engaging in "issue advocacy" or "speech that does not expressly advocate the election or defeat of a specific candidate." Ibid., 284.

191. Ibid., 288.

192. The court explained:

Political contributions and express-advocacy expenditures are an integral aspect of the process by which Americans elect officials to federal, state, and local government offices. Political contributions and express-advocacy expenditures finance advertisements, get-out-the-vote drives, rallies, candidate speeches, and the myriad other activities by which candidates appeal to potential voters. . . . We think it evident that those campaign activities are part of the overall process of democratic self-government. Moreover, it is undisputed that the government may bar foreign citizens from voting and serving as elected officers. . . . It follows that the government may bar foreign citizens (at least those who are not lawful permanent residents of the United States) from participating in the campaign process that seeks to influence how voters will cast their ballots in the elections. Those limitations on the activities of foreign citizens are of a piece and are all "part of the sovereign's obligation to preserve the basic conception of a political community."

Ibid.

193. As explained in the footnote that precedes section VII of this chapter, there may be considerable tension between these two goals. In *Blumen* the Court unambiguously held that the goal of electoral integrity trumps the goal of informed public decision making.

194. *See* note 147 above. Recent work suggests that because commercial corporations prefer to influence politics by lobbying rather than by determining which candidate is elected, *Citizens United* may not affect overall corporate independent expenditures on elections. *See* Samuel Issacharoff & Jeremy Peterman, *Special Interests After* Citizens United: *Access, Replacement, and Interest Group Response to Legal Change,* 9 Ann. Rev. L. & Soc. Sci. (Feb. 21, 2013), *available at* http://papers.ssrn.com/sol3/papers.cfm?abstract_id=2222063. Of course this work raises the question of whether the protection of electoral integrity might also require regulatory approaches to lobbying. *See* Gerken, note 74.

195. Crawford v. Marion Cnty. Election Bd., 553 U.S. 181, 197 (2008) (opinion of Stevens, J.).

196. First Amendment rights that protect public discourse have this same structure.

197. Reynolds v. Sims, 377 U.S. 533, 565 (1964).

198. *See* text accompanying notes 89–91 above; text accompanying notes 253–254 in Chapter 1.

199. On the nature of political judgment, *see* RONALD BEINER, POLITICAL JUDGMENT (1984).

200. In reviewing campaign finance legislation aimed at enhancing electoral integrity, courts might do well to keep in mind the Court's decision in *Turner Broadcasting System v. FCC*, 520 U.S. 180 (1997). In *Turner*, the Court reviewed a federal statute that required cable television systems to dedicate channels to local broadcast television stations in order to promote "the widespread dissemination of information from a multiplicity of sources." Ibid., 189. Although the legislation compromised the asserted First Amendment rights of cable owners, it was intended to serve an important First Amendment interest. Viewing the legislation as a content-neutral regulation that advanced important governmental interests unrelated to the suppression of free speech, the Court held that substantial deference ought to be given to congressional findings involving predictive judgments:

> In reviewing the constitutionality of a statute, "courts must accord substantial deference to the predictive judgments of Congress." Our sole obligation is "to assure that, in formulating its judgments, Congress has drawn reasonable inferences based on substantial evidence." As noted in the first appeal, substantiality is to be measured in this context by a standard more deferential than we accord to judgments of an administrative agency. . . . We owe Congress' findings deference in part because the institution "is far better equipped than the judiciary to 'amass and evaluate the vast amounts of data' bearing upon" legislative questions. . . . This is not the sum of the matter, however. We owe Congress' findings an additional measure of deference out of respect for its authority to exercise the legislative power. Even in the realm of First Amendment questions where Congress must base its conclusions upon substantial evidence, deference must be accorded to its findings as to the harm to be avoided and to the remedial measures adopted for that end, lest we infringe on traditional legislative authority to make predictive judgments when enacting nationwide regulatory policy.

Ibid., 195–196.

I note that congressional legislation regulating corporate campaign expenditures for the purpose of enhancing electoral integrity, like the legislation at issue in *Turner*, would serve important First Amendment interests that are unrelated to the suppression of expression. Such legislation would thus be content neutral, at least under many of the definitions of content neutrality that the Court has advanced in its doctrine. *See* City of Renton v. Playtime Theatres, Inc., 475 U.S. 41 (1986); Madsen v. Women's Health Ctr., Inc., 512 U.S. 753 (1994); Post, note 9 above, at 1265–1270. Section 441b is content-neutral legislation according to those cases that define content neutrality as legislation "aimed not at the content" of the speech, but rather at its "secondary effects." *Renton,* 475 U.S. at 47. It is also content-neutral legislation according to those cases that define content-discriminatory legislation as adopted "because of disagreement with the message" of the regulated speech. Ward v. Rock Against Racism, 491 U.S. 781, 791 (1989); *see* Sorell v. IMS Health Inc., 131 S. Ct. 2653, 2664 (2011). *Turner* thus suggests that legislation regulating corporate campaign expenditures in order to secure electoral integrity and based upon cogent congressional fact-finding should receive "substantial deference."

201. As Chief Justice William Howard Taft once wrote in a letter to the newly appointed Justice George Sutherland:

> I do not minimize at all the importance of having Judges of learning in the law on the Supreme Bench, but the functions performed by us are of such a peculiar character that something in addition is much needed to round out a man for service upon that Bench, and that is a sense of proportion derived from a knowledge of how Government is carried on, and how higher politics are conducted in the State. A Supreme Judge must needs keep abreast of the actual situation in the country so as to understand all the phases of important issues which arise, with a view to the proper application of the Constitution, which is a political instrument in a way, to new conditions.

Letter from Chief Justice William Howard Taft to Justice George Sutherland (Sept. 10, 1922), *microformed on* William H. Taft Papers, Reel 245 (Library of Cong., 1969).

202. *See* Samuel Issacharoff & Pamela S. Karlan, *The Hydraulics of Campaign Finance Reform,* 77 Tex. L. Rev. 1705, 1710–1711 (1999).

203. *See* 65% *in Poll Back U.S. Campaign Aid,* N.Y. Times, Sept. 20, 1973. Consider Henry George back in 1883: "[P]opular government must be a sham and a fraud" so long "as elections are to be gained by the use of money, and cannot be gained without it." Henry George, *Money in Elections,* 316 N. Am. Rev. 201, 201 (1883).

204. Caperton v. A.T. Massey Coal Co., 556 U.S. 868, 888–890 (2009); *see* James L. Gibson, *Challenges to the Impartiality of State Supreme Courts: Legitimacy Theory and 'New-Style' Judicial Campaigns,* 102 Am. Pol. Sci. Rev. 59, 69 (2008); James L. Gibson, *"New-Style" Judicial Campaigns and the Legitimacy of State High Courts,* 71 J. Pol. 1285, 1294 (2009). Justice Kennedy has in the past stressed the analogy between judicial elections and other types of elections for purposes of the First Amendment. *See* Republican Party of Minn. v. White,

536 U.S. 765, 794–795 (2002) (Kennedy, J., concurring) ("The State of Minnesota no doubt was concerned, as many citizens and thoughtful commentators are concerned, that judicial campaigns in an age of frenetic fundraising and mass media may foster disrespect for the legal system. . . . [But t]he State cannot opt for an elected judiciary and then assert that its democracy, in order to work as desired, compels the abridgment of speech.").

205. *But see* note 193 above.

206. For example, Canada regulates "electoral expenses," including expenses for "election advertising," during a discrete election period, defined as the period between the issue of a writ of election and polling day, a period that must be at least thirty-six days. Canada Elections Act, S.C. 2000, c. 9, § 2, § 57(c). "Electoral expenses" are defined as "any cost incurred, or non-monetary contribution received, by a registered party or a candidate . . . used to directly promote or oppose a registered party, its leader or a candidate during an election period." Ibid. § 350. The Supreme Court of Canada upheld these regulations in *Harper.* Harper v. Canada, [2004] 1 S.C.R. 827, at para. 115 (Can.). "Election advertising" is defined as "the transmission to the public by any means during an election period of an advertising message that promotes or opposes a registered party or the election candidate." Canada Elections Act, S.C. 2000, c. 9, § 319. The election-advertising ceiling is revised annually to reflect inflation. Ibid. § 405. The current limit can be found at the website of Elections Canada, the agency that oversees the country's federal elections. For the 2013 limit, see *Limit on Election Advertising Expenses Incurred by Third Parties,* Elections Canada (Aug. 9, 2013), http://www.elections.ca/content.aspx?section=pol&document=index&dir=limits/limit_tp&lang=e.

The United Kingdom sets limits on "campaign expenditures," otherwise known as party expenditures, a year prior to a general election up to polling day. Political Parties, Elections, and Referendums Act [PPERA], 2000, c. 41, § 72, § 79, sch. 9, paras. 1(3), 3(7). Since 2011, the UK has adopted fixed-term elections every five years. Fixed-term Parliaments Act, 2011, c. 14. Because Parliament still retains power to call for early elections, and because this power creates uncertainty about the timing of elections, political parties must continually maintain records of their expenditures. Ibid. § 2. UK law also limits "election expenditures," or candidate expenditures, during the period immediately following the Parliament's dissolution, or generally seventeen days before an election. Representation of the People Act [RPA], 1983, c. 2, § 73, § 76, § 118A. "Controlled expenditures," or third-party expenditures, are similarly subject to limits for any election "whether imminent or otherwise." PPERA, 2000, c. 41, § 85(3). Third parties may apply for recognition by the Electoral Commission, in which case they are subject to a larger limitation applicable to spending across constituencies in the 365 days preceding a general election. Ibid. § 94, sch. 10, para. 3.

France defines official election periods for both presidential and National Assembly elections. With respect to presidential elections, an election period lasts the two weeks preceding the first ballot and, if no candidate receives a majority of votes in the first round, the week between the first and second ballots. CODE ÉLECTORAL, art. R26. With respect to National Assembly elections, the election period begins twenty days prior to the first ballot. Ibid. art. L164. France authorizes election contributions beginning only one year preceding the first day of the month of the election, with these contributions being subject to limits. Ibid. art. L52–4, L52–11. Election expenditures are subject to limitations commencing the year prior to the first day of election month. Ibid. art. L52–11. France also regulates "election propaganda" broadly defined, prohibiting such propaganda through the press or by audiovisual means, in the six months preceding an election. Ibid. art. L48–1; L52–1.

Israel limits party expenditures during an election period defined as the 101 days before an election. Political Parties (Financing) Law [PP(F)L], 5733–1973, 27 LSI 48 (1972–1973), § 7. It also regulates election-related speech during a set period: parties and candidates are prohibited from publishing more than 10,000 inches of ads in newspapers in the three months preceding an election. Election (Means of Propaganda) Law, 5719–1959, SH No. 138, cl. 10(b)(4), 10(b)(5). Political parties are allotted free campaign advertisements in both television and radio, taking place in the sixty days before an election. Ibid. cl. 5(a)(1); ibid. art. 15.

Germany, via state and local laws, restricts political advertisements through billboards to the month preceding an election. *See* Edith Palmer, *Campaign Finance: Germany,* LAW LIBRARY OF CONG., *available at* http://www.loc.gov/law/help/campaign-finance/germany.php.

207. For example, French law entitles each presidential candidate to an equal amount of public television and radio advertisement time during the campaign. The amount of time is approved by a government council (in consultation with the candidates) and applies to all candidates regardless of popularity. Nicole Atwill, *Campaign Finance: France,* LAW LIBRARY OF CONG., *available at* http://www.loc.gov/law/help/campaign-finance/france.php. During the 2007 election, the council approved forty-five minutes of advertisement per station for each presidential candidate on the first ballot. Conseil supérieur de l'audiovisuel décision 2007–142 du 3 avril 2007 [High Council on Audiovisual Decision 2007–142 of April 3, 2007], JOURNAL OFFICIEL DE LA RÉPUBLIQUE FRANCAISE [J.O.] [OFFICIAL GAZETTE OF FRANCE], Apr. 5, 2007, p. 6453. Similar rules—mandating equal time and space—apply to the activities of political parties and the placement of posters. *See* Bruce Crumley, *France's Stringent Election Laws: Lessons for the America's Free-for-All Campaigns,* TIME (Apr. 20, 2012), http://world.time.com/2012/04/20/frances-stringent-election-laws-lessons-for-the-americas-free-for-all-campaigns.

During an election, Canadian law requires that every broadcaster make six and a half hours of prime time available for purchase to all registered political parties. Canada Elections Act, S.C. 2000, c. 9, § 335. New parties are also entitled to broadcasting time. Ibid. § 339. In addition to offering time for purchase, certain networks must also make free broadcasting time available. Ibid. § 345. During the 2011 election, for example, six networks needed to allocate between 62 and 214 minutes of free airtime to all registered parties. The Broadcasting Arbiter, Broadcasting Guidelines: Federal General Election (2011), *available at* http://www.elections.ca/abo/bra/bro/guidelines2011.pdf.

Israel also entitles parties and candidates to broadcasting time. *See* Ruth Levush, *Campaign Finance: Israel,* Law Library of Cong., *available at* http:// www.loc.gov/law/help/campaign-finance/israel.php. A national law guarantees each party ten minutes of airtime, with three additional minutes for each member already serving in Parliament. Election Law, 5719–1959, SH No. 138 (Isr.). A national council of cable broadcasters has adopted its own rules that attempt to balance public debates. Among other things, these rules mandate that when broadcasters focus on issues of public significance, at least two opinions should be presented, in equal form and with equal time. When a broadcaster cannot obtain a competing viewpoint, the public should be notified that a request for such a viewpoint was made. *See* Amit M. Schejter, *The Fairness Doctrine Is Dead and Living in Israel,* 51 Fed. Comm. L.J. 281, 289–290 (1999).

In the United Kingdom, political parties receive a certain amount of broadcasting time on national television and radio free of charge, using a formula developed by the Office of Communications. *See* Communications Act, 2003, c. 21, § 333. The Office of Communications' rules state: "Due weight must be given to the coverage of major parties during the election period. Broadcasters must also consider giving appropriate coverage to other parties and independent candidates with significant views and perspectives." The Ofcom Broadcasting Code, 2013, § 6.2 (U.K.).

208. Justice Stevens seems to have verged on explicitly recognizing elections as managerial domains. *See* Davis v. FEC, 554 U.S. 724, 751–752 (2008) (Stevens, J., dissenting).

209. Richard Briffault, *Issue Advocacy: Redrawing the Elections/Politics Line,* 77 Tex. L. Rev. 1751, 1753 (1999). The considerable and thoughtful First Amendment scholars cited in note 9 of Chapter 1 all explore the possibility of creating a domain for elections that is distinct from that of politics.

210. C. Edwin Baker, *Campaign Expenditures and Free Speech,* 33 Harv. C.R.-C.L. Rev. 1, 25 (1998).

211. Briffault, note 209 above, at 1772–1774; *see also* 2 U.S.C. § 434(a)–(b) (2006) (requiring campaign committees to disclose certain contributions and expenditures and requiring speakers unaffiliated with a campaign to disclose

certain contributions and expenditures if those speakers expressly urge the election or defeat of particular candidates).

212. Although the Court struck down BCRA's ban on "electioneering communications" by unions and corporations, BCRA's disclosure rules for "electioneering communications" remain in effect. *See* 2 U.S.C. § 434(f) (2006) (requiring disclosure of certain contributions and expenditures for "electioneering communications").

213. Media outlets must comply with four special rules during "elections." Under the "reasonable access" rule, commercial broadcasters must provide legally qualified candidates for federal office with "reasonable access" to all "classes and dayparts" of advertising time available. 47 C.F.R. §§ 73.1944 (2010). Under the "equal opportunities" rule, broadcasters and cable stations must not preclude any candidate running for any office from appearing on a station as often as and during the same general time periods as another candidate for that same office. 47 C.F.R. §§ 73.1941, 76.205 (2010). Under the "no censorship" rule, broadcasters and cable stations are forbidden from censoring the content of an advertisement purchased by legally qualified candidates for any office. 47 C.F.R. §§ 73.1941, 76.205 (2010). Under the "lowest unit rate" rule, which applies only during the forty-five days preceding a primary election and sixty days preceding a general election, the rates that broadcasters and cable stations charge candidates for purchases of advertising time cannot exceed the lowest rates charged to commercial advertisers for identical purchases. 47 C.F.R. §§ 73.1942, 76.206 (2010).

214. FEC v. Wisc. Right to Life, Inc. *(WRTL),* 551 U.S. 449, 457–458 (2007).

215. *See* notes 211–213 above. BCRA attempted to ban unions from using general treasury funds to pay for electioneering communications. *Citizens United,* 558 U.S. at 310.

216. *WRTL,* 551 U.S. at 464 (opinion of Roberts, C.J.).

217. *See* Robert Post, *Regulating Election Speech Under the First Amendment,* 77 Tex. L. Rev. 1837 (1999).

3. Out-Posting Post

1. Zachary Brugman, *The Bipartisan Promise of 1776: The Republican Form and Its Manner of Election* 33 (2012) (citations omitted), *available at* http://papers.ssrn.com/sol3/papers.cfm?abstract_id=2192705.

2. *See, e.g.,* Robert Post, Democracy, Expertise, and Academic Freedom (2012); Robert Post, Constitutional Domains (1995).

3. Buckley v. Valeo, 424 U.S. 1 (1976).

4. David A. Strauss, *Corruption, Equality, and Campaign Finance Reform,* 94 Colum. L. Rev. 1369, 1373 (1994).

5. *See* 18 U.S.C. § 201(b)(2)(A) (covering bribery); 18 U.S.C. § 3559(a)(3) (describing classification as a class C felony).

6. Arizona Free Enter. Club's Freedom Club PAC v. Bennett, 131 S. Ct. 2806 (2011).

7. Lisa Hill, *Adam Smith and the Theme of Corruption*, 68 REV. POL. 636, 636–637 (2006).

8. The data are accessible at http://ocorruption.tumblr.com.

9. *See* LAWRENCE LESSIG, REPUBLIC, LOST 127–130, 226–247 (2011).

10. Technically, "Congress" is broader than the Framers would have meant. Madison is speaking of the House in *Federalist 52*. At the Founding, the Senate was selected by the states, meaning it was not "dependent upon the People alone." But after the Seventeenth Amendment, making senators directly elected, I synthesize Madison's conception to include the Senate as well as the House.

11. THE FEDERALIST NO. 52, at 324 (James Madison) (Clinton Rossiter ed., 1961).

12. *See* LAWRENCE LESSIG, LESTERLAND (2013).

13. Frederick Schauer, *Categories and the First Amendment: A Play in Three Acts,* 34 VAND. L. REV. 265, 267 (1981).

14. Elena Kagan, *Private Speech, Public Purpose: The Role of Governmental Motive in First Amendment Doctrine*, 63 U. CHI. L. REV. 413, 465 n.143 (1996).

15. *See, e.g.,* Snepp v. United States, 444 U.S. 507, 516 (1980).

16. *Buckley,* 424 U.S. 1.

17. McCutcheon v. FEC, 893 F. Supp. 2d 133 (D.D.C. 2012), *prob. juris. noted,* 133 S. Ct. 1242.

18. SpeechNow.org v. FEC, 599 F.3d 686 (D.C. Cir. 2010).

19. As I describe in my book *One Way Forward,* former senator Evan Bayh (D-Ind.) offered the most compelling testimony about this dynamic. Bayh had been challenged during a television show to demonstrate exactly how Citizens United had affected the political process. Bayh rolled his eyes in response to the question, and as I described his answer:

> The single most frightening prospect that an incumbent now faces is that, thirty days before an election, some anonymously funded super PAC will drop $500,000 to $1,000,000 in attack ads in the district. When that happens, the incumbent needs a way to respond. He can't turn to his largest contributors—by definition, they have all maxed out and can't, under the law, give any more. So the only protection he can buy is from super PACs on his own side.
>
> That protection, however, must be secured in advance: a kind of insurance, the premium for which must be paid before a claim gets filed. And so how do you pay your premium to a super PAC on your side in advance? By conforming your behavior to the standards set by the super PAC. "We'd love to be there for you, Senator, but our charter requires that we only support people who have achieved an 80 per-

cent or better grade on our Congressional Report Card." And so the rational senator has a clear goal—80 percent or better—that he works to meet long before he actually needs anyone's money. And thus, without even spending a dollar, the super PAC achieves its objective: bending congressmen to its program. It is a dynamic that would be obvious to Tony Soprano or Michael Corleone but that is sometimes obscure to political scientists. . . .

LAWRENCE LESSIG, ONE WAY FORWARD 67–68 (2012).

4. Legitimacy, Strict Scrutiny, and the Case Against the Supreme Court

1. In support of it, Post refers to writings of theorists including, among others, Jürgen Habermas, Bernard Manin, Claude Lefort, and Nadia Urbinati.

2. For example, Post writes (after recounting the relevant history of First Amendment doctrine): "If the historical account I have . . . offered is accurate, [First Amendment] controversies should be adjudicated according to the needs of democratic legitimation."

3. See HARRY KALVEN, JR., A WORTHY TRADITION: FREEDOM OF SPEECH IN AMERICA (Jamie Kalven ed., 1988); Harry Kalven, Jr., *Ernst Freund and the First Amendment Tradition*, 40 U. CHI. L. REV. 235 (1973).

4. Baker v. Carr, 369 U.S. 186, 217 (1962).

5. *See* Chapter 2:

In these lectures I shall not explore whether electoral integrity is in fact at risk, or whether campaign finance reform will in fact ameliorate that risk. I argue only that the protection of electoral integrity constitutes a compelling state interest, and that the need for such protection depends upon the relevant facts of the matter. . . . When government acts to preserve electoral integrity, it acts for the right reasons. Tailoring state action to the maintenance of electoral integrity is thus unlikely to produce counterintuitive results.

"Compelling state interest" and "tailoring," you'll notice, are the argot of strict scrutiny.

6. *See* Chapter 2: "Because government restrictions on public discourse potentially impair democratic legitimation, courts may properly prevent the state from restricting public discourse unless in the service of the most compelling interests."

7. Elections "give citizens good reason to participate in public discourse," but they "do not displace ongoing processes of public opinion formation."

8. *See* Part IIA, above.

9. Marbury v. Madison, 5 U.S. 137, 177 (1803). Chief Justice Marshall immediately continued: "Those who apply the rule [of law] to particular cases, must of necessity expound and interpret that rule." Ibid.

10. *See, e.g.,* MARK TUSHNET, WEAK COURTS, STRONG RIGHTS 18 (2008).

11. Fisher v. Univ. of Texas at Austin, 631 F.3d 213, 231 (5th Cir. 2011), *vacated and remanded,* 133 S. Ct. 2411 (2013).

12. 133 S. Ct. 2411 (2013).

13. Because the Supreme Court was reviewing the lower court's grant of summary judgment in favor of the University, it put its holding in slightly different form. Before granting such a judgment, the Court wrote, the lower court should have satisfied itself that "the University has offered sufficient evidence to prove that its admissions program is narrowly tailored to obtain the educational benefits of diversity." Ibid., 2421 (emphasis supplied).

14. Ibid.

15. *See, e.g.,* ibid., 2418–2419.

16. "To understand First Amendment doctrine, . . . and especially the kind of doctrine that is relevant to a decision like Citizens United, we must conceive First Amendment rights as designed to protect the processes of democratic legitimation required for discursive democracy."

17. *See* RONALD DWORKIN, LAW'S EMPIRE 239, 255–256 (1986).

18. "Because government restrictions on public discourse potentially impair democratic legitimation, courts may properly prevent the state from restricting public discourse unless in the service of the most compelling interests."

19. COREY BRETTSCHNEIDER, DEMOCRATIC RIGHTS: THE SUBSTANCE OF SELF-GOVERNMENT 18 n.23 (2007).

20. *See* Richard H. Fallon, Jr., *Legitimacy and the Constitution*, 118 HARV. L. REV. 1787, 1796, 1798 (2005) (describing "minimal" conceptions of legitimacy, using the latter term in "a moral sense").

21. Ibid., 1790–1791, 1795 (defining a "sociological" usage for "legitimacy").

22. At one point in his text, Post might seem to be sliding toward acceptance of an objective test of impartial (judicial) reason. "The point of First Amendment rights," he affirms, is "to guarantee that each person is equally entitled to the possibility of democratic legitimation." "The possibility of democratic legitimation" could be read to mean the state is obliged to act so as to make that possibility available to right-reasoning persons—an "objective" standard. But the whole thrust of the essay is toward a different reading: the state must act so that persons as they are do not find themselves rendered incapable in fact of imagining themselves as "owners," in the manner supposed by the model of discursive democracy.

23. *See, e.g.,* Jürgen Habermas, *Richard Rorty's Pragmatic Turn, in* ON THE PRAGMATICS OF COMMUNICATION 343, 355–356 (Maeve Cooke ed., 1998).

24. Am. Tradition P'ship, Inc. v. Bullock, 132 S. Ct. 2490 (2012).

25. *See Baker,* 369 U.S. 186.

26. Ibid.

27. *See* Robert C. Post, *Fashioning the Constitutional Culture: Culture, Courts, and Law,* 117 HARV. L. REV. 4, 4, 8, 9 (2003) (defining constitutional culture as "the beliefs and values of nonjudicial actors" regarding "the substance of the Constitution," and positing "a continuous exchange between constitutional law and constitutional culture").

28. *See* ROBERT POST, CONSTITUTIONAL DOMAINS 291–331 (1995).

29. "Whether to encase elections in such a managerial domain ought to depend upon whether the dangers to electoral integrity of government inaction outweigh the risks to democratic legitimation of potential government regulation. This is a difficult, fraught, empirically based calculus."

30. *See* Frank I. Michelman, *Reflection,* 82 TEX. L. REV. 1737, 1741–1748, 1758–1761 (2004); Robert C. Post, *Prejudicial Appearances: The Logic of American Antidiscrimination Law*, 88 CALIF. L. REV. 1, 37–40 (2000).

5. Free Speech as the Citizen's Right

1. BERNARD MANIN, THE PRINCIPLES OF REPRESENTATIVE GOVERNMENT 220 (1997) (arguing that the death of party democracy and the birth of audience democracy is "a change" yet not a "departure" from democracy).

2. "The aspect more cherished by the Athenian democrats was *isegoria,* not *isonomia.* Now, whereas *isonomia* implies natural equality as well as equality of opportunity, *isegoria* is really about equality of opportunity. No Athenian expected that every one of the 6000 citizens who attended a meeting of the Assembly could—or would—address his fellow citizens. *Isegoria* was not for everyone, but for anyone [who] cared to exercise this political right. Each citizen must have equal opportunity to demonstrate his excellence, but he deserved reward according to what he actually achieved." MOGENS HERMAN HANSEN, THE ATHENIAN DEMOCRACY IN THE AGE OF DEMOSTHENES 83–84 (J.A. Crook trans., 1993).

3. "On this view, the First Amendment signifies what Michel Foucault has called a 'parrhesiastic contract,' through which the sovereign people acquire the truth they need for self-government, in exchange for a promise not to punish speakers who speak the truth, 'no matter what this truth turns out to be.'" Keith Werhan, *The Classical Athenian Ancestry of American Freedom of Speech,* 2008 SUP CT. REV. 293, 322 (2008).

4. HANSEN, note 2 above, at 84.

5. "A democracy without public opinion is a contradiction in terms. Insofar as public opinion can arise only where intellectual freedom, freedom of speech, press and religion, are guaranteed, democracy coincides with political—though not necessarily economic—liberalism." HANS KELSEN, GENERAL THEORY OF LAW AND STATE 287–288 (1945) (Anders Wedberg trans., 1999).

6. MANIN, note 1 above, at 188–190.

7. CHARLES R. BEITZ, POLITICAL EQUALITY 192 (1989).

8. Athens, which was a genuine democracy, is the touchstone for a procedural interpretation of democracy. Born as a compromise between the newly empowered "common people" and the already powerful wealthy ("a strong shield around both parties"), it took several revolutions to become the rule of the many (poor or "ordinary"). Democracy meant that poverty was neither something the people had to be ashamed of nor a reason for political and civil disempowerment. *See* Solon, *Fragments, in* EARLY GREEK POLITICAL THOUGHT: FROM HOMER TO THE SOPHISTS 26 (Michael Gagarin & Paul Woodruff eds., 1995); THUCYDIDES, THE PELOPONNESIAN WAR 145–147 (Moses I. Finley trans., 1972) (Pericles' funeral oration).

9. Jean Bodin and Robert Filmer strictly distinguished between the legislative act and the debate that preceded it; the former only consisted in the sovereign act of promulgation; the latter was held by the "counselors" whose opinion or judgment the king decided to listen to or ignore. *See* JEAN BODIN, ON SOVEREIGNTY: FOUR CHAPTERS FROM THE SIX BOOKS OF THE COMMONWEALTH (Julian Franklin ed., 1992); ROBERT FILMER, *Patriarcha, in* PATRIARCHA AND OTHER ESSAYS 47 (Johann P. Sommerville ed., 1991).

10. On the "punctuated" short-term logic implied in direct votes on issues, see Yannis Papadopoulos, *Analysis of Functions and Dysfunctions of Direct Democracy: Top-Down and Bottom-Up Perspectives,* 23 POL. & SOC'Y 421, 438–439 (1995). I discussed monoarchic and diarchic conceptions of democracy in REPRESENTATIVE DEMOCRACY: PRINCIPLES AND GENEALOGY (2006).

11. NORBERTO BOBBIO, THE FUTURE OF DEMOCRACY 93 (Roger Griffin trans., Richard Bellamy ed., 1984).

12. E. EDWIN BAKER, MEDIA CONCENTRATION AND DEMOCRACY: WHY OWNERSHIP MATTERS 7 (2007).

13. One of the most substantial themes in twentieth-century political science has been precisely that of distinguishing public opinion from the initiatives of government—this distinction makes communication between the two possible. This is technically speaking the meaning of "government by means of opinion," which was systematically studied (particularly in the United States) in the years in which Europe experienced despotic and plebiscitarian mass regimes. See the classic work of Emil Lederer, *Public Opinion, in* POLITICAL AND ECONOMIC DEMOCRACY 284–293 (Max Ascoli & Fritz Lehmann eds., 1937); and also HAROLD D. LASSWELL, DEMOCRACY THROUGH PUBLIC OPINION 19–31 (1940).

14. "Elections are not only instruments for choosing governments; they are also media for sending messages about the democratic process," which means that although we accept that people decide not to exercise their right to vote, this should not make us "neglect a salient empirical fact," that the opportunity to exercise the right to vote and voice messages are not equal, and sometimes this inequality is felt by citizens as a reason for futility in voting. Thus, paying

attention to the conditions in which opinions are formed is an essential component of our respect for procedures and rules. DENNIS F. THOMPSON, JUST ELECTIONS: CREATING A FAIR ELECTORAL PROCESS IN THE UNITED STATES 28 (2002).

15. Bernard Yack, *Democracy and the Lover of Truth, in* TRUTH AND DEMOCRACY 171 (Jeremy Elkins & Andrew Norris eds., 2012).

16. Thus Hobbes defined democracy as an "aristocracy of orators" because popular consent is consent on arguments or speeches that citizens make in view of persuading the larger number. THOMAS HOBBES, THE ELEMENTS OF LAW NATURAL AND POLITIC (J.C.A. Gaskin ed., 1994). But for more on this issue see MICHAEL WALZER, SPHERES OF JUSTICE: A DEFENSE OF PLURALISM AND EQUALITY 304 (1983).

17. Adam Przeworski, *Minimalist Conception of Democracy: A Defense, in* DEMOCRACY'S VALUE 34–45 (Ian Shapiro & Cassiano Hacker-Cordón eds., 1999).

18. Ibid.

19. DAVID HUME, *On the First Principles of Government, in* POLITICAL ESSAYS 16 (Knud Haakonssen ed., 1994).

20. The expression "paper stones" was coined by Friedrich Engels; I borrow it from Przeworski's "Minimalist Conception of Democracy." I discussed this aspect in REPRESENTATIVE DEMOCRACY, note 10 above, at 30–33. The problem of "circularity" between opinion and government was studied early on in CHARLES E. LINDBLOM, POLITICS AND MARKETS: THE WORLD'S POLITICAL ECONOMIC SYSTEM (1977).

21. PIERRE ROSANVALLON, LA LÉGIMITÉ DÉMOCRATIQUE. IMPARTALITÉ, RÉFLEXIVITÉ, PROXIMITÉ 47–53 (2008).

22. Yasmin Dawood, *The New Inequality: Constitutional Democracy and the Problem of Wealth,* 67 MD. L. REV. 147 (2007). On the growth of economic inequality in the last decades and its negative effects on democracy, see JOSEPH M. SCHWARTZ, THE FUTURE OF DEMOCRATIC EQUALITY: REBUILDING SOCIAL SOLIDARITY IN A FRAGMENTED AMERICA (2009); and Kay Lehman Schlozman et al., *Inequality of Political Voice, in* INEQUALITY AND AMERICAN DEMOCRACY 19 (Lawrence R. Jacobs & Theda Skocpol eds., 2005).

23. Mark Warren, *What Does Corruption Mean in a Democracy?,* 48 AM. POL. SCI. REV. 328 (2004).

24. I made this claim in REPRESENTATIVE DEMOCRACY, note 10 above, at 226–228.

25. THOMPSON, note 14 above, at 22.

26. BAKER, note 12 above, at 8.

27. DARA STROLOVITCH, AFFIRMATIVE ADVOCACY: RACE, CLASS, AND GENDER IN INTEREST GROUP POLITICS 200–212 (2007). On the formulation of elections as enabling citizens to control policy makers and to influence them, see G. BINGHAM POWELL, JR., ELECTIONS AS INSTRUMENTS OF DEMOCRACY: MAJORITARIAN AND PROPORTIONAL VISIONS 4–7 (2000).

6. Citizens Deflected: Electoral Integrity and Political Reform

1. James A. Gardner, *Shut Up and Vote: A Critique of Deliberative Democracy and the Life of Talk*, 63 TENN. L. REV. 421 (1996).

2. New York Times Co. v. Sullivan, 376 U.S. 254, 270 (1964).

3. Quoting THE FEDERALIST NO. 57, at 277 (James Madison) (Terence Ball ed., 2003).

4. Citizens United v. Federal Election Commission, 558 U.S. 310 (2010).

5. *See also* Pamela S. Karlan, *Foreword: Democracy and Disdain*, 126 HARV. L. REV. 1, 31 (2012). In that article, I explain how the Court's later decision in *American Trading Partnership, Inc. v. Bullock*, 132 S. Ct. 2490 (2012) (per curiam), confirms the conclusion that "the Court's decision in Citizens United reflected a philosophical, rather than an empirical, position on money's effect on politics." Karlan, above, at 35.

6. *See generally* THOMAS E. MANN & NORMAN J. ORNSTEIN, IT'S EVEN WORSE THAN IT LOOKS (2012); Richard H. Pildes, *Why the Center Does Not Hold: The Causes of Hyperpolarized Democracy in America*, 99 CALIF. L. REV. 273 (2011).

7. Samuel Issacharoff & Pamela S. Karlan, *The Hydraulics of Campaign Finance Reform*, 77 TEX. L. REV. 1705, 1734 (1999).

8. Federal law requires the use of these districts for the House of Representatives. *See* 2 U.S.C. § 2c. As a practical matter, although each state formally constitutes a multimember district with respect to the Senate, having two senators, the fact that their terms are staggered means that any senatorial election selects only one senator.

9. *Cf.* Michael S. Kang, *Voting as Veto*, 108 MICH. L. REV. 1221, 1273 (2010) (suggesting that elections using proportional representation may be less likely to produce negative advertising).

10. *See* Nathaniel Persily & Kelli Lammie, *Perceptions of Corruption and Campaign Finance: When Public Opinion Determines Constitutional Law*, 153 U. PA. L. REV. 119, 146 (2004); David M. Primo & Jeffrey Milyo, *Campaign Finance Laws and Political Efficacy: Evidence from the States*, 5 ELECTION L.J. 23, 26 (2006).

11. *See* Persily & Lammie, note 10 above, at 147.

12. *See* ibid., 148.

13. In this vein, consider Eben Moglen's question about the tangled relationship between telecommunications firms that have been awarded pieces of the public airwaves and the political process: "Is it relevant that those holding the privileges then sell to politicians the communications advantages awarded to them, as well as donate money to the campaigns and personal fortunes of the legislators?" Eben Moglen, *The Invisible Barbecue*, 97 COLUM. L. REV. 945, 952 (1997).

14. *See* Letter from Laura W. Murphy et al., Am. Civil Liberties Union, to Senator Richard Durbin & Ranking Member Lindsey Graham 3 (July 24, 2012), *available at* http://tinyurl.com/post-tanner1. David Strauss long ago suggested that the phenomenon that many corporate-affiliated donors contribute to both candidates in political races may be a sign that a soft form of extortion motivated their conduct. *See* David A. Strauss, *What Is the Goal of Campaign Finance Reform?*, 1995 U. CHI. LEGAL F. 141, 152–155. This suggests—and several conversations I've had with lawyers who specialize in campaign regulation reinforce the premise—that large, publicly traded corporations would prefer to have a ban on corporate political contributions because it protects them.

15. Persily & Lammie, note 10 above, at 143.

16. Primo & Milyo, note 10 above, at 34.

17. Ibid., 38.

18. *See* FairVote Releases Projections for the 2014 Elections (Apr. 26, 2013), *available at* http://tinyurl.com/post-tanner3.

19. *See* Samuel Issacharoff & Pamela S. Karlan, *Where to Draw the Line?: Judicial Review of Political Gerrymanders*, 153 U. PA. L. REV. 541, 572–574 (2004).

20. Daniel R. Ortiz, *Got Theory?*, 153 U. PA. L. REV. 459, 487 (2004).

21. 549 U.S. 1 (2006) (per curiam).

22. Citing Burson v. Freeman, 504 U.S. 191, 200–205 (1992); and ELIHU ROOT, ADDRESSES ON GOVERNMENT AND CITIZENSHIP 69 (Robert Bacon & James Brown Scott eds., 1916).

23. J. MORGAN KOUSSER, THE SHAPING OF SOUTHERN POLITICS: SUFFRAGE RESTRICTIONS AND THE ESTABLISHMENT OF THE ONE-PARTY SOUTH, 1880–1910, at 51–52 (1974).

The white supremacist Arkansas Democratic Party actually used a campaign song to celebrate this feature:

> The Australian ballot works like a charm,
> It makes them think and scratch,
> And when a negro gets a ballot
> He has certainly got his match.
>
> . . . .
>
> They go into the booth alone
> Their ticket to prepare.
> And as soon as five minutes are out
> They have got to git from there.

John William Graves, *Negro Disfranchisement in Arkansas*, 26 ARK. HIST. Q. 199, 212–213 (1967). Under current federal law, every voter has the right to the assistance of her choice (except for assistance by her employer or union) within the voting booth. *See* 42 U.S.C. § 1973aa-6 (1994).

24. *See* MICHAEL SCHUDSON, CHANGING CONCEPTS OF DEMOCRACY (1999), *available at* http://tinyurl.com/post-tanner5. Interestingly, at the cusp of this change—which coincides roughly with the rise of the commitment to discursive democracy on which Post focuses—Elihu Root notably opposed New York's decision at its 1915 constitutional convention to impose a literacy test for voting, despite arguments by its supporters that the restriction was necessary to maintain electoral integrity. *See Literacy Test Wins in Wild Convention,* N.Y. TIMES, Aug. 26, 1915, *available at* http://tinyurl.com/post-tanner4.

25. *See* Bolden v. City of Mobile, 542 F. Supp. 1050, 1061, 1065 (S.D. Ala. 1982) (noting that in Mobile, where abandonment of districted municipal elections was characterized as an anticorruption measure, "good government reform was considered synonymous with the elimination of black political influence" and that "the disfranchising constitution of 1901 and the white primary were also promoted as good government reforms").

26. *See generally* FRANCES PIVEN & RICHARD CLOWARD, WHY AMERICANS DON'T VOTE 5 (1988); Dayna L. Cunningham, *Who Are to Be the Electors? A Reflection on the History of Voter Registration in the United States,* 9 YALE L. & POL'Y REV. 370 (1991).

27. Ariz. Rev. Stat Ann. §§ 16-166, 16-579 (2006).

28. In *Arizona v. Inter Tribal Council of Arizona, Inc.,* 133 S. Ct. 2247 (2013), the Supreme Court held that Arizona's evidence-of-citizenship requirement was preempted with respect to applicants for registration who used the uniform form for voter registration promulgated by the federal Election Assistance Commission pursuant to the National Voter Registration Act of 1993, 42 U.S.C. § 1973gg-4(a)(1).

29. *Purcell,* 549 U.S. at 7 (quoting Dunn v. Blumstein, 405 U.S. 330, 336 (1972)).

30. Ibid.

31. Ibid. (quoting Eu v. San Francisco County Democratic Cent. Comm., 489 U.S. 214, 231 (1989)).

32. Ibid.

33. 553 U.S. 181 (2008).

34. Ibid., 189–190 (opinion of Stevens, J.) (quoting Anderson v. Celebrezze, 460 U.S. 780, 788 (1983)).

35. Ibid., 194.

36. Ibid., 197.

37. Stephen Ansolabehere & Nathaniel Persily, *Vote Fraud in the Eye of the Beholder: The Role of Public Opinion in the Challenge to Voter Identification Requirements,* 121 HARV. L. REV. 1737, 1739 (2008).

38. For a typical example, see http://voterintegrityproject.com/.

39. 377 U.S. 533, 565 (1964).

40. *Purcell,* 549 U.S. at 4.

41. For one version of this oft-repeated quotation, see Lynn Langway, *Huckstering the Candidates*, Newsweek, Apr. 12, 1976, at 87.

7. Representative Democracy

1. *See* Robert Post & Reva B. Siegel, *Originalism as a Political Practice: The Right's Living Constitution*, 75 Fordham L. Rev. 545 (2006); Reva B. Siegel, *Dead or Alive: Originalism as Popular Constitutionalism in* Heller, 122 Harv. L. Rev. 191 (2008).

2. Justices Scalia and Thomas jettison their originalism whenever it is inconsistent with their constitutional convictions, as for example in the area of affirmative action. *See* Post & Siegel, note 1 above. The remaining three justices in the majority in *Citizens United* have never professed any particular allegiance to originalism.

3. I am attracted to Lessig's distinction between the "Public Domain" and the "Republic Domain." The difficulty, however, is that communication in public discourse is often precisely "targeted at government officials, not ordinary citizens." As Nadia Urbinati rightly observes, "The right to take part in the formation of public opinion is a right that produces power, not only a right that protects from power." As a practical matter, then, I would not know how to implement the distinction that Lessig advances.

4. *See* Robert Post, *Theories of Constitutional Interpretation*, Representations, No. 30, Spring 1990, at 13.

5. Korematsu v. United States, 323 U.S. 214 (1944).

6. McLaughlin v. Florida, 379 U.S. 184 (1964).

7. Regents of Univ. of California v. Bakke, 438 U.S. 265 (1978); Grutter v. Bollinger, 539 U.S. 306 (2003). The difference between "weak-form" and "strong-form" strict scrutiny does not concern the formal tests that a court applies. It rather concerns the spirit or rigor that a court brings to bear in its application of these tests.

8. Fisher v. Univ. of Tex. at Austin, 133 S. Ct. 2411 (2013). The Court was actually deliberately ambiguous about the standard it was imposing. "Strict scrutiny must not be 'strict in theory, but fatal in fact.' But the opposite is also true. Strict scrutiny must not be strict in theory but feeble in fact." Ibid., 2421.

9. NAACP v. Button, 371 U.S. 415, 433 (1963).

10. Robert Post, Constitutional Domains: Democracy, Community, Management 1–20 (1995).

11. *See, e.g.*, Robert Post, *The Social Foundations of Privacy: Community and Self in the Common Law Tort*, 77 Calif. L. Rev. 957 (1989).

12. *See, e.g.*, Chiarella v. United States, 445 U.S. 222 (1980) (confirming that liability for insider trading arises "from a relationship of trust and confidence

between parties to a transaction"); *see also* BLACK'S LAW DICTIONARY 564 (5th ed. 1979) (describing actions in a "fiduciary capacity" as "necessitating great confidence and trust").

13. RESTATEMENT (THIRD) OF TRUSTS § 82 (2006).

14. Ibid., § 81. The *Restatement of Agency* analogously suggests that an agent is obliged "to act reasonably and to refrain from conduct that is likely to damage the principal's enterprise." RESTATEMENT (THIRD) OF AGENCY § 8.10 (2006). *See* Meinhard v. Salmon, 249 N.Y. 458, 463–464 (1928).

15. Post, note 11 above.

16. *See* Robert Post, *Federalism in the Taft Court Era: Can It Be "Revived"?*, 51 DUKE L. J. 1513, 1589–1605 (2002).

17. Post, note 4 above; POST, note 10 above; Robert Post, *Foreword: Fashioning the Legal Constitution: Culture, Courts, and Law*, 117 HARV. L. REV. 4 (2003).

18. City of Ontario v. Quon, 130 S.Ct. 2619, 2630–2631 (2010).

19. United States v. Windsor, 133 S.Ct. 2675, 2692 (2013).

20. Miller v. Alabama, 132 S.Ct. 2455 (2012).

21. Gonzales v. Carhart, 550 U.S. 124, 146 (2007).

22. At some points Karlan seems to express doubt whether campaign finance reform is even relevant to electoral integrity. Karlan asserts that the public's trust in government appears to "float independently of what is going on with respect to [the] legal regulation of political spending." Yet the very paper Karlan invokes to question the need for campaign finance reform affirms that our campaign finance system spawns massive distrust of elections. It unequivocally states, "No one can dispute that the public perceives a great deal of corruption and undue influence arising from campaign contributions." Nathaniel Persily & Kelli Lammie, *Perceptions of Corruption and Campaign Finance: When Public Opinion Determines Constitutional Law*, 153 U. PA. L. REV. 119, 143 (2004). It is of course a separate question whether recent legislative efforts to repair campaign finance have failed to sustain public trust or whether future efforts to reform our campaign finance system can succeed.

23. *See, e.g.*, Vieth v. Jubelirer, 541 U.S. 267 (2004). Karlan's lovely observation that it may be more accurate to say that partisan gerrymandering allows "legislators (and their political allies) go into a room to select their constituents than to pretend that every two years voters go into a booth to elect their representatives," chimes with Bertolt Brecht's mordant poem, *The Solution:*

> After the uprising of the 17th June
> The Secretary of the Writer's Union
> Had leaflets distributed in the Stalinallee

Stating that the people
Had forfeited the confidence of the government
And could win it back only
By redoubled efforts. Would it not be easier
In that case for the government
To dissolve the people
And elect another?

24. CLERK OF H. REP., 113TH CONG., STATISTICS OF THE PRESIDENTIAL AND CONGRESSIONAL ELECTION OF NOVEMBER 6, 2012, at 72–73 (2013). The number of seats awarded to the Republican Party in part reflects a concerted effort to draw favorable districts during the reapportionment process following the 2010 Census. *See 2012 REDMAP Summary Report,* REDISTRICTING MAJORITY PROJECT (Jan. 4, 2013), http://www.redistrictingmajorityproject.com/?p=646; *The Great Gerrymander of 2012,* N.Y. TIMES (Feb. 2, 2013), http://www.nytimes .com/2013/02/03/opinion/sunday/the-great-gerrymander-of-2012.html.

25. 549 U.S. 1 (2006) (per curiam).

26. 553 U.S. 181 (2008).

27. *Purcell,* 549 U.S. at 7. *See Crawford,* 553 U.S. at 197 ("Public confidence in the integrity of the electoral process has independent significance, because it encourages citizen participation in the democratic process.").

28. 528 U.S. 377 (2000).

29. Ibid., 390 (2000).

30. I discuss *Crawford* and not *Purcell,* and likely Souter did not dissent in the latter, because *Purcell* is a decision whose proper analysis is complicated by the special procedural rules that apply to the issuance of interlocutory injunctions.

31. *Crawford,* 553 U.S. at 235 (Souter, J., dissenting).

32. On balancing, see Konigsberg v. State Bar, 366 U.S. 36 (1961); Bartnicki v. Vopper, 532 U.S. 514 (2001); Watchtower v. Village of Stratton, 534 U.S. 1111 (2002).

33. On proportionality, see United States v. Alvarez, 132 S. Ct. 2537, 2551–2552 (2012) (Breyer, J., concurring); Ysursa v. Pocatello Educ. Ass'n, 555 U.S. 353, 367–368 (2009) (Breyer, J., concurring in part and dissenting in part). On the use of proportionality to adjudicate tension between two "principle-shaped constitutional rights," see AHARON BARAK, PROPORTIONALITY: CONSTITUTIONAL RIGHTS AND THEIR LIMITATIONS 87–97 (Doron Kalir trans., 2012).

34. Reynolds v. Sims, 377 U.S. 533, 565 (1964).

35. I should add that so long as we conceive electoral integrity on the model suggested by Michelman, which depends upon a normalized account of intersubjective norms, electoral integrity can no more be captured by arbitrary subjectivity than can the conclusions of the "reasonable" man.

36. The principle of self-governance is both necessary and evanescent. Its character is well captured in Wallace Stevens's great poem, *Angel Surrounded by Paysans:*

I am the angel of reality,
Seen for a moment standing in the door. . . .

I am one of you and being one of you
Is being and knowing what I am and know.

Yet I am the necessary angel of earth,
Since, in my sight, you see the earth again,

Cleared of its stiff and stubborn, man-locked set
And, in my hearing, you hear its tragic drone

Rise liquidly in liquid lingerings,
Like watery words awash; like meaning said

By repetitions of half-meaning. Am I not,
Myself, only half a figure of a sort,

A figure half seen, or seen for a moment, a man
Of the mind, an apparition appareled in

Apparels of such lightest look that a turn
Of my shoulder and quickly, too quickly, I am gone?

ACKNOWLEDGMENTS

I am deeply grateful for the research and assistance of a sterling group of students: Joshua Bone, Rob Cobbs, Bridget Fahey, Jed Glickstein, Marvin Lim, and Erin Miller. Even in the best of times it would have been difficult to explore the new and challenging material in these lectures; but in the midst of deaning a great and demanding institution, it would have been simply inconceivable. The persistently imaginative, informative, and insightful scholarship of this remarkable team of students made these lectures possible. I have merely followed where they have led. Kevin Lamb was also of great assistance, as were Rachel Bayefsky, Lauren Bilsacky, Conor Clarke, Daniel Schuker, Josh Silverstein, and Wanling Su. I am also grateful for the generous and helpful comments of Floyd Abrams, Bruce Ackerman, Jean Cohen, Heather Gerken, Jeffrey Gordon, Dieter Grimm, Michael Ignatieff, Sam Issacharoff, Christine Jolls, Alexander Keyssar, Alvin Klevorick, Elizabeth Knoll, Christine Landfried, Sandy Levinson, Justin Levitt, Rick Pildes, Sasha Post, David Pozen, David Rabban, Judith Resnik, Reva Siegel, Dennis Thompson, Larry Tribe, Daniel Viehoff, James Weinstein, and John Witt.

COMMENTATORS

PAMELA S. KARLAN is Kenneth and Harle Montgomery Professor of Public Interest Law at Stanford University.

LAWRENCE LESSIG is Roy L. Furman Professor of Law at Harvard University.

FRANK MICHELMAN is Robert Walmsley University Professor, Emeritus, at Harvard University.

NADIA URBINATI is Kyriakos Tsakopoulos Professor of Political Theory at Columbia University.

INDEX